THE
ENCYCLOPEDIA
OF THE
Cat

THE ENCYCLOPEDIA OF THE Cat

Angela Sayer

Pauline Thompson, US Consultant Editor
Michael Findlay, BVMS, MRCVS, Veterinary Consultant Editor

CRESCENT

First English edition published
in United Kingdom in
1979 by Octopus Books Limited,
59 Grosvenor Street, London W1

© MCMLXXIX by Octopus Books Limited
All rights reserved

This edition published by Crescent Books.
A division of CROWN PUBLISHERS INC.

Library of Congress Cataloging
in Publication Data

Sayer, Angela.
    The encyclopedia of the cat.

Includes index.
1. Cats. 1. Title.
SF442.2.S29 636.8 78-21668

ISBN 0-517-27338-1

Printed in Hong Kong

The Cat in Context

The Eocene period on Earth was one of violent change as active volcanoes moulded rock into new mountain ranges, and immense ravines filled with water, forming seas, including the Atlantic and Indian Oceans. Although glaciers were evident on the highest peaks of the North American land mass, much of the Earth was experiencing tropical conditions, with a hot, damp climate encouraging the growth of lush, fronded palms and flowering deciduous shrubs. This period began 70 million years ago and lasted for more than 30 million years in all. It was about two-thirds of the way through the Eocene that *Miacis*, ancestor of the domestic cat, first made its appearance. *Miacis* was a tenacious little mammal, short of leg and with a long, slender body, rather like a weasel in looks and in character. It was a carnivorous creature, and a perfect product of evolution for its era. This small creature was destined to become the ancestor of several groups of mammals known today, including the bear, the dog, the hyena, the mongoose, the raccoon, the civet and all the members of the cat family.

After the Eocene the Oligocene began, and lasted 15 million years, during which time great tracts of land were formed, mountain ranges, including the Alps, rose up and pleasantly warm conditions prevailed on Earth.

In some regions the weather patterns fell into a yearly cycle with hot summers and cooler winters, and this led to the dwindling of some of the dense forests, allowing development of pampas grasslands. This, in turn, led to the evolution of more species of herbivore, some resembling the deer of today and some like small elephants, with short trunks for pulling down high foliage. For the first time a primitive tail-less ape appeared, living safely in the high branches of the huge forest trees. The carnivorous creatures preyed upon the herbivores and, in evolutionary terms, rapidly developed new characteristics which enabled them to adapt to each and every change in conditions.

At this time two distinct groups descended from *Miacis*. One was *Hoplophoneus*, a group of powerful animals with unusually developed skull structures. The powerful lower jaw was hinged in such a way that it could open almost at right angles to the upper jaw, and the canine teeth were very long and sharp. A relative of *Hoplophoneus* was *Smilodon*, the legendary sabre-toothed tiger. This great beast was not directly related to the tiger of today, but was as large as a lion and was a very powerful cat. Its six inch long canine teeth were set in immense jaws which enabled it to seize, stab and kill the largest of the lumbering planteaters that grazed the vast plains. The second group was *Dinictis*, and it was from this group that the true cat-like animals evolved.

During the Miocene the climate became more varied. Some regions were dry and arid, while others became wet and cool. This affected the evolutionary paths of many animals and plants as they adapted gradually in step with the slowly changing conditions. More powerful earth movements occurred, forcing the Asian, African and European land masses together and virtually locking in the Mediterranean Sea. Many areas of land were isolated as island groups, while other land masses were linked by land bridges. On the islands flora and fauna diversified as they evolved, while linked continental masses enabled migration of many species and dispersal over great areas. It was in this most formative age, which lasted for 14 million years, that some of the early apes descended from their arboreal homes and became partly ground-dwelling. *Dinictis* subdivided considerably and some 95 species appeared, all directly related to present-day cats, 40 of which still exist in similar, recognizable forms.

Some of the species of *Dinictis* bore a striking resemblance to the civet family of the present time, but had more pointed noses and shorter tails.

Lynx.

marine
carnivores

raccoons

bears

dogs

weasels

civets

hyenas

cats

miacis

The family tree of the
cat family, showing how
the family has descended
from one common
ancestor – MIACIS.

Left A reconstruction of Smilodon, the sabre-toothed tiger, showing the well-developed upper canine teeth after which scientists named this long extinct member of the cat family.

The skull and jaws of a typical cat *left* compared to the sabre-tooth *right*.

Other members of the civet tribe, such as the mongoose and the genet, have skeletal structures very similar to some fossil remains of *Dinictis*, and a comparison of the bones is quite fascinating. The most successful sub-division of the group, however, was that of an animal rather like a stream-lined lynx, long in the leg and with a small head and forward-facing eyes. This creature had newly evolved retractile claws, and this adaptation improved its hunting ability and so ensured its survival. With the claws sheathed, the animal could run swiftly and quietly over the hard ground, and also spring high and wide in attacking its prey. With the claws extended, each paw became a deadly weapon equipped for grasping, holding and tearing the victim. The extended claws were also useful for climbing the densely growing forest trees to escape from larger predators, or to reach a vantage post for waiting in ambush for passing prey. The development of this character was effective in extending the range of *Dinictis* to include both forest and plain.

In the Pliocene, which began 11 million years ago and lasted for 10 million years, great changes took place. Violent storms raged, sifting and sorting the soil, eroding mountain tops and filling valleys. Then, at last, the climate settled down and became very similar to that of the present time, but with a broader temperate zone. Most of the giant land and sea creatures died out, but mammals continued to thrive. Although the number of species dwindled considerably, those that survived continued to develop well and some of the large apes began to walk upright upon the Earth.

All the catlike mammals went quietly and efficiently about their business, making the most of other creatures' misfortunes – all, that is, except for the highly specialized *Smilodon*. With the gradual extinction of the giant herbivores, he also met his demise. His clumsy bulk and strange skull formation could not adapt sufficiently quickly to enable him to catch the smaller, swifter prey, and so the sabre-toothed tiger, after millions of successful years on Earth, also became extinct.

After the Pliocene, a mere million years ago, the Pleistocene age began. It was the era of the great Ice Ages, which ensured that only the fittest and most adaptable forms of life survived on this planet. In those testing centuries the great lakes and fjords of the world were formed and land masses successively sank and rose again as ice sheets froze, then melted over the eons of time. Many mammals finally emerged as we know them today, including some 40 species of the cat family, highly tuned for survival under these most rigorous and changeable conditions. The upright apes developed greater brains and started to fashion stone implements to use as weapons and tools for killing and skinning other animals.

Ten thousand years ago the Holocene period began and climatic conditions improved on Earth as the last of the ice retreated to the Poles. The sea levels rose and great tracts of tundra were replaced by fertile zones, while forests of hardwood trees sprang up. Man emerged at last from his apelike foundations and began to cultivate plants for food. He domesticated useful animals, drew symbols on the walls of his cave dwellings and discovered fire. None of the cave paintings found to date depict any animal vaguely resembling our domestic cats, so it is safe to assume that they were not hunted for food at this time.

It is pleasant to imagine the first timorous tabby slinking ever nearer to the warmth and comfort of the early caveman's cooking fires, and foraging for food scraps. What was it about those early cats that prevented them from being clubbed, skinned and eaten, like most other animals? Perhaps when early man became a successful farmer and learned to store his grain, the cat frequented the stores and lived off marauding rodents. This is the most likely story of the cat's domestication; it would have been encouraged, even if it could not, at that time, be tamed. The veil of mystery persists, however, from the extinction of *Smilodon* until the authenticated emergence of the cat as protector of the granaries and deity in the Egypt of five thousand years ago.

An Ancient Egyptian tomb-painting showing a family hunting-party in the Nile marshes. The cat, which has caught three of the water-fowl, is an ancestor of the Mau.

Right These cats have been deliberately bred in Britain since 1964 to resemble the cats of Ancient Egypt. What began as an exercise in genetics has now produced a charming, intelligent breed of cat.

It is not known for certain just when the cat was first sanctified in Ancient Egypt, and it was never officially considered to be a sacred animal. The art of the period, however, establishes the fact that the cat, like many other animals, was treated with the utmost care and respect and was worshipped as a god by the Egyptian people.

Cats were kept in the house to guard against rats and mice invading the precious food stores, and also to protect the family from poisonous snakes. Cats also patrolled the cities' granaries, as well as being used for hunting game. A beautiful fresco now housed in the British Museum, London, is of interest to all cat lovers. It shows an Ancient Egyptian family enjoying a day out in their light papyrus boat. Nebamen steers the boat into the reeds, putting up flocks of waterfowl which are immediately seized by the family's hunting cat, while his wife Hatshepsut and their daughter gather lotus blossoms from the water's edge. The cat, a strikingly marked tabby, is shown with one large bird gripped in its jaws and two others held tightly in its claws.

Most of the frescoes and tomb paintings of the time show tabby or spotted cats, often reddish brown in colour and with long, elegant bone structure.

From mummified remains of the period, two main species of cat have been identified, *Felis chaus*, the Jungle Cat, probably used mainly for hunting and in the granaries, and *Felis lybica*, the African Wild Cat, known today as the Egyptian or Kaffir Cat.

A cult developed in Egypt which was to last for more than two thousand years in which the cat, in all its forms, wild or tame, was treated with love and reverence by people from all walks of life. Very strict laws were instituted to protect all cats, and the penalty for killing one was death. One day a Roman soldier who accidentally killed a cat narrowly escaped being lynched in retribution by an angry crowd, who had witnessed the incident. The affair reached diplomatic levels and is thought to have been one of the provocative acts which led to wars between Egypt and Rome.

The Egyptians' regard for the welfare of cats was used against them by Cambyses, son of Cyrus the Great of Persia. When he marched on the port of Peluse, guarded by a garrison of Egyptian soldiers, he made his troops carry live cats in their front line as they attacked the city walls. Rather than risk killing any of the sacred animals, the Egyptians surrendered, and Cambyses won a bloodless victory.

Although the cat was originally associated with Isis, wife of Osiris, Lord of the Underworld, gradually a new cat goddess emerged. This was Bast or Bastet, the Lady of Life, sister of the lion-headed goddess Sekhemet. Bast was also known as Pasht, and it is likely that our word 'puss' comes from this name. The great goddess is usually depicted as a tall, slender woman with a cat's head, and carries her three emblems, a musical sistrum and an aegis or shield, held across her chest, and a basket in the crook of her left elbow. Quite often the basket contains one or more kittens, or there are kittens at her feet. In the museum in Cairo an inspiring portrayal of Bast may be seen, drawn on a papyrus dated to the twenty-first dynasty. At that time she took precedence over all other gods and goddesses, and a vast temple was built in her glory at Bubastis, east of the Nile delta. Herodotus the Greek historian gave a long account of this goddess and her temple. He wrote: 'Here is a temple of Bubastis deserving of mention; other temples are larger and more magnificent but none more beautiful than this. . . .' It was a splendid construction standing lower than the foundations of the encircling buildings, and was built of red granite blocks to form an enormous square. On either side canals, one hundred feet wide, were fed by the waters of the Nile and in the centre a grove of tall trees protected by a stone wall surrounded the shrine of the goddess. The interior walls were all richly decorated in relief with various scenes and inscriptions. One of these, inside the shrine, shows King Osorkon the Second presenting gifts to the cat goddess. The inscription says: 'To thee I give every

Bast, the Lady of Life, and an important member of the Ancient Egyptian's pantheon of deities. In this model the goddess, part woman part cat, holds a sistrum in her right hand, perhaps using its music to summon her followers to the cult centre at Bubastis.

land in Obeisance. To thee I give all power like Ra' – direct evidence of the cat's importance.

Bast represented the sacred eye of the God of Light, Horus, and was worshipped as both a solar and a lunar goddess. Feasts and holidays were held regularly in her honour, and her sacred statue was brought from its shrine on such occasions, so that her spirit could join in the revelry. There was an annual festival at Bubastis at which the statue was carried forth with great pomp and ceremony and then transported by barge along the Nile. Herodotus wrote of the long pilgrimage made by thousands of men and women each year, who would leave their homes in April or May, setting sail on the great river in order to take part in the festivities. The long voyage to Bubastis gave the excuse for much merrymaking and drinking. As each town was reached, the pilgrims would tie up to the bank and entertain the local people in singing and dancing. The following day they would set sail again, playing flutes and cymbals, called crotala. On arrival in Bubastis many victims were sacrificed to the goddess, and there was feasting for several days.

The Ancient Egyptians' cat as they depicted it *far right* and the appearance of today's Oriental Spotted Tabby or Egyptian Mau *right*.

Below One of the many thousands of mummified cats discovered by archeologists in Egypt. Dating from the time of the Ancient Egyptians, they are a vivid demonstration of the veneration in which the cat was held.

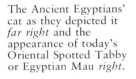

While all cats were venerated during the reign of the great cat goddess, house pets were given the very best of care and attention that their owners could afford. Sick cats were tended with the care usually only afforded to ailing children, and no expense was spared in trying to obtain medicines and potions to effect a cure. Pet cats were adorned with jewelled collars, and pendants were hung about their necks with silver, bronze or golden chains. Sometimes the ears of the cat would be pierced to take gold ear-rings or jewelled studs. Hunting cats were given the best of food and comfortable beds. Even stray, wild cats were treated with respect and the finest food was left out for them.

When a cat died of illness or old age, the whole family went into a period full of mourning and shaved off their eyebrows as a mark of respect for the dead animal. They would wail, chant and pound their chests to show their grief, then beat death gongs. The master of the house would then wrap the cat's body carefully in a linen sheet and carry it, with lamentations, to the sanctified house of an embalmer. The cat's body would be treated according to the finance available, but even poor people would pay as much as, or more than, they could afford to ensure that their cat was treated in the accepted manner.

The body of the cat was rubbed with many precious aromatic oils, then wrapped in layers of fine linen cloth. The cats of poor people were treated with as much respect as those belonging to the wealthy, and in all cases particular attention was given to the support and wrapping of the ears in a natural, upright position. After the wrapping the body would be put in some sort of case or outer binding. The most simple would be a binding of plain, narrow strips of cloth. A little more elaborate binding was possible by dying the cloth in two rich colours, and alternating them to form an intricate pattern around the body. Other fairly simple cases were made from coloured straw. Wealthy owners would have wonderful mummy cases carved for their dead cats. Wood of all types would be used and shaped carefully before being inlaid with gold and jewels. Often, tiny carved cats and kittens would be used to adorn the lid of the casket. Some cat coffins were box-shaped, some cat-shaped. Some were formed of a type of pâpier-mache, resembling the cat's body, with great attention paid to the modelling of the head and ears, the eyes being indicated by meticulously painted circles of linen cloth.

After the embalming and encapsulating of the small body was completed, the bereaved family would take it, accompanied by an entourage of wailing mourners, to a special cat cemetery for a ritual burial. There were many such cemeteries along the banks of the Nile and an enormous one at Bubastis. Cats' remains were sent from all over Egypt to be placed there.

At the turn of this century a cat cemetery was excavated at Beni Hassan in central Egypt and was found to contain more than 300,000 mummified

The sacred cat cuts off the head of the serpent of the night. One of the many Ancient Egyptian myths in which the cat played a prominent part. The serpent could also represent the darkness of death and this papyrus painting may show one of the very many ways which, over the centuries, man has tried to come to terms with his own mortality.

cats. Many of the bodies were dug out by mechanical diggers and dumped into the holds of waiting ships, then taken to England, where they were to be used on agricultural land as fertilizer. Luckily the importance of the discovery was realized just in time for a few specimens to be saved for study and research. It is largely due to these intact remains that we have our present knowledge of the methods of mummification of the Ancient Egyptian cats.

It is interesting to note that the Ancient Egyptian word for cat is *mau*, which means 'to see'. Bast was presented with an amulet of the sacred eye, known as the *utchat*, meaning 'possessed of mental and physical health'. The utchat represents the solar eye of the god Horus, the source of all human health and happiness.

The Egyptians made cat amulets in all shapes and sizes and of every conceivable material. They were made as decorations for the home, to place in shrines and to wear as personal adornments. Many cat amulets have the utchat engraved upon them; sometimes the utchat itself is a large eye with tiny cats filling the spaces between the outer eye and the central pupil. Large cat figures in bronze and other metals often have the utchat engraved as a pendant around the cat's neck. The cat and the utchat were both considered to have

remarkable powers, and when found in conjunction formed a powerful talisman against sickness and evil. Cat amulets were thought to have greater power if engraved with the name of Bast, and were often set to guard the dead. A special amulet was popular in Ancient Egypt among newly wed couples. This was the charm depicting a cat family. The couple would decide upon the number of children they hoped to have, then search for an amulet showing a mother cat with the same number of kittens.

Cat family amulets were made of faience with blue or green glaze. The mother cat was usually made in a reclining position with her kittens all around her, suckling, playing with her paws or climbing over her back or head. A cat might have shy kittens peeping out from between her legs, or sometimes the cat would sit up with her litter at attention by her feet. These amulets were designed to be worn as pendants. Other cat family amulets in bronze were much larger, and were placed on shelves or hung on the wall of the house or temple.

The cult of the cat lasted for centuries in Egypt, and the sacred animal was jealously guarded by its masters. But although the export of cats was strictly forbidden, gradually cats were taken by travelling monks and Phoenician traders west towards Europe and east to the Orient.

During the days of the cat's worship in Egypt, cats of very similar type are known to have existed in China and India, in a semi-wild state. Cats were smuggled out of Egypt by returning Roman armies, and soon became established as vermin controllers, taking over from the small non-venomous snakes and weasels that had been previously used. Cats were probably kept as house pets in Italy too, although there is little in the art of the time to substantiate this. A beautiful mosaic dated at about 100 B.C. was excavated at Pompeii. It shows a large, strikingly marked tabby cat seizing a bird in its mouth, but there is nothing to indicate whether this was a pet cat or a wild creature with its natural prey. Pompeii was destroyed in A.D. 79, and it was about this time that the history of language was undergoing changes along with the paths taken by the intrepid Roman armies.

Our word *cat* most probably came from the Nubian word *kadīs*, for in the early centuries A.D. a similar word travelled through the Baltic, Slavic, Mediterranean and Atlantic countries, along the trade routes over which the increasingly popular cat was carried. The cat is called similar names in these countries, most of which have only minor differences in spelling or pronunciation.

Holland and Denmark	kat
Sweden	katt
Germany	katze
Poland	kot
Russia	kots
Portugal and Spain	gato
Italy	gatto

Also: catt, chat, cath, catus, cattus, cait, katte, katti, kottr, kazza, kattos, kate and kotu.

Pliny, writing in the first century A.D., made several observations on cats in general, and they refer to the cat as we know it today and certainly not to any similar, related species such as weasels, mongooses or civet cats. There is little in Greek art to suggest that much store was set by the domestic cat, although it is known that cats took over from weasels in controlling vermin in the grain stores. One Ancient Greek vase shows a cat being led by a slave. Other art of the time shows dogs being kept as pets, and other small animals such as cicadas were kept in tiny, specially made cages, so it would seem that cats were merely tolerated for their usefulness. The Romans, however, valued their cats, having been greatly impressed by the veneration of the animals in Egypt. The Egyptian cults made a great impact on the Romans generally, and so it was perhaps inevitable that cats worshipped in Egypt would be kept as pampered pets in Rome.

At first only wealthy households kept cats, but, owing to the animal's prolific nature, it would only have taken a few years for cats to multiply to such an extent that there were sufficient kittens to pass on to the common people.

Wherever the Roman armies marched, they took their animals, including cats. Some were left behind in certain regions and possibly intermated with local wild cats. Some kittens were captured

and tamed and taken on to replace those lost on the route. The cat was important to the Romans, and this fact is indicated by some of the towns they named after them. The old stronghold of Cat Vicense in Holland is now called Kattewyk, or Cat's Town. Caithness in Scotland is the County of the Cats. It is possible that the Romans also brought their cats through Europe and into Britain, but the first cats known to have been introduced to the British Isles were brought by Phoenician traders, in exchange for tin from the Cornish mines.

Cats seemed to prosper and thrive wherever they found a comfortable niche in which to establish themselves. They also had the knack of endearing themselves to people as well as proving their worth as working animals. Humans were quick to appreciate the value of the cat and to respect the animal's complete independence.

In the year 936 Howell the Good, a king of Wales, drew up laws to protect the cat. The worth of a kitten from its birth until it had opened its eyes was put at one legal penny, from the time it opened its eyes until it was capable of killing mice it was worth two pence, and when it had reached hunting age it was worth four pence. The *tiethi* or qualities of a cat were to see, hear and kill mice, to have sharp claws and to rear kittens without devouring them. If anyone bought a cat and found it to be deficient in any one of these qualities, he was entitled, under Howell's law, to have one third of the purchase price returned. The law also covered the stealing and killing of cats. The worth of such an animal was determined by holding it by the tail tip so that the head just touched a clean and even floor, then threshed wheat was poured over

Right A striking Roman mosaic dating from *c* 100 B.C. showing a cat catching a bird which looks remarkably like a farmyard hen.

Left 'The Cat's Dream', a charming Chinese print showing what all cat-owners, at one time or another, must have believed their pets to be dreaming about!

Right The cat merchants beside the quay of a busy Chinese harbour. This scene was drawn in the eighteenth-century by an early European visitor to China, who may not have realized the fate that awaited the cats.

the cat until the tip of the tail was covered, and the corn was said to be equal to the animal's value. If grain was not available, a milch ewe, her fleece and her lamb was said to be equal to the value of the cat.

In Japan, in A.D. 999, a breeding programme for domestic cats was drawn up, the first record of such a plan. It was instituted after a cat gave birth to five kittens in the Imperial Palace of Kyoto, Japan. Apparently the Emperor found the kittens so entrancing when they were born on the tenth day of the fifth moon that he ordered special care and feeding arrangements for the family, and instructed that they must be protected from all outside interference so that similar kittens could be bred in the future. Cats were very valuable at that time in Japan, as they were used for killing the plagues of mice that attacked the silkworm cocoons. Very soon others followed the Emperor's plan and tethered their cats on silken leads, feeding them on delicacies and treating them royally. The silk industry, deprived of its protective cats, soon reached the point of collapse as the workrooms and breeding rooms became overrun with mice. The granaries and food stores of the cities were also alive with vermin, and the economy was at a critical level when at last the government took action. It decreed that all cats must be set free and that a fine would be imposed on anyone who bought or sold cats. Eventually the cats brought matters back under control, and once more proved their worth in killing rodents.

As the cities of the world grew and people began to live closer together in cramped conditions, so the rat population also increased. Wherever humans went, the rats followed, their paths keeping track of the routes of invasion, explor-

ation and commerce. The rat not only devastated food stores, it also carried disease, including the terrible Black Death that ravaged Europe and Asia in the fourteenth century. In 1660 the black rat, living and breeding in the sewers of London, was responsible for the outbreak of bubonic plague in the city which killed half the inhabitants. Man's only ally against this menace was the cat, which rose in esteem and value. The church, however, outlawed the cat at this time owing to its connection with pagan rites and rituals, so, for the next few generations, the animal was encouraged on the one hand as protector and friend, and persecuted on the other as a devil.

The Crusaders, returning from the Holy Wars, brought with them plague and pestilence, but they also carried home strange, long-coated cats of various colours. How these cats developed in the first instance is a matter for conjecture, because the long coat is the result of a recessive mutant gene. When a cat with long hair is mated to one with short hair, only shorthaired kittens are produced. The shorthaired offspring, mated together, however, will produce a proportion of longhaired kittens.

It is believed that the cats of Eastern temples, being carefully confined and breeding under very controlled conditions, possibly produced the first longhaired varieties. Starting with a mutant kitten, perhaps taken to the temple and treasured for its unusual appearance, plain-looking offspring would eventually have bred more longhaired kittens.

Zoologists hypothesized that the manul (*Felis manul*) or Pallas' Cat might be the ancestor of the longhaired breeds of today. This beautiful creature has long, fine hair patterned with spots on a

Above The cat is a good luck symbol in many countries, including China from where this advertising motif comes.

Right A cat trying its luck at catching goldfish in the village fountain, watched by three ducks who dare not go too close – just in case!

Far right The festival of the cats in Cairo.

greyish background. Its range extends from the Caspian Sea to Tibet, and north to Siberia, and it lives in mountainous areas of low temperature. The Caspian Sea forms part of the northern frontier of Iran, formerly called Persia. Today's longhaired cats, often called Persians, probably originated in this area.

It would be pleasant to build a legend around the longhaired cats, but there are strong reasons for discounting the hypothesis. The manul has different dentition from that of the domestic cat, and its ear size and placement are quite unlike that of any of the tame species of feline. Most important of all, though, is the difference found in the structure of the eye. All domestic cats have a pupil which, when closed down, forms a vertical slit. In the manul the pupil contracts to a disc.

Other longhaired cats from Persia had much thicker fur. When first seen in sixteenth-century Europe, they were described as being beautiful to behold, ash-coloured, dun and speckled. These cats had long silky fur, long heads and pointed ears, whereas the Persian had much thicker fur, broad heads and long bushy tails. The two types were apparently mated quite freely together, and the traits of the Angora were inclined to be overcome by those of the heavier Persian type.

It was perhaps the shipboard cats that accelerated the spread of cats throughout the world. The holds of all ships teemed with rats, and the only way to have any control at all over the pests was to install ships' cats. Even the courts recognized the worth of these cats in rat control and some maritime insurance companies would only

indemnify for rat damage if they were certain that cats were carried on board the ship. The absence of cats was held to be negligence on the part of the captain of the vessel, and the shipping company had to bear the loss.

Ships' cats were a law unto themselves. They came aboard and went ashore at will, although they were usually loyal to their own ship. Kittens were often born at sea, and, when independent, might well disembark to start a new life in a port far from the land of their conception. In this way new colours and shapes of cat were distributed around the world.

In the eighteenth century Europe suffered a serious threat. It was invaded quietly and methodically by the Brown Rat. Versatile and voracious, this disease-ridden creature swept in waves across the continent, even taking over from the indigenous Black Rat. Only the cat was capable of keeping this new enemy under control, and good hunting cats were in great demand everywhere. Cats were taken on in offices, shops, warehouses, ministerial buildings – anywhere that rats might be found. Every farm, bakery, food store and shop had its cats and took a pride in the prowess of its little hunters. The cat was thus confirmed as an acceptable part of the home and workshop in most countries of the world, and accepted on its own terms. Despite its independence the cat insinuated itself into the lives and hearts of many, eventually establishing itself firmly and irrevocably, first as a fireside pet, and later still as an object of acquisition as specific breeds developed and the first cat shows came into being.

The fishmongers of Mytilene, Greece, with the inevitable cat in attendance.

The Eye of the Cat

Cats have been associated with many super-stitions, religious ceremonies and magical rites since the earliest days of their domestication. It is a matter for conjecture why the cat above all other animals should have become so important in so many forms of worship, in various cultures from the days of the Pharaohs until the present day.

Perhaps it was the expressive eye of the cat, with its variable pupil, sometimes full and lustrous and sometimes narrowed to a tiny slit, that captured human imagination. The cat, like the snake, will stare, unblinking, into human eyes, and can produce a strange and almost hypnotic effect in some people. All through the ages strange beliefs have arisen concerning the eyes of the cat. The Chinese believe that the pupil size is determined by the position of the sun above the horizon, and so lift the eyelids of the animal in order to tell the time of day. Others believe that the state of the tides is reflected in the pupil size: a tiny vertical slit pupil indicates a flood tide, while a full pupil means that the tide is ebbing. A semi-precious stone known as 'cat's eye' is so called because it can change colour and lustre, like the eyes of the cat in dim light, and is often worn as a lucky charm.

There was a Celtic belief that cats were at one with the fairy world and that their eyes were the windows of the fairy rulers' palace. By looking deep into the cats' eyes, a strangely illuminated world could be seen, while the fairies could look out, keeping a close watch on the activities of the humans. This belief probably arose because of the uncomfortable feeling often experienced from the deep gaze of the cat, as if it is peering into the soul. Conversely, looking back into the calm eyes of a contented cat can have a therapeutic effect on anyone suffering from overwork, tiredness or stress.

The eyes of the cat have been used in many magic charms and potions, and the cat's repu-tation for second sight has caused it to suffer terrible tortures at the hands of those wishing to acquire the gift for themselves. Not only was the cat considered to provide a cure for blindness, but also those who were deranged or mentally blind were treated by strange rituals involving the use of cats' eyes. It was thought that the eyes of a black cat mixed with the gall of a human would form a charm giving second sight to its wearer. And to perceive devils the Jewish Talmud instructed that a placenta from the litter of a black cat should be burned to charcoal, beaten to a powder, then rubbed into the eyes. English children of long ago were encouraged to play with tortoiseshell cats in order to develop clairvoyant powers.

The Healer

Many superstitions arose concerning the healing powers of the cat. Even Pliny, historian of the Roman Empire, considered cats' faeces to be medically efficacious. Mixed with mustard the dung was said to cure ulcers of the head, while added to resin and oil of roses it cured uterine ulcers. To draw out thorns, it was mixed to a thick paste with a little wine. Centuries later, in his

Left The UTCHAT or sacred eye associated with the Ancient Egyptian goddess, Bast.

Right Another artist's view of a fishmonger. The time and place are different: Flanders in the eighteenth century, not Greece in the twentieth, but the cat is there, ever hopeful, and in this picture looking very healthy and well-fed.

Left To introduce a more homely note into his *Annunciation*, Lorenzo Lotto added a cat. He depicted its fear of the angelic messenger so clearly that he obviously knew and understood cats well.

Historie of Foure-Footed Beastes and Serpentes, Edmund Topsell recorded that the dried powdered liver of a cat was a good cure for bladderstones in humans, while fat rendered from the cat cured gout. For curing blindness he gave a full description of how to take the head of a black cat, burn it to a powder and apply to the affected eyes with a quill.

The cat's tail is the part of its anatomy most commonly used for healing purposes, and even today, in many country districts of England, it is believed that a stye in the eye will be cured if rubbed with the tail of a black cat. In Northamptonshire the stye is stroked nine times with a single hair plucked from the tail of a black tomcat.

Many old diseases caused acute itching which was apparently so unbearable that drastic measures were necessary. A black cat was whirled by a left-handed man, three times around his head, then three drops of blood were let from its tail, to be mixed with the ashes of nine baked barleycorns. This potion was applied to the affected area with a gold wedding ring, while the Trinity was invoked, and, hopefully, the irritation ceased.

Whitlows were cured by winding the tail of a black cat in an intricate pattern through the fingers of the affected hand, on each of three successive days. Three drops of blood from a cat's tail provided a cure for the falling sickness or epilepsy, and in Mark Twain's *Tom Sawyer*, Huckleberry Finn explained how a cat was used to cure warts. The cat had to be taken to a graveyard in the middle of the night when '. . . Devil follow corpse, cat follow Devil, wart follow cat, that will fetch any wart.'

Burying the tail of a black cat under the doorstep of the home was thought to protect the

entire family from any kind of sickness. The Celts believed that the tail of the cat was very potent, and should anyone tread on one, a serpent would rise up and strike him dead.

Cats' fur was used extensively for treating burns suffered by Londoners in the Great Fire of 1666. Dead cats were skinned and the soft fur placed next to the badly burned areas. By insulating the wound against the air, the pain was somewhat relieved. In Holland and elsewhere skins of freshly killed cats were used to treat sore throats and severe skin infections. In Japan the fur of a live black cat placed across the stomach was said to cure severe gastric disturbances and also epilepsy.

The Corn Cat and the Rainmaker

An association between the cat and the cornfield has lingered through the ages and still exists in some parts of the world. Freya, the Nordic goddess of love and fertility, rode in a chariot drawn by grey cats. Farmers would leave out offerings of fresh milk for her cats, hoping to ensure good crops and protection from bad weather. William Morris portrayed Freya as:

'Freya, thin robed, about her ankles slim
The grey cats playing.'

Remnants of old beliefs passed down the generations, and children of rural areas were warned against trampling the growing corn for fear that the 'corn cat' would get them. Cats were garlanded with flowers, ribbons and ears of corn at the start of the harvest in Briançon, France, and were the centre of celebrations until the crop was safely gathered in, when the decorations were ritualistically removed. Any reaper cutting himself with the scythe during the harvesting would have the wound licked clean by the cat.

In other parts of France the final sheaf to be cut and tied was called the 'cat's tail', and in Silesia the man who cut it was given a tail of stalks to wear, and called Tom Cat. A second reaper was chosen as She Cat, and together the two would chase the other harvesters, beating them ritualistically.

The corn crop in some mountain regions of

Below Indian children from Otavalo, Ecuador, playing cat's-cradles, a game found among many races and in widely scattered parts of the world. It is so ancient that its origins are lost in the mists of time.

Europe was known as 'the cat', and was described as being fat or lean according to the quality of the grain. The reaper who cut the last sheaf was called 'the catcher of the corn cat' and presented with a small, decorated fir tree.

Sacrificing a cat was thought to bring a good harvest the following year. The cat was bound within the last sheaf, then ceremoniously beaten to death with the flails used to thresh the corn from the husks. Originally the ceremony ended with the cooking and eating of the cat's body, but this later gave way to the burial of the cat in the cornfield. Later still the rite of 'killing the corn cat' consisted of merely beating the last sheaf with the flails, then carrying it in procession to the traditional harvest home supper, which was known as 'the cat'.

The Chinese *Book of Rites* tells of the worship of the cat god Li Shou, to whom sacrifices were

made after a successful harvest. In Malaya cats were used in rainmaking rituals to ensure good crops. The cat was immersed in a large earthenware pan filled with water and repeatedly doused until it was almost drowned, while the onlookers prayed and played musical instruments.

In Java a similar ritual existed in which the cats were repeatedly dipped in pools, and in the Celebes the cat, tied securely in a sedan chair, was carried three times around a parched field before being doused with water to bring the rain. Sumatran ceremonies required a black cat so that the sky would darken with rain-clouds. The cat was carried into the river, then released to swim ashore, being chased and splashed before making its escape.

Cat's-Cradles

An ancient game known as 'cat's-cradle' is known all over the world. String or cord is wound in intricate patterns around the fingers and passed between two people. Tribesmen of the Congo used the string figures and designs to cause the sun to rest and cease its blinding glare, while the Eskimos tried to snare the solar cat within the strings to hold back the sun from setting in its long winter rest. In New Guinea the game was played by adults and children, then the strings were undone and used to tie up the stalks of the yam crop, the staple diet of the area. It was believed that the magic of the strings would encourage the yam leaves to spread and intertwine, producing more fruit.

Nautical Cats

In the old days bad weather and strange pheno-mena at sea were thought to be due to witchcraft, and the responsiveness of cats to changes in the atmosphere gave rise to many superstitions. Seamen are notoriously superstitious, so it is not surprising that so many nautical terms have feline connotations. A small boat with a single mast is called a 'cat-boat' and its rigging the 'cat-rig'. The anchor beam is called a 'cathead', while securing the anchor to this is known as 'catting the anchor'. A 'cat-hairpin' is an iron piece which clamps the rope into place. A light breeze at sea is a 'cat's-paw', and when the wind is changeable, it is watched carefully 'to see how the cat jumps'. A narrow bridge or planking walkway on board ship is called the 'cat-walk'. In the bad old days punishments at sea would be meted out by whippings performed with a lash of nine knotted leather thongs. This was the legendary 'cat-o'-nine-tails', which was wetted and applied with practised force to the offender's back, quickly

Left and right Children and cats make an appealing subject for the artist, almost as irresistible as skeins of wool for cats and kittens. Eighteenth-century cats were, in many ways, little different from todays'.

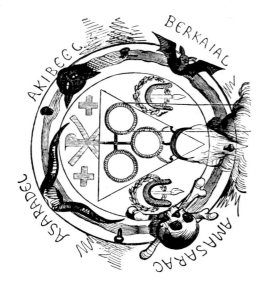

Fairly or not, cats have played a prominent part in the rituals of black magic and witchcraft, *top*. Probably it is due to their aloofness and habit of disappearing, so that perhaps the cat and wolf *right* really were a witch and devil in other form.

opening the flesh right through to the bone.

Seamen were usually very kind to the ships' cats, believing them to be good luck charms as well as giving warning of bad weather. When a sailing vessel was becalmed, a ceremony for raising the wind was performed in which the cat was placed under an iron pot on deck. To throw a cat overboard, especially a black cat, was a certain way to invoke a violent storm.

Weather Cats

Even on shore cats were used to forecast the weather. In China cats were said to wink an eye to signify coming rain. Cats washing behind their ears also indicate rain, and if they sit with their backs to the hearth, a hard frost can be expected. In Scotland a cat scratching at a table leg presages high winds of gale force, while in other parts a cat scampering about wildly and mewing indicates a severe storm. Cats can certainly foretell the coming of a storm, for they become restless and nervous of sudden noises a few hours before the storm breaks.

A Slavic myth has us to believe that cats' bodies are inhabited by demons during thunderstorms and that the thunderclaps bring forth angels' prayers, while the cat devils mock them. Lightning is aimed by the angels at the cats to cast out the demons, so cats must be chased well away from the house in a storm to prevent a strike by lightning.

The Familiar

Witchcraft trials first took place in the thirteenth century in Europe and many involved cats as the witches' familiars. For some four hundred years thereafter, the unfortunate cat was persecuted and regarded as evil. Even normal behaviour of cats was regarded as the work of the Devil. One man, seeing a cat using its paw to lift a door latch, killed it immediately, believing it to be possessed, and a

woman was hanged, having been accused of witchcraft when a neighbour saw her cat jump through her window one evening.

Witches' cats are often depicted as being black, but it is more likely that they were tabby-patterned, and this is one reason why tabbies are so rarely seen in some rural areas. Black cats were always used in the terrible Taigheirm rituals, however, which were adapted from ancient pagan ceremonies. The cats were dedicated to the Devil, placed on a spit and slowly roasted to death. As each tormented creature ceased its howling and died, another was placed over the fire so that there was no break in the continuity of the ritual for four days and nights. The operator would then demand

his reward from the spirits, usually the gift of second sight. The location of the last recorded Taigheirm ritual is still marked on the Island of Mull, where it took place in the middle of the seventeenth century.

In the Taigheirm cats were sacrificed to the Devil, but there were many cases in which they were offered to God. On Corpus Christi, in Aix, Provence, the best male cat was caught and swaddled in linen, then placed in a beautifully appointed shrine for public worship. Incense was burned and prayers chanted; then, at the close of the day, the bound cat was put in a wicker basket and thrown alive into the heart of a bonfire in the city square. As its death cries rang out, the priests sang anthems and marched off in procession.

Most of the rites involving cats included some form of burning as a form of purification. In England, at the coronation of Elizabeth the First, a wickerwork effigy of the Pope was filled with live cats, carried ceremoniously through the streets and then burned. The screams of the dying cats were said to be the cries of the devils in the body of the Holy Father.

Witches were identified when they had wounds known to have been inflicted on cats. A typical case was that of a Scottish laird whose stock of wine was slowly diminishing. He hid in his cellar armed with a sword, and later found himself surrounded by menacing black cats. Wielding his sword he cleared the cellar of cats, seriously mutilating one in the process. The next day a villager long suspected of witchcraft was discovered to have a leg missing.

Right The Cat-Woman, or is it the Woman-Cat? Chagall captures the mystery of his subject in a way so apt that it is almost disturbing.

Left Cats on the tiles, an archetypal view of cats, brilliantly caught by the French artist Manet.

Basque farmers believed that witches appeared as black cats, and bewitched their cattle. One man waited in the byre, and at midnight cut an ear from one of the cats that entered the building. The next morning the ear of a woman, complete with ear-ring, was found in the straw on the floor of the cowshed where he had attacked the cat.

In confessions some witches told how they changed into cats. A French witch rubbed her body with black ointment and was then able to pass unobserved through the darkness as a black cat. A Scottish witch on trial in 1662 recited part of a spell which enabled her to change into a cat at will. The members of a coven were able to transform each other into cats. If one witch met another, she would call 'The Devil speed thee and go thou with me', whereupon the second witch would also assume the form of a cat.

In Baldwin's book of 1584, *Beware of the Cat*, it is stated that a witch could only take on feline form nine times. Nine is a mystical number, being composed of a trinity of trinities, and it is said that a cat has nine lives. To take even one of the cat's nine lives could have dire consequences, for it is held that the cat will haunt the taker of its life and work its vengeance on him.

Witches not only assumed feline form, but also kept cats as familiars. Some witches were said to possess an extra nipple on which they suckled their cats. The cat-familiars shared the witches' powers and took part in all magical rites. At her trial in 1579 one witch told the court how she fed her cat on her own blood mixed with milk. At another trial in Essex the witch confessed to allowing her cat to suck blood from her arms at night. Blood was usually provided for the cats by the witches pricking themselves on the arms or face and encouraging the cats to lick and suck the wounds.

Anne Baker.   Ioane Willimot.   Ellen Greene.

No picture of witches or demonology was complete without a cat. It made no difference whether the artist was an unknown seventeenth-century Englishman *above* or the great eighteenth-century Spanish painter Goya *right*.

Gatherings of witches, known as sabbats, were connected with phases of the moon and took place at crossroads, on high mountains or in deep caves. Presided over by the Devil, usually in the form of a black cat, the sabbats, at dead of night, were occasions at which many strange rites took place. Novices were initiated and given their familiars, and, often, sacrifices were made. Sometimes even the cat-familiars were sacrificed to make a Dead Man's Candle. The grease and fat was rendered from a black cat to make the body of the candle and the wick was twisted from the hair of a dead man. The candle was fixed in the hand of an executed murderer, severed at the wrist at the time of an eclipse of the moon. The light from this candle was said to have the power to totally paralyse anyone on whom it shone.

The Charm

Ordinary folk contrived many types of charms, talismans and amulets against witchcraft and cat-familiars. It was thought that the most powerful safeguard was to invoke the Holy Trinity. A rowan tree was considered to possess great power against witches too: a rowan branch was tied to a baby's crib to protect it through the night, and if a rowan branch was shaken at a witch's cat, it was said to cause it to disappear from sight.

Cats themselves became charms, the most famous and prolific being the Maneki Neko or Beckoning Cat of Japan. This delightful cat charm is modelled in a sitting position with one paw raised to the left ear. The cat has a benign, smiling face and kind eyes. Maneki Neko is a symbol of an ancient Japanese legend and brings good luck to its owner. The raised and beckoning paw brings wealth and prosperity.

Cats were sometimes used as charms in a ceremony known as the building sacrifice. It was

thought that the incorporation of the body of a cat within the walls of a new building would ensure its protection against vermin and, in some areas, also against witchcraft. In the demolition of some old buildings the bodies, often well preserved by smoke or chemicals, have been found singly, or arranged in small groups. In one building in Southwark the mummified body of a cat was excavated. It held a rat in its jaws and had another pinned beneath its forefeet. During alterations to the Tower of London, a cat's body thought to be at least two hundred years old was removed from a wall, and at Hay Hall a very well preserved cat with a small bird was discovered, dating to the fourteenth century. Several English museums, including those at Salisbury and Peterborough, have exhibits of this old, macabre rite.

Live cats are kept as charms in Chinese shops. They are kept safe with collars and chains, and the older and uglier they are, the more luck they bring their owners. In Europe black cats are thought to be lucky and white cats unlucky. In Scotland tortoiseshell cats bring health to the home. An old Buddhist belief states that all cats are bringers of luck and prosperity, and dark cats bring gold, while light cats bring silver. Whatever their colour, cats have made their peace and taken their place as permanent members of the family, and no matter how humble their beginnings, always retain a certain air of mystery.

In contrast, the cat is also a symbol of domesticity and homeliness, even though Percy *above* looks ever hopeful that a bird may land on the balcony. And in 'Homage to the Cat' *left* a twentieth-century artist depicts, in the current idiom, exactly the same theme as did the artists of the pictures on pages 22 and 23.

All species of cats today, from the majestic lion to the fireside pet, belong to the order Carnivora, which embraces all the flesh-eating mammals. The Carnivora have two sub-orders: the Arctoidea, which covers dogs, weasels, bears and raccoons, and the Aeluroidea, which covers hyenas, civets and the cats. The cat family or Felidae can be further broken down into three groups or genera, *Felis, Panthera* and *Acinonyx*. The first two are further divided into species. Sometimes the species themselves consist of a number of subspecies. An extreme example of this is the puma, with some 29 recorded subspecies. Animals are grouped by zoologists into species on their interbreeding abilities and on whether or not such interbreeding produces fertile offspring. For example, all the varieties and breeds of the domestic cat, *Felis catus*, may look different, but they will freely intermate and produce viable offspring, and therefore they all belong to the same species. Lions and tigers, on the other hand, rarely mate in the wild, although they have been encouraged to do so in captivity. The offspring of the cross is either sterile or only weakly fertile, and therefore the lion and tiger are classed as quite separate species.

Cats are sorted in groups or genera on basic structural criteria. The only member of the genus *Acinonyx* is the Cheetah. *Acinonyx* differs from all other cats in having non-retractile claws and an unusual skull structure. The Cheetah has a wide range and is found in both Africa and Asia.

The genus *Panthera* has six separate species: the Clouded Leopard, the Snow Leopard and the Tiger are found only in Asia, while the Leopard and the Lion inhabit both Africa and Asia. The Jaguar, however, is found only in the American continent. During the evolution of the cat family, a variation occurred in the hyoid bones of the head which connect the larynx to the skull. Instead of the usual tight bony structure, members of the *Panthera* have a strong, flexible ligament holding the voice-box in place. This enables the larynx to vibrate and gives rise to the distinctive roar of all the big cats. In the genus *Felis* all the bones of the skull are present and intact, and the larynx is firmly attached. *Felis* can emit howling cries and purrs, but cannot roar.

Cats of the genus *Felis* are found in 31 species, although there could of course be some rare species still undiscovered in the most remote regions of the world. Of these, only *Felis catus*, the domestic cat, is found in all of the continents, having been spread far and wide by the intervention of man.

Cats large and small are native to all parts of the

Left N. American racoon.
Below left N. American bear.
Below Cheetah.

world, with the exception of the continent of Australasia and some island groups. These areas obviously split away from the original vast land mass of Gondwanaland at a key time in the evolution of mammals, a point borne out by the variety of placental mammals, unique to Australia and New Zealand.

The cat family is well equipped for survival, and its members are perfect carnivores, completely adapted to their natural place in the order of things. Some species have become extinct or are threatened by extinction only because of the greed of man and not because of natural causes. Cats most at risk today are those with beautifully spotted coats which are still in demand to make garments for women. Until the female of the human species can be sufficiently educated to realize that the skin looks far better on the cat than it does on her, these cats are in danger of being lost forever. Other species are threatened as their natural habitat is destroyed and more tracts of land are taken for human use. Pesticides have also taken their toll of feline life by getting into the food chain, poisoning the systems of the animals and reducing or destroying their fertility. Even *Felis catus* is affected in this way, as many veterinary surgeons will confirm.

Above Borrowed skins always look just that.

Below Clouded leopard.

Left Jaguar (Leo onca).

Only three members of the cat family are confined solely to the continent of Africa. They are the African Golden Cat, the Black-footed Cat and the Serval.

African Golden Cat: *Felis (Profelis) aurata* (Temminck, 1827)

Characteristics: head and body 29 in, tail 12 in, weight 30–40 lb

Twice the size of the domestic cat and sturdily built with long legs, large paws, a small head and a long tail. Very variable in colour, it ranges through all shades of chestnut to silver-grey. The cheeks, chin, chest, belly and inside the legs are white. Some Golden Cats have brown or grey spots, some have spotting only on the belly and inside the legs. The ears have dark thumbprints and the tail has a dark central line dorsally.

Habitat: high deciduous forest.
Habits: nocturnal or crepuscular. Terrestrial.
Prey: rodents, small ungulates, game birds.

Distribution: W and Central Africa.
Felis aurata aurata Congo to Uganda.
Felis aurata celidogaster W Africa

Black-footed Cat: *Felis nigripes* (Burchell, 1822)

Characteristics: head and body 14–18 in, tail 6–7 in, weight 4 lb

The smallest of all African cats, possibly the smallest wild cat in the world, the Black-footed Cat is a sandy, ochre colour, slightly darker on the back, and lighter under the belly. Dark brown or black spots are streaked on the cheeks, throat, chest and belly, and there are transverse bars of dark colour on the forelegs and haunches. The backs of the rounded ears are dark brown and the feet have black soles.

Habitat: dry sandy plains to grassy savannahs.
Habits: mainly nocturnal, also hunts at dawn and twilight. Terrestrial.
Prey: ground squirrels, small rodents, birds and reptiles.

Distribution: S Africa (Kalahari region).
Felis nigripes nigripes S and SW Africa
Felis nigripes thomasi E Cape Province

Serval: *Felis (Leptailurus) serval* (Schreber, 1776)

Characteristics: head and body 32 in, tail 16 in, weight 35 lb

Lightly built, with very long legs and very large oval ears. The coat is a pale buff or reddish yellow, with black markings giving a speckled appearance. The tail is spotted with a black tip and the backs of the ears are black with distinctive white spots.

Habitat: always near water and with dense cover such as reed-beds, scrub or high grass.
Habits: nocturnal, but will also hunt in the daytime if hungry. Terrestrial.
Prey: rats, lizards, small game birds, small ungulates.

Distribution: Algeria, Africa S of Sahara.
Felis serval serval Cape Province
Felis serval beirae Mozambique
Felis serval brachyura Sierra Leone to Ethiopia
Felis serval constantina Algeria
Felis serval hamiltoni E Transvaal
Felis serval hindeio Tanzania
Felis serval ingridi S Rhodesia; Botswana; SW Africa
Felis serval kempi Uganda
Felis serval kivuensis Congo; Angola
Felis serval liposticta N Angola
Felis serval lonnbergi SW Angola
Felis serval mababiensis N Botswana
Felis serval robertsi W Transvaal
Felis serval togoensis Dahomey; Togo

African lynx.

Four other species of *Felis* found in Africa are also found in Asiatic countries. These are the African Wild Cat, the Caracal Lynx, the Jungle Cat and the Sand Cat. Two of the *Panthera*, the Leopard and the Lion, as well as the *Acinonyx*, are also found in both Asia and Africa.

Right Serval.
Below African wild cat.
Bottom Black-footed cats.

African Wild Cat: *Felis lybica* (Forster, 1780)

Characteristics: head and body 14 in, tail 12 in, weight 10–18 lb

Slightly larger than the domestic cat and more sturdily built, the African Wild Cat is yellowish to grey-brown in colour and may have a pattern of tabby markings, pale or well-defined, depending on the sub-species. Cats with dark markings are found in forest areas, paler specimens in the desert regions.

Habitat: all types of country, high or low, open or wooded.
Habits: mainly nocturnal. Hunts mainly on the ground but a good climber.
Prey: small mammals, lizards, insects, birds.

Distribution: Africa; W Eurasia.
Felis libyca libyca Morocco to Egypt
Felis libyca brockmani Somalia
Felis libyca cafra Rep. South Africa
Felis libyca caudata Turkey to Iran; Afghanistan
Felis libyca foxi Guinea to Cameroon
Felis libyca griselda North Botswana; SW Africa
Felis libyca iraki Arabia; Iraq
Felis libyca issikulensis E Russia; Turkestan
Felis libyca kozlovi E Tianshan Mountains
Felis libyca matschiei Transcaspia
Felis libyca mellandi Malawi; E Zambia

Caracal Lynx: *Felis (Caracal) caracal* (Schreber, 1776)

Characteristics: head and body 28 in, tail 9 in, weight 37 lb

Slender animal with long dainty legs and a short, sharply tapered tail. Uniformly reddish brown in colour, the Caracal has a strong, lynx-like head with narrow pointed and tufted ears. There are white markings round the eyes and on the throat, chin and belly.

Habitat: desert, savannah, scrub, stony ground, mountain ranges.
Habits: mainly nocturnal, terrestrial, but a good climber and jumper.
Prey: small and large birds, rodents, small ungulates, fawns of larger ungulates.

Distribution: Africa and Asia.
Felis caracal caracal Sudan to Cape Province
Felis caracal algira N Africa
Felis caracal damarensis Damaraland
Felis caracal limpopoensis N Transvaal; Botswana
Felis caracal lucani Gabon
Felis caracal michaelis Turkmenia
Felis caracal nubicus Sudan; Ethiopia
Felis caracal poecilictis Niger; Nigeria
Felis caracal schmitzi Central India to Arabia

Jungle Cat: *Felis chaus* (Güldenstaedt, 1776)

Characteristics: head and body 24–30 in, tail 9–12 in, weight 16–30 lb

A powerful cat with true cat characteristics. The coat is sandy-grey to tawny-red, and the tabby markings of kittenhood fade in the adult, leaving faint bands on the limbs and a dorsal stripe on the tail. Both tail and ears have black tips.

Habitat: woodlands, reed-beds, cornfields and near human habitation.
Habits: hunts by night and day. Terrestrial.
Prey: hares, birds, porcupines, frogs and snakes.

Distribution: N Africa and Asia.
Felis chaus chaus Turkestan to Iran
Felis chaus affinis Kashmir to Sikkim
Felis chaus fulvidina Indochina; Thailand; Burma
Felis chaus furax S Syria; Iraq
Felis chaus kelaarti Ceylon; S India
Felis chaus kutas Bengal
Felis chaus nilotica Egypt
Felis chaus oxian Russia
Felis chaus prateri Sind; W India

Sand Cat: *Felis margarita* (Loche, 1858)

Characteristics: head and body 20 in, tail 12 in, weight 5–6 lb

A small cat with short limbs and a broad head adorned with low-set ears and full cheeks. The coat is a sandy colour, slightly darker towards the spine and lighter under the belly. Slightly tabby bars may be seen on the limbs and along the flanks and the tail is ringed, with a black tip. The feet are unusual in having dense mats of hair hiding the pads, to protect them from the scorching sand.

Habitat: arid, sandy regions. Sand-dunes overgrown with desert plants.
Habits: mainly crepuscular or nocturnal. Terrestrial.
Prey: Jerboas, other small rodents and small reptiles.

Distribution: N Africa; SW Asia.
Felis margarita margarita Algeria to Arabia
Felis margarita airensis Niger
Felis margarita meinertzhageni Sahara
Felis margarita thinobius Turkestan

Leopard: *Panthera pardus* (Linnaeus, 1758)

Characteristics: head and body about 48 in, tail about 24 in, weight 70–120 lb

A massive, graceful cat with a long lithe body and long tail. The coat ranges from a pale straw colour through all shades of ochre to light chestnut. Striking rosettes and spots of

Above Jungle cat.
Left Black leopard.

black adorn the coat, in an overall pattern. Sometimes the melanistic gene is present and the population will produce animals which are jet black, sometimes referred to as black panthers.

Opposite Cheetahs.

Habitat: widely distributed over every type of country, and up to the snow line of mountains.
Habits: hunts in the morning, late afternoon and at night.
Prey: very varied: all types of deer and antelope, baboons, jackal, hares, large birds.

Distribution: Africa to SE Asia.
Panthera pardus pardus Sudan; Congo; Ethiopia; Kenya
Panthera pardus ciscaucasica Siberia
Panthera pardus delacouri Indochina
Panthera pardus fusca Kashmir to Ceylon; Burma; S China
Panthera pardus japonensis N China
Panthera pardus jarvisi Sinai
Panthera pardus leopardus W Africa
Panthera pardus melanotica S Africa
Panthera pardus nimr Arabia
Panthera pardus orientalis Korea to Amur
Panthera pardus panthera Algeria; Egypt
Panthera pardus pernigra Sikkim to Nepal; Kashmir
Panthera pardus saxicolor Iran
Panthera pardus sindica Sind-Baluchistan
Panthera pardus tulliana Asia Minor

Right Sand cat.

Below Lionnesses.

Lion: *Panthera leo* (Linnaeus, 1758)

Characteristics: head and body 8–9 ft, tail 2–3 ft, weight 300–400 lb

The lion is a very large cat, with a large head and a well-proportioned, muscular body. The coat varies in colour from light silvery-yellow through to a deep yellow-brown, and the underparts are always lighter. The tail tip is always black and there are distinctive black patches on the ears. Male lions carry heavy manes of gold, brown or very dark hair. Cubs are usually spotted until they reach puberty, although the spots become very pale at weaning.

Habitat: semi-desert, grassy plains, open woodlands, bush.
Habits: hunts by day or night. Terrestrial and territorial.
Prey: usually the larger ungulates.

Distribution: Africa S of Sahara; NW India.
Panthera leo azandica Congo
Panthera leo bleyenberghi Angola; Rhodesia
Panthera leo hollisteri Congo
Panthera leo massaicus Uganda; Kenya
Panthera leo persica Gir Forest, India
Panthera leo roosevelti Sudan; Ethiopia
Panthera leo senegalensis Senegal to Cameroon
Panthera leo somaliensis Somalia
Panthera leo verneyi SW Africa

Cheetah: *Acinonyx jubatus* (Schreber, 1776)

Characteristics: head and body 4–5 ft, tail 20–30 in, weight 85–140 lb

The cheetah is a tall, slim cat, built for speed in running down its prey. Its coat varies between a pale fawn and a golden brown, with round black spots. There are striking black markings pencilling the face and the ears are black with tawny margins. The long tail is spotted and has a white tip.

Habitat: dry open areas, semi-desert, light woodland, acacia scrub.
Habits: diurnal. Terrestrial.
Prey: small antelope and other ungulates, hares.

Distribution: Africa; S Asia.
Acinonyx jubatus jubatus Southern Africa
Acinonyx jubatus hecki N Africa to Dahomey
Acinonyx jubatus ngorongorensis Tanzania; Congo
Acinonyx jubatus raineyi Kenya
Acinonyx jubatus soemmeringii Nigeria to Somalia
Acinonyx jubatus venaticus S Asia

Asia has ten species of *Felis* which are confined within its borders and three species of *Panthera*. They are the Bay Cat, the Chinese Desert Cat, the Fishing Cat, the Flat-headed Cat, the Irimote Cat, the Leopard Cat, the Marbled Cat, Pallas' Cat, the Rusty Spotted Cat and Temminck's Golden Cat, plus the Clouded Leopard, the Snow Leopard and the Tiger.

Bay Cat: *Felis (Pardofelis) badia* (Gray, 1874)
Characteristics: head and body 20 in, tail about 15 in, weight about 5 lb

Also called the Bornean Red Cat, it has a bright chestnut coat with slight spots on the underparts and limbs, and faint stripes on the face. It has a round head, and small rounded ears, blackish brown in colour.

Habitat: rocky areas.
Habits: probably nocturnal.
Prey: small rodents and birds.

Distribution: Borneo.
Felis (Pardofelis) badia Borneo

Chinese Desert Cat: *Felis bieti* (Milne Edwards, 1892)
Characteristics: head and body 30 in, tail 12 in, weight about 12 lb

A fairly large, yellowish cat with faint, darker markings, and a striped tail with a black tip. The pads of the feet are very hairy.

Habitat: steppes and mountain areas with bush and forest.
Habits: probably nocturnal.
Prey: small rodents.

Distribution: Central Asia.
Felis bieti bieti Szechuan, China
Felis bieti chutuchta S Mongolia
Felis bieti vellerosa NE Shensi, China

Fishing Cat: *Felis (Prionailurus) viverrinus* (Bennett, 1833)
Characteristics: head and body 32 in, tail 12 in, weight about 25 lb

Very like a civet cat in appearance, the Fishing Cat is of clumsy build, with short, coarse grey fur. Dark brown spots run in longitudinal rows along the body, and the short, round ears are black with distinctive white spots. The feet are partially webbed and the retractile claws project considerably from the sheaths.

Habitat: marshy areas, reed-beds, mangrove swamps.
Habits: diurnal. Terrestrial.
Prey: fish, molluscs, frogs, small mammals, snakes, birds.
Distribution: S and SE Asia; Sumatra.
Felis (Prionailurus) viverrinus S and SE Asia; Sumatra

Left Leopard Cat.

Below Fishing Cat.

Flat-headed Cat: *Felis (Ictailurus) planiceps*
(Vigors and Horsfield, 1827)
Characteristics: head and body 22 in, tail 7 in,
weight about 15 lb

A very unusual cat, about the size of the
domestic, with a very long body, short legs and
a short tail. The head is broadly flattened, with
a ridge formed by the nasal bones. The coat is
reddish-brown, shading to dark brown, and the
underparts are white. A yellow line runs from
each eye to the ear, and dark lines etch the
cheeks. The thick tail is reddish-brown above
and yellow-brown underneath.

Habitat: low-lying country near human
habitation.
Habits: nocturnal. Terrestrial.
Prey: fish, frogs, fruit, sweet potatoes.

Distribution: S Asia; Sumatra; Borneo.
Felis (Ictailurus) planiceps S Asia; Borneo;
Sumatra

Iriomote Cat: *Felis (Mayailurus) iriomotensis*
(Imaizumi, 1967)
Characteristics: head and body 23 in, tail 8 in,
weight about 12 lb

Only discovered in 1964 on a small island, this
cat caused a sensation. It is about the same size
as a domestic cat, with a long body and a short
tail and legs. The coat is dark brown in colour
and has lines on the neck which end at the
shoulders. There are rows of spots which merge
into bands along the body and the round ears
are black, with white spots on the backs.

Habitat: forest.
Habits: possibly nocturnal. Arboreal.
Prey: small mammals and birds.

Distribution: Iriomote Island, Taiwan.
Felis (Mayailurus) iriomotensis Iriomote Island,
Taiwan

Marbled Cat: *Felis (Pardofelis) marmorata*
(Martin, 1836)
Characteristics: head and body 21 in, tail 15 in,
weight about 12 lb

The head of this cat is short and broad, with
short rounded ears. The coat is beautifully
marked, similar to that of the clouded leopard,
the dark spots outlined sharply in black against
the paler ground colour.

Habitat: forest dweller.
Habits: arboreal. Diurnal.
Prey: mainly birds.

Distribution: S Asia; Sumatra; Borneo.
Felis marmorata marmorata Malaya to Borneo
Felis marmorata charltoni Nepal to Burma

Flat-headed Cat.

Leopard Cat: *Felis (Prionalilurus) bengalensis*
(Kerr, 1792)
Characteristics: head and body 25–32 in, tail
10–14 in, weight 7–15 lb

This species varies considerably in colour and
markings. The ground colour is anything from
grey to red, with white or light underparts.
Dark spots extend all over the body and the
head is boldly striped with black and white
markings. The ears are black with white spots.

Habitat: forest regions of high and low
altitude.
Habits: hunts by day and night. Mainly
arboreal.
Prey: game birds, small mammals, fish,
squirrels, hares.

Distribution: Kashmir E to Siberia, China and
the Philippines.
Felis bengalensis bengalensis India to Indochina
Felis bengalensis borneoensis Borneo
Felis bengalensis chinensis China; Taiwan
Felis bengalensis euptilura E Siberia
Felis bengalensis horsfieldi Kashmir to Sikkim
Felis bengalensis manchurica Manchuria
Felis bengalensis trevelyani N Kashmir to S
Baluchistan

Right Golden Cat.

Above Clouded Leopard.

Above right Snow Leopard.

Pallas' Cat: *Felis (Otocolobus) manul* (Pallas, 1776)
Characteristics: head and body 22 in, tail 10 in, weight 7–12 lb

Pallas' cat is very similar to the lynx in its facial structure. It has a large body and short sturdy legs. The head is very short and broad, with wide-set blunt ears, and large round eyes. The coat is long and silky, and varies from light grey to russet, with white tips to the hairs, giving a sparkling appearance to the coat. There are dark cheek lines, and rings on the dark tipped tail. Lips, chin and throat are white.

Habitat: rocky plateaux and river banks.
Habits: mainly nocturnal. Terrestrial.
Prey: small mammals and birds.
Distribution: Central Asia.
Felis manul manul Mongolia; W China
Felis manul ferruginea Turkestan; Afghanistan; Iran
Felis manul nigripecta Tibet to Nepal

Rusty Spotted Cat: *Felis (Prionailurus) rubiginosa* (Geoffroy, 1834)
Characteristics: head and body 17 in, tail 9 in, weight 6–9 lb

A very small wild cat, with small, round ears and a tail that is only half the length of its body. The fur is soft and short, grey with a rufous tinge on top, pale underneath. There are spots on the belly and inside the legs, and dark stripes over the head. The face has two white and two dark streaks, and the soles of the feet are black.

Habitat: (India) scrubland, dried river beds, drainage systems near human habitation.
(Ceylon) forests and woodland.
Habits: nocturnal.
Prey: small birds and mammals.
Distribution: S Asia.
Felis rubiginosa rubiginosa S India
Felis rubiginosa phillipsi Ceylon

Tiger.

Temminck's Golden Cat: *Felis (Profelis) temmincki* (Vigors and Horsfield, 1828)
Characteristics: head and body 31–35 in, tail 19–20 in, weight 14–25 lb

A beautiful golden coloured cat only faintly marked in some sub-species, leopard-spotted in others. Occasionally a melanistic variety occurs. There is a grey patch behind each short, round ear, and white lines bordered with black run from the eyes to the crown of the head.

Habitat: forest interspersed with rocky terrain.
Habits: probably diurnal. Mainly terrestial.
Prey: mammals up to the size of small deer, birds of many kinds.
Distribution: Himalayas to SE Asia.
Felis temmincki temmincki Nepal to Malaya; Indochina
Felis temmincki dominicanorum S China
Felis temmincki tristis Tibet; N Burma

Clouded Leopard: *Panthera (Neofelis) nebulosa* (Griffith, 1821)
Characteristics: head and body 36 in, tail 30 in, weight 48 lb

This striking cat is called the mint leopard by the Chinese because the markings on its attractive coat resemble the leaves of the local mint. The coat varies from pale to rich brown and the head is marked with black bands. The short ears are round and black, with grey central patches. The underparts are pale or white, and the tail is banded with black rings.

Habitat: dense forest.
Habits: mainly arboreal, dropping onto prey from tree branches.
Prey: monkeys, deer, goats, large birds.
Distribution: S Asia; Borneo; Sumatra.
Panthera nebulosa nebulosa S China; Indochina
Panthera nebulosa brachyurus Taiwan
Panthera nebulosa diardi Borneo
Panthera nebulosa macesceloides Nepal to Burma

Snow Leopard: *Panthera uncia* (Schreber, 1775)
Characteristics: head and body about 41 in, tail about 35 in, weight 100–150 lb

Often called the ounce, this cat has a dense, smoke-grey woolly coat with a yellow tinge on the flanks and pale on the belly. Blurred rosettes cover the body, and there are round black spots on the head.

Habitat: high mountains, above the tree line.
Habits: diurnal. Terrestrial.
Prey: ungulates and large birds.
Distribution: Kashmir; Tibet; Himalayas.
Panthera uncia Kashmir; Tibet; Himalayas

Tiger: *Panthera tigris* (Linnaeus, 1758)
Characteristics: head and body 5–6 ft, tail 2–3 ft, weight very variable 250–500 lb

Massively built, the tiger is among the most powerful of the cats. The coat may be any shade from pale cream to tawny, with vertical stripes of grey, brown or black, and no two tigers have identical markings. The round ears have black backs, with white central spots.

Habitat: all types of forest; grassy jungle, bamboo thickets, rocky areas.
Habits: mainly nocturnal. Terrestrial.
Prey: ungulates, monkeys, domestic animals, occasionally birds, frogs and termites.
Distribution: India to Siberia and SE Asia.
Panthera tigris tigris India
Panthera tigris altaica E Siberia; Manchuria; Korea
Panthera tigris amoyensis S China
Panthera tigris corbetti S China; Indochina
Panthera tigris sondaica Java; Bali
Panthera tigris sumatrae Sumatra
Panthera tigris virgata Transcaucasia

Geoffroy's Cat.

The continent of America has a wide variety of wild cats, including one member of the genus *Panthera*, the Jaguar. Of the Lynx species of the genus *Felis*, only one is also found outside the Americas – the Northern Lynx, which will be discussed under Wild Cats of Europe. The other members of the genus *Felis* found only through out the American continent include the Bobcat, Geoffroy's Cat, the Jaguarundi, the Kodkod, the Margay, the Mountain Cat, the Ocelot, the Pampas Cat, the Puma and the Tiger Cat.

Bobcat: *Felis (Lynx) rufus* (Schreber, 1777)
Characteristics: head and body about 30 in, tail about 6 in, weight 15–35 lb

Also known as the Bay Lynx, the Bobcat is smaller than the Northern Lynx, with smaller body and feet and slender legs. The fairly large head has sharply pointed ears, which may be tufted in some specimens. The buff coat is barred and spotted with dark brown or black, and the backs of the ears are black.

Habitat: chaparral, semi-desert, brush, woodlands, subtropical swamp forest, open rocky terrain.
Habits: mainly nocturnal. Very territorial.
Prey: rabbits, gophers, other small mammals, some birds, deer in winter.
Distribution: British Columbia S and E to Central Mexico.
Felis rufus rufus N Dakota to E Oklahoma to E Coast
Felis rufus baileyi SE California to Durango to W Kansas
Felis rufus californicus California
Felis rufus escuinapae Central Mexico
Felis rufus fasciatus S British Columbia to NW coast of California
Felis rufus floridanus E Arkansas to S California
Felis rufus gigas Maine
Felis rufus pallescens British Columbia to Nevada and Colorado
Felis rufus peninsularis Baja California, Mexico
Felis rufus superiorensis Minnesota, Wisconsin, Michigan, S Ontario
Felis rufus texensis Texas to NE Mexico

Geoffroy's Cat: *Felis (Leopardus) geoffroyi* (d'Orbigny and Gervais, 1843)
Characteristics: head and body about 20 in, tail about 12 in, weight about 6 lb

Named after Geoffroy St. Hilaire the French naturalist, this striking little cat is known as 'gato montes' or the 'mountain cat' in Argentina. Found in various shades of ochre to silver grey, the coat is covered all over with equally placed small black spots. On the shoulders and flanks of some individuals, the spots may merge to form rosettes and bars. The rounded ears are black at the back with large white spots.

Habitat: open bush and scrubby woodland.
Habits: thought to be mainly nocturnal. Terrestrial.
Prey: small mammals and birds.
Distribution: S America.
Felis geoffroyi geoffroyi Central Argentina
Felis geoffroyi euxantha Bolivian mountains
Felis geoffroyi leucobapta Patagonia
Felis geoffroyi paraguae Paraguay; N Argentina
Felis geoffroyi salinarum NW and Central Argentina

Jaguarundi: *Felis (Herpailurus) yagouaroundi* (Geoffroy, 1803)
Characteristics: head and body about 26 in, tail about 18 in, weight about 16 lb

Often called the weasel cat, the jaguarundi looks very like an otter with its long, flat skull and compressed nose. Small, with short legs and a very long tail, this cat is found in two colour phases which readily interbreed, and produce kittens of both colours within the same litter. One phase is black to brownish-grey, and the other a chestnut-red.

Habitat: lowland forest and bush, chaparral.
Habits: sleeps at noon, hunts through the rest of the day and at night. Terrestrial but able to climb trees.
Prey: mainly birds, also small mammals.
Distribution: S USA to central S America.
Felis yagouaroundi yagouaroundi E Venezuela to NE Brazil
Felis yagouaroundi ameghinoi W Argentina
Felis yagouaroundi caomitli S Texas to Central Veracruz
Felis yagouaroundi eyra S Brazil; Paraguay; N Argentina
Felis yagouaroundi fossata Veracruz to Central Nicaragua
Felis yagouaroundi melantho Peru
Felis yagouaroundi panamensis Central Nicaragua to Ecuador
Felis yagouaroundi tolteca S Arizona to Central Guerro

Above Margays.
Right Bobcat.

Margay: *Felis (Leopardus) wiedii* (Schinz, 1821)
Characteristics: head and body about 26 in, tail about 16 in, weight 9–18 lb

Often called the 'little ocelot', margay or marguey is translated more literally as 'tiger cat'. Slimly built, with long legs and a long tail, the Margay has a light coat strikingly marked with dark brown.

Habitat: forest.
Habits: mainly diurnal, arboreal.
Prey: birds, tree frogs and lizards, small mammals.
Distribution: Central and S America.
Felis wiedii wiedii E and Central Brazil; N Argentina
Felis wiedii amazonica Amazonas, Brazil
Felis wiedii boliviae Bolivia; Mato Grosso, Brazil
Felis wiedii cooperi Nuevo Leon, Mexico; Texas border
Felis wiedii glaucula Sinaloa to North Oaxaca, Mexico
Felis wiedii nicaraguae Honduras to Costa Rica
Felis wiedii oaxacensis Tamaulipas to Oaxaca, Mexico
Felis wiedii pirrensis Panama to N Peru
Felis wiedii salvinia Chiapas; Guatamala; El Salvador
Felis wiedii vigens Orinoco to Amazon Basin
Felis wiedii yucatanica N Chiapas; N Guatamala; Yucatan Peninsula

Kodkod: *Felis (Oncifelis) guigna* (Molina, 1782)
Characteristics: head and body about 18 in, tail about 8 in, weight about $4\frac{1}{2}$ lb

Probably the smallest wild cat in the Western Hemisphere, the Kodkod is buff in colour, with heavy round black spots. The tail has black rings and the ears have black backs with white central spots.

Habitat: forest.
Habits: nocturnal. Terrestial, but an expert climber.
Prey: birds and small mammals.
Distribution: S America.
Felis guigna guigna S Chile; Patagonia
Felis guigna tigrillo Central Chile

Mountain Cat: *Felis (Oreailurus) jacobita* (Cornalia, 1865)
Characteristics: head and body about 23 in, tail about 14 in, weight 8–15 lb

Known also as the Andean Highland Cat, the Mountain Cat has a remarkable soft fine coat of 2 in long hair, pale silver-grey in colour, with darker markings. These markings may be brown or orange on the body and flanks, but almost black on the white underparts and down the legs. The tail has several blackish rings and a light tip. The backs of the ears are grey.

Habitat: arid mountainous zones, occasionally above the snow line.
Habits: believed to be mainly diurnal.
Prey: small mammals such as chinchilla and viscacha.

Distribution: S Peru to N Chile and NW Argentina.
Felis (Oreailurus) jacobita S Peru to N Chile and NW Argentina

Mountain Lion.

Ocelot: *Felis (Leopardus) pardalis* (Linnaeus, 1758)
Characteristics: head and body about 35 in, tail about 16 in, weight 12–30 lb

One of the most beautiful of all cats, the Ocelot has been driven to the point of extinction by the demand for pelts. No two animals are exactly alike, but the oblique, elongated spots are generally black with a slightly paler centre, and on a pale yellow ground colour. The Ocelot's head is boldly marked with solid black spots and cheek lines. The limbs are spotted and the tail is either ringed or barred. The rounded ears have black backs with central spots of a yellowish tone.

Habitat: dense humid jungle to thorny chaparral; any type of cover, but never in the open.
Habits: generally nocturnal. Mainly terrestrial but rests during the day in high trees. Very territorial.
Prey: birds, deer, peccary, monkey, coati mundi, agouti.
Distribution: S USA to central S America.
Felis pardalis pardalis Veracruz to Honduras
Felis pardalis aequatorialis Costa Rica to Peru
Felis pardalis albescens Texas to Tamaulipa, Mexico
Felis pardalis maripensis Orinoco to Amazon Basin
Felis pardalis mearnsi Nicaragua to Panama
Felis pardalis mitis E and Central Brazil to N Argentina
Felis pardalis nelsoni Sinaloa to Oaxaca
Felis pardalis pseudopardalis N Venezuela; N Colombia
Felis pardalis pusaea SW Ecuador
Felis pardalis sonoriensis Arizona to Sinaloa, Mexico
Felis pardalis steinbachi Central Bolivia

Pampas Cat: *Felis (Lynchailurus) colocolo* (Molina, 1782)
Characteristics: head and body about 24 in, tail about 12 in, weight 8–14 lb

Slightly larger than the domestic cat, the Pampas Cat has been known in Argentina for many years as 'gato pajero' or the 'grass cat'. It has a broad race with pointed ears. The coat colour is variable and ranges from pale silvery grey, through all tones of yellow, to brown. The sides are banded with dark yellow or brown, and the bushy tail and legs are also banded. Some sub-species are more distinctly marked than others.

Habitat: open grasslands of high pampas. Humid forest lands.
Habits: nocturnal. Terrestrial.
Prey: small mammals, especially cavies, birds.
Distribution: S America.
Felis colocolo colocolo Central Chile
Felis colocolo braccata Central Brazil
Felis colocolo budini NW Argentina
Felis colocolo crespoi NW Argentina
Felis colocolo garleppi S Peru; W Bolivia
Felis colocolo pajeros Central Argentina
Felis colocolo thomasi Ecuador; N Peru

Puma: *Felis (Puma) concolor* (Linnaeus, 1771)
Characteristics: head and body about 48–60 in, tail about 28 in, weight about 100–200 lb

The most widely distributed of all the American cats, the Puma varies greatly in size and weight. The name Puma comes from the Quechua language of Peru, but the big cat has been called many other names by early settlers, including cougar, mountain lion, panther, brown tiger and king cat. The Puma has a small blunt head, and small round ears. The body is long, lithe and narrow, and the legs strong and muscular, extra length in the hind limbs giving rise to an elevated rump. Two colour phases are found in this species, a grey phase ranging from a light silver-grey through to a dark slate-toned cat, and a red phase which may be found in all shades from pale buff to a dark tawny-red. The red phase cats are generally found in the tropical areas, while the grey phase ones inhabit the forest regions. Both phases readily intermate and can be found in the same litters. Young Pumas are distinctly spotted, with ringed tails, but lose their markings as they grow to maturity.

Habitat: variable, from coniferous forest to semi-desert.
Habits: mainly diurnal. Solitary and territorial over wide range.
Prey: deer, wild sheep and goat, peccary, beaver, ground birds, various small mammals, fish and large insects.
Distribution: N and S America.
Felis concolor acrocodia Mato Grosso to Bolivia; N Argentina

Felis concolor anthonyi S Venezuela
Felis concolor araucana Chile; Argentina
Felis concolor azteca Arizona; New Mexico
Felis concolor bangsi Columbia to Ecuador
Felis concolor borbensis Amazonas to Ecuador
Felis concolor browni Hualpai Mountains,
Arizona to Catvina, Baja
Felis concolor cabrerae W and Central
Argentina
Felis concolor californica California to N Baja
Felis concolor capricornensis SE Brazil to N
Argentina
Felis concolor coryi Arkansas; Los Angeles to
Florida
Felis concolor costaricensis Nicaragua to
Panama
Felis concolor cougar Tennessee to Michigan
Felis concolor concolor Venezuela; Guyana; N
America
Felis concolor greeni E and S Brazil
Felis concolor hippolestes N Dakota to
Wyoming; Colorado
Felis concolor hudsom S Central Argentina
Felis concolor improcera S Baja, California;
Mexico
Felis concolor incarum N Peru; S Ecuador
Felis concolor kaibabensis Nevada; Utah; N
Arizona
Felis concolor mayensis Guerro; Veracruz;
Mexico to Honduras
Felis concolor missoulensis British Columbia to
Idaho; Montana
Felis concolor oregonensis SE British Columbia;
Washington; Oregon
Felis concolor osgoodi Central to E Bolivia
Felis concolor pearsoni Patagonia; S Chile
Felis concolor puma Central Chile; W
Argentina
Felis concolor schorgeri Minnesota; Wisconsin;
Kansas
Felis concolor staleyana Oklahoma; Texas to
New Mexico
Felis concolor vancouverensis Vancouver Island

Tiger Cat: *Felis (Leopardus) tigrina* (Schreber,
1775)
Characteristics: head and body about 22 in, tail
about 13 in, weight 5–8 lb

Very similar to the Margay, but with slightly
smaller spots and a rougher coat texture, the
Tiger Cat is a typical forest-dwelling feline.

Habitat: dense forest.
Habits: arboreal. Probably diurnal or
crepuscular.
Prey: birds, small rodents.
Distribution: Central America to central S
America.
Felis (Leopardus) tigrina Central and S America
Felis tigrina tigrina E Venezuela to NE Brazil
Felis tigrina guttula E and Central Brazil to N
Argentina
Felis tigrina pardinoides W Venezuela to W
Ecuador

Above Jaguar.
Left Tiger Cat.

Jaguar: *Panthera onca* (Linnaeus, 1758)
Characteristics: head and body 6 ft, tail about
22 in, weight variable, males 110–300 lb,
females 90–125 lb
A powerful and heavily built cat, the Jaguar has
a massive, deep-chested body, sturdy limbs and
a large, round head. The ground colour of the
body can be any shade of yellow through to
tawny-red, and is patterned with spots forming
large rosettes. Markings are very variable, and
the spots along the spine often run together
into a stripe. Melanistic specimens also occur.

Habitat: tropical forest, savannah, near water.
Habits: hunts at dawn and at dusk,
occasionally totally nocturnal.
Prey: peccary, capybara, coypu, otter, fish.
Distribution: S USA to Central and S America.
Panthera onca onca Venezuela to E and Central
Brazil
Panthera onca arizonensis Arizona to N Mexico
Panthera onca centralis Mexico to Colombia
Panthera onca goldmani Yucatan Peninsula; N
Guatamala
Panthera onca hernandesii Mexico
Panthera onca palustris S Bolivia; Mato Grosso
to Central Argentina
Panthera onca peruvianus Peru
Panthera onca veraecrucis S Texas to N Mexico

European Wild Cat.

Of the three wild cat species found in Europe, only one, the Spanish Lynx, is confined solely to that continent. The European Wild Cat, despite its name, is also found in Asia, and the Northern Lynx is quite widely distributed in Asia and America, as well as in European countries.

European Wild Cat: *Felis sylvestris* (Schreber, 1777)
Characteristics: head and body 22–28 in, tail about 12 in, weight 10–30 lb

About one-third larger than a domestic cat, the European Wild Cat is sturdily built, with long legs. It has a broad head with a blunt nose and wide-set ears. The fur is thick and dense, yellowish grey in colour on the flanks, darker on the back, and lightening almost to cream under the body. Four or five long stripes run from the forehead down the back of the neck, and merge into a dorsal line which runs to the root of the tail. From the dorsal stripe, transverse lines run down the body in solid or slightly broken bars. The tail is banded and has a very dark tip. All four legs are also banded, and there are strong tabby markings on the face and forehead. The eyes are usually amber or yellow, the nose leather is flesh-coloured and the throat and lips are white.

Habitat: woodland and high, rocky terrain; occasionally on heathland, moors and marshes if there is an abundant food supply.
Habits: mainly crepuscular, also hunts in early morning.
Prey: small rodents, birds, squirrels, rabbits, young deer.
Distribution: Europe to W Eurasia.
Felis silvestris silvestris Central Europe to SW Russia
Felis silvestris caucasica Asia Minor
Felis silvestris euxinia Rumania
Felis silvestris grampia Scotland
Felis silvestris molisana Italy
Felis silvestris morea S Greece
Felis silvestris tartessia S Spain

Northern Lynx: *Felis (Lynx) lynx* (Linnaeus, 1758)
Characteristics: head and body about 40 in, tail about 7 in, weight 30–65 lb

A large, powerfully built cat with a very short tail and short sturdy legs, the Northern Lynx has a large head, side whiskers and large tufted ears. The coat is yellow-brown, often marked with darker spots. The spotted pattern varies considerably between the sub-species. The eyes of the Northern Lynx are clear, bright yellow and the nose leather is usually brick-red.

Habitat: pine forests, thick scrub.
Habits: mainly nocturnal. Terrestrial.
Prey: rabbits and hares, birds, rodents, fish, deer, sheep.

Left Northern Lynx.

Distribution: N America; Europe to Siberia.
Felis lynx lynx Europe to Siberia
Felis lynx canadensis Canada and N USA
Felis lynx dinniki N Caucasus; Iran
Felix lynx dozlowi Irkutsk
Felis lynx isabellina Kashmir to Russia; Central Asia; Mongolia
Felis lynx sardiniae Sardinia
Felis lynx stroganovi Russia
Felis lynx subsolanus Newfoundland
Felis lynx wrangeli Siberia

Spanish Lynx: *Felis (Lynx) pardina* (Linnaeus, 1758)
Characteristics: head and body about 38 in, tail about 5 in, weight about 54 lb

A beautiful cat with very keen eyesight, the Spanish Lynx is pale-coated, with clearly defined black spots. Slightly smaller than the Northern Lynx, it has a typically short, stocky body, long powerful legs and a short tail. The broad head has long side whiskers in both male and female cats, and the pointed triangular ears have long tufts at the tips. The cat's large round paws grow thick pads of hair in winter.

Habitat: pine forests.
Habits: mainly nocturnal. Terrestrial.
Prey: rabbits, hares, squirrels, birds, fish, wood-boring insects, deer and sheep.
Distribution: Iberian peninsula.
Felis (Lynx) pardina Iberian peninsula

Left Young Lynx.
Bottom Spanish Lynx.

Cats are part of the everyday scene almost everywhere in the world. The colours and conformation may vary a little, but the attitudes are the same. Whether looking for food, taking the air, or just quietly observing the world go by, cats are an integral part of our world, even though at times they appear to be doing us a favour by keeping us company.

The domestic cat is the most successful and widely distributed of all the Felidae, and is found all over the world. Cats are kept for a variety of reasons. Some are expected to earn their living, either as pest controllers or as breeding stock. Others are kept for prestige, cosseted, pampered and groomed so that they can uphold the honour of their breed at cat shows. Some are just kept as pets and accepted for what they are, beautiful, graceful and independent creatures. The cat is kept for company by the lonely, and imparts a sense of peace and tranquillity in a stressed, chaotic world. The cat is an opportunist and has the best of two worlds. Free to slide through the shadows of twilight and dawn in pursuit of prey or romance, equally free to share the comforts of home, food and a warm fire. Even after more than two thousand years of so-called domestication *Felis catus* remains aloof, friendly and tame, but independent; politely tractable and clean, but virtually untrainable. The cat is quite unique in its effect upon human beings; it is either loved or loathed, and never thought of with indifference. It is said that one household in every four throughout the developed world keeps one or more cats and for a variety of reasons. One survey resulted in a variety of reasons given for having a cat in the home. Almost half of those questioned kept a cat for company; about a quarter regarded the cat as a deterrent to rats and mice; and the rest kept cats because they loved them, as companions to their children or just to complete the family. Those who did not keep cats gave a variety of reasons. About one-third actively disliked the animals; another one-third were unable to have a cat because of restrictions imposed by landlords, or similar factors; and the rest were either prevented owing to the allergy of a member of the family, or just did not have any particular reason.

In some instances cats have been found to give stability and a sense of purpose to old or lonely people. Such owners have confessed to enjoying the planning of their pet's menus for the week, buying and preparing the food, and the discipline of regular mealtimes. Owners insist that their cat will only eat certain brands or flavours of cat food, and have to be given specific delicacies on certain days. The veterinary surgeons' waiting-rooms are often packed with anxious owners with their pet cats, mostly genuine cases of illness or accident, but quite often the pet is presented for a check-up when it is in blooming health – it would seem that a form of pet hypochondria is growing in affluent societies.

Even with modern pesticides, the cat remains the most efficient controller of vermin on farms and in warehouses and stores. Not only is it an expert hunter, but also its presence alone acts as something of a deterrent. Cats are often on the official payroll of government departments, and there are railway cats and post office cats, library cats and museum cats. Sometimes the working cat is well fed in return for his pest-patrolling duties. Occasionally things get out of hand and there is a population explosion among working felines resulting in masses of feral cats living in pitiful conditions, half-starved and disease-ridden. To help control and re-house such cats, and to improve their conditions, charitable organizations such as Britain's Cats in Industry have been formed.

Animal societies do their best to help and control cats in distress or in bad conditions, but it is up to the ordinary person to do his bit to help whenever possible. Entire pets should not be allowed to roam free to procreate and add to the problems, and kittens should only go to reliable, caring homes.

Even though an alley cat must resort to scavenging in the gutter, reminders of the cat's wild, regal ancestry are never far away. The lion's feet in stone, a cat's paws in fur, flesh and blood demonstrate man's centuries old fascination with these graceful independent animals in all their beauty.

Perhaps the most important role of today's domestic cat is its contribution to science, no matter how repugnant this may be to many of us. The cat's physiological make-up makes it the perfect experimentee for research purposes. The cat has been a favourite subject for scientists for one hundred years, especially in the field of behavioural psychology, where its reactions are very similar to those of man. The brain of the cat is very similar to that of man, and has been studied more closely than that of any other animal. Many experiments performed on cats have led directly to new methods of treating brain-damaged humans and the mentally sick.

Laboratory animals are properly housed and cared for and are operated on under anaesthetic. If they have to be destroyed for an experiment, this is done humanely. Their treatment is covered by legislation in Great Britain, Europe and America, with severe penalties for violation of the law. Many experiments on cats, however, could easily be carried out by other methods, and there are societies petitioning for the replacement of live animals in experiments wherever possible.

What is a Cat?

Grace, speed and co-ordination combine in the cat to produce the perfect predator.

In common with all other living creatures, the cat's body is composed of the tiny units of life known as cells. Each cell is a complete and discrete system, and is so small that it can only be seen under a powerful microscope. The millions of cells that make up the body of the cat cluster together in specialized groups, each with its own function. Some cells form into tissues such as muscle, skin or hair, while others form into various types of bone. **The skeleton.** Although the cat is so much smaller than Man, its skeleton contains more bones, having a total of 230, to Man's 206. The cat's skeleton consists of a semi-rigid framework which supports the other, softer structures. A system of efficient levers is provided by the bone of the spine, limbs, shoulders and pelvis, connected and geared by powerful attached muscles. Other bones, such as the skull and arched rib-cage and pelvis, encase and protect the vital organs.

Four distinct types of bone make up the skeleton of the cat: they are known as long bones, short bones, irregular bones and flat bones.

Long bones are roughly cylindrical and have hollow shafts containing the vital bone marrow in which the manufacture of blood cells takes place. These bones form the cat's limbs. In the forelimb the long bones are the humerus, which runs from the shoulder-blade to the elbow, and the thick radius, connected by strong ligaments to the thinner ulna. In the hind-limb, the femur, or thigh-bone, is very long and rather fragile. It fits into the pelvis with a ball-and-socket joint, and at the lower end is joined to the tibia, a strong bone, reinforced down its entire length by the thinner fibula.

Short bones consist of a spongy core surrounded by compact bone. They are found in the cat's feet and knee-caps or patellae. The patella is found where the femur joins the tibia. It glides freely over the smooth end of the femur and adds to the graceful movement of the cat in action. The forepaws of the cat are made up of sets of three small bones, each of which forms a digit corresponding to the finger of the human hand. The tiny bones at the end of each digit are highly specialized, however, and articulate so that the claws may be extended or contracted at will. The cat has no 'thumb' as such, and the corresponding digit consists of two bones only which form the dew claw. In the hind-feet the bones are longer and the first toe is absent altogether. If one looks at the diagram of the cat's skeleton, it can be seen that the animal walks right up on its toes, adding to its speed and accuracy of movement.

Irregular bones are so called because of their varying, irregular shapes. They are similar in structure to the short bones. A long string of these bones make up the vertebral column, or spine, of the cat. Attached to the skull at one end with the atlas and axis bones of the neck, the spine continues with the hollow cervical, thoracic and lumbar vertebrae which contain the spinal cord. Then, gradually, smaller and smaller bones extend to the tip of the cat's tail. The irregular projections of the bones of the vertebral column serve as attachment points for the various muscles of the back.

Flat bones are made of two layers of compact bone with a spongy layer sandwiched in between

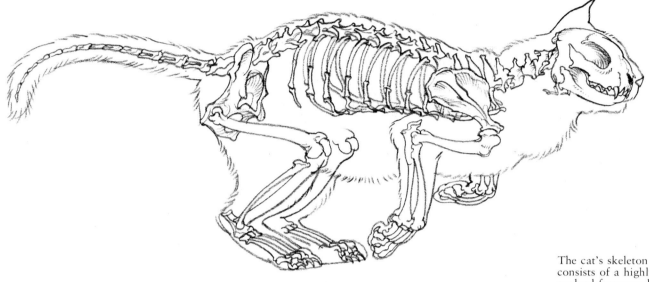

The cat's skeleton consists of a highly evolved framework of efficient levers connected by powerful muscles.

them. Such bones make up the skull, the pelvis and the shoulder-blades or scapulae. The skull consists of many pieces of flat bone connected together. At birth, however, the flat plates are separated in some places, and it is important to avoid injury to the kitten's head. The flat pieces of bone are pierced by numerous holes for the passage of blood-vessels and nerves. The scapula is a flat bone, roughly triangular in shape, which is jointed to the upper end of the humerus. Unlike Man, the cat does not have a fully-developed collar-bone, and there is a great deal of free movement in the animal's shoulder. The hip-bone, too, is connected to the spine in such a way that it allows fluid and flexible movement, making the cat one of the most agile of animals.

Flattened and elongated bones make up the cat's thirteen pairs of ribs. These bones are not hollow, but their spongy interiors contain a substantial amount of marrow and produce a proportion of the animal's blood cells. The volume of the chest cavity is controlled by the strong muscles attached to the ribs, causing the lungs to empty and refill.

Skeletal abnormalities are not very common in the cat, but those seen include bent or shortened tails, cleft palates, flattened chests, polydactylism and split-foot. A bent or kinked tail may be caused by injury at birth or later and is fairly common in the cat. Other cases are due to genetic factors. A shortened tail is due to the presence of a simple recessive gene, while kinked tails are caused by a more complicated pattern of inheritance. The early Siamese cats were noted for their shortened,

thick and kinked tails, but this defect has been eliminated in most strains by selective breeding methods.

Cleft palates and hare-lip in the kitten are caused by the failure of the two halves of the hard palate and upper lip to fuse. The anomaly has been caused in experiments, by the use of drugs administered to pregnant queens, and it is also thought to be a hereditary problem in the cat. Kittens with this defect are unable to suckle and usually die soon after birth.

A deficiency of vitamin A in the diet is thought to be a causative factor in the production of kittens with flattened rib-cages and other skeletal abnormalities. Flat-chested kittens have difficulty in breathing properly, being unable to fully expand their lungs. Polydactylism is a hereditary defect, fairly common in the cat. It is the presence of extra toes on the feet, and varies from one extra toe in some cats to an appearance of double sets of feet in extreme cases. In the split-foot condition there is a cleft in the centre of one or both forefeet and the toes may be fused together, possessed of double claws, or entirely missing. This defect is thought to be inherited through a dominant gene.

One other skeletal problem appears to be on the increase, especially in Siamese-derived varieties. The end of the sternum projects so far that it forms a lump, often mistaken for a hernia, under the cat's body. In extreme cases, the cat or kitten may catch the protrusion while jumping or climbing and injure itself. The piece of bone can be removed surgically, and as the condition is hereditary, the animal should be neutered at the same time.

Massive muscles in the hindquarters enable the cat to balance its body and provide energy for accurate and perfectly controlled jumping movements.

Overlying the skeletal framework of the cat is a complex network of muscles which afford the animal its typical graceful movement and pad the bones to give it its sinuous shape. There are three types of muscles in the body of the cat. The first are the striped or striated fibres attached to the limbs and other parts of the anatomy which are under the voluntary control of the cat. These are known as *voluntary muscles*. The second group consists of smooth or unstriated tissue, which carries out muscular functions not under voluntary control, such as the muscles of the intestines and the walls of blood vessels. These are known as *involuntary muscles*. Finally, there is the specialized cardiac muscle which has adapted to carry out the functions of the heart and possesses unique powers of rhythmic contraction.

The voluntary muscles are usually attached to the bones which form a joint. The *extensors* are those which extend and straighten a limb, while the *flexors* flex and bend the joint. The muscles that move a limb away from the body are called

abductors, and *adductors* draw the limb back again.

Muscles are attached directly to bone by fibrous attachments at points known as *origins*, which usually occur at the point nearest the cat's spine. At the other end of the muscles the attachments are called *insertions*, and the muscles are secured by strong cords of fibres which form the *tendons*. A muscle may have more than one origin and insertion, and the variety of the voluntary muscles – there are more than five hundred in the cat – enables it to be almost fluid in its movements.

The cat can turn its head from side to side, as the cervical vertebrae are supported by exceptionally strong muscles in the neck, enabling the animal to position the head accurately for searching out prey, by sight, sound and smell. The strength of these muscles can be seen clearly as a mother cat carries her young, or the hunting cat carries prey as large as himself.

The rib-cage is lifted by powerful involuntary muscles of the chest. The diaphragm contracts, causing air to be drawn into the lungs through the cat's nasal passages and windpipe.

Arching of the back and strong springing movements are made possible in the cat by the arrangement of the large groups of muscles running down and along the back, and attached to the

Right: from left to right In the walk or lope of the cat the legs move in four-time. The sequence being right foreleg; left hindleg; left foreleg; right hindleg.

In climbing, the cat uses the specialised muscles of the claws for grip and the powerful muscles of the hindlimbs for impetus.

thoracic, lumbar and sacral vertebrae. The only powerful muscles in the tail are near the root, and the rest of the appendage is controlled by small muscles and tendons down to the tip. Though small and delicate, these muscles enable the cat to use the tail expressively, as well as in balancing the weight of the body in running and jumping. In the limbs the muscles of the foreleg enables the forepaw to be rotated as the radius moves around the ulna; the wrist bones being fixed, this enables the cat to grasp small objects and to use its paw as a scoop.

The head of the humerus, held only in a shallow groove in the scapula, can also move freely and is held by muscles to the chest wall. Thus the whole forelimb is extremely flexible and can move forwards and backwards for running, as well as across the chest or up above the head for climbing, washing and grasping prey.

The hind-limb is less flexible and can basically only move forwards and backwards. The muscles are immensely strong, and form the spring mechanism that enables the cat to pounce from its waiting position with such strength, speed and accuracy.

Perhaps the most interesting and specialized muscles of the cat are those found in the paws. The voluntary muscles attached to the claws enable the cat to extend or retract these at will. The cat uses its claws for climbing and in hunting to grip prey. It also uses them as weapons of defence when cornered and of attack when fighting. The claws are often extended and retracted rhythmically in time with purring, when the cat is very happy and contented, as, for example, when a mother cat is suckling her kittens. Kittens also perform the same action when suckling, kneading with their paws at either side of the breast.

The operation of onychectomy has become fashionable among cat owners whose regard for their furnishings exceeds that for their pet. The procedure consists of the total removal of the cat's claws by surgical means. A general anaesthetic is used and the claw is removed so that no regrowth occurs. Although it is generally believed that no ill-effects are suffered by cats having had this operation, the animal is no longer able to climb or protect itself from attack. Such declawed cats often make the normal stropping motions with their non-existent claws, and may undergo a change of personality after the operation. Most countries ban declawed cats from entry to their cat shows and most cat-lovers deplore the practice of depriving the cat of its claws.

Left On reaching an obstacle the cat is able to keep its body at virtually the same profile by employing its unique shoulder action as it glides smoothly across.

Right At rest the cat's body is relaxed and suspended from the hips and shoulders, weight equally spread on all four paws and the tail acting as a counterbalance to the head and neck.

The skin of the cat is made up of two layers of tissue. The inner layer is known as the *dermis* and the outer layer as the *epidermis*. The epidermis is constantly being replaced as the outer surface dies and sloughs away into tiny flakes of dandruff. The skin can be used to monitor the health of the cat in many cases. In the healthy, fit animal the skin is soft and pliable. It is possible to take a fold of skin on the neck, scruff or back, then release it and watch it immediately regain its normal position. In a sick cat, or one that is in the process of dehydrating, the skin is stiff and unyielding. It may be impossible to lift even the smallest fold, and that which is pinched up appears to have lost its elasticity, remaining in the pinched fold for some moments. A sudden change in the colour of the skin points to severe illness in the cat, as some diseases can induce deficiencies of pigment. A pallid appearance can point to infestation by parasites, a lack of some vital dietary requirement or an acute case of shock. Reddening of the skin can indicate an inflammatory disease of the skin or its underlying tissues, while a blue tone can suggest heart trouble, poisoning or the onset of respiratory disease.

Jaundice, one symptom of several serious illnesses, produces a yellowish effect in the skin of the cat. Any change in the colour of the cat's skin is usually noticed first on the ear-flaps and nose, lips and gums. The skin of the cat contains some sweat glands, but these seem to exist mainly for excreting impurities from the body, rather than playing a major role in controlling the animal's temperature. The true sweat glands of the cat are in the pads of its feet, and this is why most cats leave a slightly damp trail of pawmarks on surfaces such as laminated worktops. The cat has sebaceous glands in the skin which open into the hair follicles and produce a semi-liquid, oily substance known as *sebum*, the purpose of which is to coat each new hair as it grows. Occasionally these glands become over-active and small spots like blackheads may appear around the chin, whisker-pads and on the top of the tail. If neglected, these areas can become

Above If neglected, the coat of the longhaired cat becomes matted and unkempt.

Right Daily attention is required to keep the hairs separated and clean, and the ruff, which may grow rather like the mane of a lion, often becomes soiled as the cat eats from its dish.

infected, especially the greasy regions of the tail, and a condition known as 'stud tail' may develop. Washing away the excess sebum with soap and water keeps the skin clean and prevents the pores from clogging up, even in cats such as working stud males which may have overactive sebaceous glands.

The skin of the cat's nose leather is extremely sensitive to touch, while that of the pads of the paw is more sensitive to pressure. The epidermis of the pads is very thick and rough, providing a surface with perfect friction for running, jumping and climbing. The claws are formed of layers of keratin and grow continuously from the base, like human finger-nails. Hair is derived from the outer layer of the skin and acts as an insulatory cover, keeping the cat warm in cold weather and cool in hot weather. Hair forms a dense pelt over the entire body of the cat, and is modified in certain areas, forming eyelashes and whiskers. Each individual hair is a long thin cylindrical structure, pointed at one end and ending in a tiny bulb at the root end which is embedded in the dermis. Each hair is formed quite separately in its follicle, and pigment cells called melanocytes inject tiny granules of colour into the hair as it grows, giving the coat its genetically determined colouring. Special muscles attached to the large follicles enable the hairs to become erect and stand out at right angles to the skin, whenever the cat is startled or angry. The coat may also stand out when the animal is ill, with a subnormal temperature.

It is quite interesting to watch a cat using its whiskers or *vibrissae*. These long neat hairs which protrude from either side of the animal's upper lip are very sensitive. The slightest touch at the tip transmits a message to a nerve in the lip, then on through a larger nerve directly to the brain. The whiskers are used for emotional gestures of various kinds, for touching objects and obstacles and for sensing changes in the environment.

In laboratory tests cats are sometimes blindfolded before being set to traverse obstacle courses of narrow ledges, paths, mazes and tunnels. Most of them find their way accurately and confidently, feeling their way by means of the vibrissae. It is quite possible that cats use their whiskers during their nocturnal hunting pursuits. Coupled with their specialized eyes, which can utilize every atom of available light, the cat is a successful creature of the night even if it cannot truly see in the dark.

Moulting or shedding is the term given to the regular or irregular loss of the animal's dead hair. Some cats shed such hair very lightly throughout the year, others have a considerable change of coat during the spring and autumn months, and even the appearance of the summer and winter coats can vary in some varieties. Hair loss can also occur in some diseases, or when the cat has been poisoned by some toxic substance. Neutered cats occasionally have bare patches on the thighs due to a hormonal imbalance, or thin patches of hair along the spine. In some skin diseases the hair is lost in clumps or circles, and any noticeable change in the skin or hair of the cat should be discussed with the veterinary surgeon.

Top In this picture of a Devon Rex it is possible to see the typical looseness of a cat's skin where it covers the powerful muscles of the body.

Centre The healthy cat has a dense shining coat and in varieties such as the Oriental Shorthair, it forms a thick, close-lying coat over the entire body.

Below A mutant gene produced the unique coat of the Cornish Rex which covers the animal in deep, marcelled waves of soft fur.

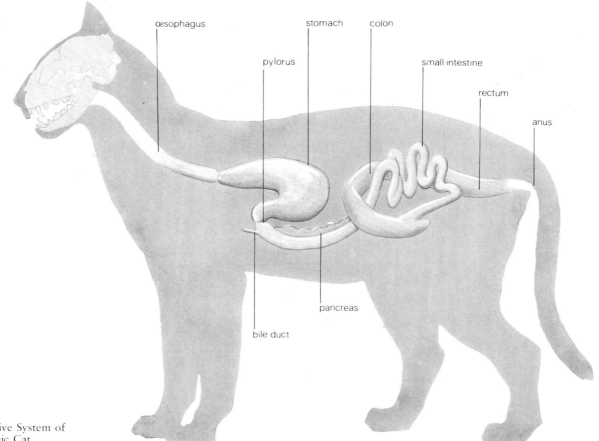

oesophagus   stomach   colon

pylorus   small intestine

rectum

anus

pancreas

bile duct

The Digestive System of
the Domestic Cat.

Fresh meat is sliced
with a chopping action
of the cat's premolar
teeth.

The cat is a very successful carnivore, with specialized dentition, highly adapted for stabbing, slicing, tearing and biting, but not for chewing its prey.

In the adult cat there are 12 incisors, 4 canines, 10 premolars and 4 molars, giving a total set of 30 teeth. When kittens are born, the teeth are just visible inside the gums. They soon erupt, and by the time the kittens have reached six weeks of age the teeth are strong and needle-sharp. It is at this stage that the queen will naturally become increasingly reluctant to feed the youngsters, who should be given thin strips of raw meat to chew on. Kittens eventually shed their baby teeth as the permanent ones come through. This usually happens without any problems at 5–6 months. Occasionally double dentition is seen when the early teeth are not shed, and the kitten develops a sore mouth. The veterinary surgeon can quickly ease out the temporary teeth and the condition soon rights itself.

As the cat cannot chew, it has a specialized process of digestion. Having caught its prey, the cat tears or bites a piece from the carcase and swallows it so quickly that the salivary juices in the

Right Eating grass is thought to aid digestion and the material is often regurgitated together with bile fluids.

Far right Free-ranging cats often prefer to drink water green with algae even when fresh drinking water is readily available.

mouth have virtually no time to start breaking down the food. The salivary glands of the cat produce little or no ptyalin, which is the powerful enzyme present in human saliva necessary for the preliminary breakdown of starches into blood sugars. Any starches present in the cat's diet are, therefore, of little food value to the animal. The gastric juices of the cat are much more powerful than those found in the human stomach, in fact they are strong enough to soften bone. The cat is able to swallow large chunks of rodents and birds, and any parts such as feathers, hair and bones that are not quickly broken down in the stomach may be regurgitated.

In the stomach itself protein material is broken down in the first stage of its reduction to simple amino acids, before being combined again to form the building blocks necessary for replacement of cells throughout the cat's body.

From the stomach the partly digested food passes through a valve called the pylorus, to the small intestine. Here further digestive changes take place aided by secretions from accessory glands such as the pancreas and liver. Fats are broken down and extracted, sugars are changed structurally, ready for storage, and minerals are absorbed. From the small intestine the now fluid contents pass into the large intestine, where they are acted upon by the specialized bacteria that are present there. Water is drawn off, and finally the remaining waste material passes into the colon to be voided as faeces.

Although cats are usually fastidious in their eating habits, kittens are not always so careful and they do not always eat sensibly. They all keep their coats and paws clean by grooming with their rough tongues, swallowing loose hair, dirt, dust and grease in the process. It seems inevitable, therefore, that both cats and kittens suffer from digestive upsets now and again. The most common cause of trouble in the digestive tract is stale, tainted or unsuitable food. Cats given complete freedom often scavenge in neighbours' dustbins, eating things they would refuse if offered at home on a dish.

They are fond of eating the fat of roast joints, often complete with string, and the bones carefully removed from fish, chicken and rabbit. Cats are also fond of drinking from garden pools, and the greener the water the better they seem to like it. They will also drink from water vases, goldfish bowls and oily puddles, often with dire results. Bouts of diarrhoea and sickness in the cat can often be traced to this craving for drinking unsuitable or tainted water. To help guard against this, clean, fresh drinking-water should be provided at all times for all cats.

Owing to the unnatural diet often fed to pet cats, the condition known as gingivitis is commonly seen these days. This is a severe inflammation of the gums, and can be seen as a thin red line along the junction between the teeth and gums. Cats and kittens with gingivitis often drool excessive strings of saliva, and lose condition fast owing to their reluctance to eat. Antibiotics and attention to dental hygiene help to alleviate the condition, and after this treatment chunks of raw meat and hard complete foods in biscuit form should be given to keep the teeth and gums in good order.

Other gastric upsets in the cat can often be traced to infestation with intestinal worms or to a quite unsuitable diet. Feeding too much fish can result in great ropes of the food being returned almost as soon as it is swallowed. In some cats milk can cause a persistent and offensive diarrhoea. Whole minced poultry may cause problems when tiny slivers of bone damage the lining of the bowel, causing internal bleeding and signs of blood in the stool.

A cat with a long, loose coat may swallow so much hair during self-grooming that a fur ball is formed in the stomach or intestines. Fur balls in the stomach are usually vomited up after a few days of dullness, lethargy and loss of appetite. Fur balls sometimes move down to the bowel and cause the cat some sickness, complete loss of appetite, indigestion and constipation. The veterinary surgeon will prescribe some form of laxative in these cases and suggest special care of the cat's coat. The secret of keeping the cat's digestion in good working order is to feed a sensible varied diet, and to ensure that the food is prepared in hygienic conditions and served on clean dishes.

The respiratory system of the cat is fairly complex. Like other mammals, the cat has a pair of lungs, which are situated within the chest or thoracic cavity and separated from the abdomen by a strong muscle known as the diaphragm. Each lung is divided into three lobes and consists of the bronchi, smaller branching bronchioles and a mass of tiny air sacs.

During respiration, the cat draws in air through its paired nasal cavities, which then passes through the pharynx or throat, down the *trachea* or windpipe and then on through the *bronchi* into the lungs. When the air fills the air sacs, gaseous exchange takes place. Carbon dioxide from the blood filters into the air sacs as oxygen passes from the air to replenish the blood. The used air is then exhaled by the cat and another breath is then drawn in.

The process of breathing is quite automatic, as the chest muscles contract and relax, acting rather like a pump on the ribs and diaphragm, driving the air in and out of the lungs. The breathing rate varies from cat to cat, and is affected by exercise, emotion or environmental temperature. The normal respiration rate of a resting cat is, however, put at 20–30 breaths per minute.

Every cell in the body of the cat needs a supply of nourishment, and it is the function of the blood to deliver the nutrients and to take away the cell's waste products. The blood consists of red blood cells and white blood corpuscles contained in a fluid known as blood plasma. Red blood cells contain haemoglobin, a compound which trans-

Above Even a stifled yawn expels excess carbon dioxide from the lungs to be replaced with oxygen.

Below During sleep, the respiration rate slows down and breathing becomes quietly rhythmic.

ports oxygen. White blood corpuscles pick up and transport impurities and bacteria which have invaded the cells. Plasma contains specialized platelets which cause cuts and wounds to clot.

The blood is pushed around the body by the heart, a muscular pumping organ which consists of four chambers. The blood's journey starts in the left auricle, or upper chamber, of the heart. Enriched with oxygen from the lungs, the bright rich blood passes into the left ventricle, or lower chamber, and then it is forced out into a great artery, the *aorta*, to run its course through all the arteries and arterioles and into the fine network of capillaries that infiltrate the cat's body, distributing its store of oxygen as it goes. As the blood gives up its oxygen, it collects a great deal of waste matter. Leaving the capillaries, it enters into tiny veins or venules, before passing into the great veins which transport the stream back to the heart.

Muscular movements of the cat and the expansion and contraction of its chest muscles during normal breathing help the transport of the blood back towards the heart. The blood moves quickly in the main arteries, but the rate is reduced by one-half on its return journey through the main veins.

Extra blood with its nutrients is required by different parts of the body at different times. After a heavy meal, for example, the cat's abdomen draws in extra blood to aid digestion, at the expense of the supply to the brain and other parts of the body. When the deoxygenated blood, with its wastes and impurities, returns to the heart, it passes through large veins, the *venae cavae*, into the *right auricle*. A valve allows the blood to enter the *right ventricle*, and then it is driven, under pressure, through the pulmonary artery to the lungs for ventilation and purification. Carbon dioxide is given off, oxygen is collected and the clean, enriched blood passes into the heart's left auricle to run its course again.

Blood passing through the aorta causes its walls to expand, and a pressure wave passes down the arteries. This wave is known as the *pulse*. It is usual to take the pulse rate of the cat by placing a finger on the femoral artery on the inside of the animal's thigh. The frequency of the pulse beats are recorded. In a calm, healthy, adult cat the rate is approximately one hundred beats per minute. Excitement or fear accelerates the pulse rate, and kittens have a higher rate than adult cats.

As the newborn kitten emerges from the birth canal, the mother cat in licking its face ruptures the amniotic sac and the tiny creature draws in its very first breath of air.

The male cat. In the male cat paired testes, enclosed within a bag, the *scrotum*, are situated outside the abdominal cavity just below the anus. The testes produce the male hormone, *testosterone*, and sperms, the production of which requires a temperature slightly cooler than that of the cat's body.

The sperms develop to maturity as they pass down the long tubes coiled over the surface of the testes, and then pass into the cat's abdomen through the *vas deferens*, where other nutrients and secretions are added by the prostate and urethral glands, forming seminal fluid. The spermatic cord carries the semen to the urethra, from which it is ejaculated through the penis during mating.

The testes descend from the abdominal cavity into the tiny sacs of the scrotum, either when the kitten is still within the uterus of its mother or shortly after birth. Very occasionally, however, one or both testes fail to descend in the normal way, resulting in a sterile, or partially sterile, male cat.

A cat with only one testicle is known as a monorchid, and a cat without descended testicles is known as a cryptorchid. If such cats are fertile, they can be a menace, for they may pass on the condition to their offspring. Monorchids and cryptorchids should be neutered as soon as they are old enough for the operation, for when adult they may have all the usual characteristics of the normal tom-cat, including the pungent odour of the urine, the habit of 'spraying' and the urge to fight for queens and territory. The neutering operation can be complex, and veterinary advice should be sought as soon as the defect is noticed in a young, male kitten.

The female cat. In the female cat paired ovaries lie on either side of the spine, just behind the kidneys. The ovaries produce the female hormone, *oestrogen*, and following the stimulus of mating, may expel several ova. These pass down into the coiled fallopian tubes, where they may be fertilized by the sperm from the male cat. This process of fertilization can take place up to three days after mating. The tiny, fertilized egg cells spend five or six days in the fallopian tubes, during which time they divide, forming blastocysts. This is a critical time in the development of the embryos, for it is during this stage that the ovaries of the mother cat begin to secrete another hormone, *progesterone*, which is required for their successful implantation in the uterine wall. If the queen is taken ill or suffers an accident, stress or shock at this stage, implantation may not take place, and some or all of the kittens may be lost. Having become implanted in the lining of the uterus, the kittens gradually develop to their full birth size. Around the 45th day of the pregnancy, the ovaries cease production of progesterone, and the mother cat should be protected from any chance of accident, stress or shock at this time, or she may well give premature birth to her litter. This is considered by the experts to be a form of protective mechanism to ensure the survival of the mother in times of danger or food shortage.

kidney

anus
testicle
penis
vas deferens
bladder

kidney   uterus
ovary   cervix

anus
vulva
vagina
bladder

The Reproductive Systems of the Domestic Cat.
Top The Male Cat.
Bottom The Female Cat.

Right The typical stance of the male cat as he uses droplets of distinctive urine to spray markers around his territory.

The gestation period is sixty-five days in the cat, and kittens born before the fifty-seventh day are unlikely to survive. Queens sometimes go several days over term, and live kittens have been known to arrive up to seventy-two days after mating. An average litter consists of four kittens, which are born with fur, claws and whiskers but are deaf and blind, opening their eyes at 2–12 days from birth. They feed on their mother's milk for about eight weeks, although they are capable of eating solid food from the age of four weeks. As the litter develops and becomes independent, the queen spends less time with them, and soon her hormones ensure that she starts another breeding cycle.

Female cats can become sexually mature from the age of 4–6 months, but usually have their first period of heat at 9–10 months. The onset of oestrus (estrus) in the maiden queen is often determined by the season of the year. Many female kittens start their distinctive 'calling' in the early weeks of the first February which follows their birth.

Even though they may not be fully grown or mature, it is quite possible for them to become pregnant and to produce a litter. This is not advisable, for having a litter too early in life may seriously deplete the young queen's calcium reserves at a highly critical stage in her own development.

Top left A typical battle-scarred feral tom rests warily in the sun on the island of Lanzarote.

Top right The pet male, when neutered, fails to develop the jowled head of the full tom, but grows a lustrous coat and exhibits a firm, well-fed appearance.

Below The entire female spends her life in an endless cycle of kitten production, happily ensuring the survival of the species. Here a contented tabby nurses her four kittens.

Seeing. Although the cat cannot see in total darkness, it has excellent vision even in subdued light, due to the ability of its pupil to expand and contract. This controls the amount of light available, and explains why the cat's eye looks different each time we look at it. In dim light conditions the iris becomes relaxed and the pupil dilates. The light passes through the transparent, curved cornea and lens to the retina at the back of the eye, to be reflected by a special layer of iridescent cells called the *tapetum lucidum*. This causes the familiar effect of the cat's eyes shining yellow, green or red at night. It is thought that either the tapetum or the retina itself may have a photomultiplying effect on the received light. The delicate mechanisms in the back of the eye are shielded from strong light during the day-time by the contraction of the iris, which closes down to form a slit-like pupil.

The eyes of the cat face forward, causing the fields of vision to overlap, and giving stereoscopic vision. This makes the cat extremely accurate in judging distances for jumping or springing and pouncing while hunting.

Being comparatively large and set in deep sockets in the skull, the cat's eyes do not move freely, so the animal turns its head and sometimes its body, too, in order to bring objects into sharp focus. Cats are said to be colour-blind, but many cat-owners have noticed a preference in their pets for food dishes, bedding and furniture of certain colours.

As well as the upper and lower lids, the cat has a third eyelid, known as the *nictitating membrane* or 'haw'. This is a sheet of pale tissue situated in the inner corner of each eye and normally tucked away out of sight. Any inward movement of the eye within its socket causes the membrane to move diagonally upwards and across the front of the eyeball. The function of the 'haw' is to remove dust and dirt from the cornea and to keep the eye moist and lubricated. When a cat is out of condition or incubating an illness, a tiny pad of fat beneath the eyeball contracts and causes the eye to

retract slightly into its socket, then the nictitating membrane is extended part of the way across the eye. The appearance of the 'haw' is often taken to be an early warning of disease in the cat.

Cat's eyes are very useful in diagnosing illness, for a change in their appearance is often the first sign that there is something wrong. Discharging eyes may be symptomatic of illnesses such as pneumonitis, while a distinct colour change may indicate jaundice.

Hearing. The hearing of the cat is exceptionally well developed, and the animal can pick up the high-pitched sounds of its prey, as well as many other noises quite inaudible to the human ear. Research has indicated that the hearing of the cat may be superior to that of the dog. The ear of the cat consists of three sections. Outside, the pinna, or ear-flap, is naturally erect and forward-pointing. It is flexible enough to move forwards, sideways or back, in order to catch the slightest sound and to pinpoint the direction of its source. The sound waves are collected by the pinna, which acts as a funnel leading down to the eardrum, which is tautly stretched across the ear-canal. In the middle ear three small bones transmit the sound waves to the cochlea of the inner ear. Here they are analysed and converted into nerve impulses which are passed along the acoustic nerve to the auditory cortex of the brain. Here the signals are decoded and recognized by comparison with stored sounds in the memory bank.

The cat's ear is capable of registering frequencies two octaves higher than can be managed by the human ear, but it is less sensitive to the lower frequencies. Acuity of hearing may diminish with age, and many old cats are very deaf. Deafness can be the result of a severe disease of the ear, and may be partial or complete. The condition can be hereditary, and is often linked to white coat colour and blue eyes in cats. In such cats the genetic factors which cause the coat and eye colour appear to be linked with changes in the cochlea which are severe enough to prevent the normal passage of sound waves.

Far left Being naturally adaptable, the cat soon learns to adjust to unusual situations. Having lost one eye in an accident, this black neuter turns his head to enable him to make best use of his monocular vision.

Left Cats use their eyes to signal intent and here a Russian Blue queen is literally staring-out a companion and causing her to back away.

Right The young feral kitten soons learns the art of survival by using his senses to the full. Eyes, ears and nose are employed in conjunction here as he hunts his next meal.

The same use of the sense organs is apparent as the tabby stalks its prey.

Smelling. In the cat the sense of smell is well developed, and is stimulated as minute particles of odorous substances in the atmosphere are drawn in during normal breathing, or are deliberately sniffed in by the cat. Highly sensitive nerve endings within the nasal cavities take the form of fine olfactory hairs, and are linked with nerve cells connected directly to the brain. The olfactory organ of the cat is much larger than expected in an animal of its size, and indicates how important is the sense of smell to animals of this species. This sense is related to the sexual life of the cat as well as being essential in its search for food and hunting activities. In the roof of the cat's mouth is situated a small pouch lined with receptor cells. This is known as the Jacobson's organ. A cat that receives a new, subtle or interesting smell opens its mouth and raises its head as if to savour the scent. This strange grimace, with wrinkled twitching nose and drawn-back lips, is called the *flehmen reaction* and enables the odour to reach the Jacobson's organ for identification. Other wild carnivores also exhibit this curious attitude, and, as in the domestic cat, it is most likely to be seen when they are investigating an area where another animal has urinated, or which has been marked with scent glands.

Cats rarely eat carrion, and most of them find the smell of tainted food highly offensive. Some cats appear to be very fond of perfume, and like to nuzzle into the shoulder or chin of a human wearing after-shave lotion or cologne. The catnip plant emits an odour which most cats find irresistible, and the diluted oil of the plant has been used in the trapping of wild cats such as the puma and

Above The cat has a surprisingly well developed sense of touch and is often seen to touch objects in passing as well as in hunting-play behaviour.

Right Most cats also enjoy being touched and will solicit a stroke with this typical tail raised posture.

the lynx. Just how catnip affects cats is a matter for conjecture, but the effect is plainly visible. The plant appears to excite the cat sexually while having a simultaneous and contradictory soothing effect on the nervous system. Given the opportunity, even neutered cats and young kittens will roll in the plant, purring ecstatically.

Tasting. It is extremely difficult to distinguish between the senses of smell and taste in the domestic cat, but it seems that the cat's tongue can differentiate between things that are salt, sour, bitter or sweet.

Most felines seem to like salty tastes but vary considerably in their reaction to sweet foods. The very positive response that the cat shows towards fresh meat is more likely to be evoked by smell than by taste.

Tiny kittens, on first leaving the nest, test most new surfaces and objects by taste, licking carefully and methodically, and with great concentration. Just how the information they receive in this way is analysed and stored is not known, but it occurs only during the most sensitive period of learning in the young cat.

Touching. Cats use their noses, paws and whiskers for examining objects by touch, generally after having first checked the items out by smell. Cats rarely burn their noses or mouths with hot food or liquids, as they use their noses as thermometers, approaching the dish closely and appearing to sniff, they are, in fact, testing for temperature, and will step back if it is too hot.

Affectionate cats often pat at their owner's face to attract attention. Hunting cats touch prey with a paw to see if it is dead or alive. Mother cats often touch their kittens with their paws and faces. And cats use their faces, whiskers and paws to touch each other.

Centre, left and right In eating and drinking the sense of taste is important and the cat rarely eats tainted food. The cat that really enjoys its food may well close its eyes while eating and drinking, seemingly to savour the taste.

Left Cat companions are often seen to touch one another, and appear to gain comfort from close contact while at rest.

The domestic cat has a highly evolved brain with a deeply convoluted surface, remarkably similar to the brain of Man.

The central nervous system of the domestic cat consists of the brain and spinal cord, and controls and coordinates all the animal's activities. Information received by the cat's sensory organs are constantly monitored by the system and dealt with according to their degree of importance. Vitally urgent information is acted upon immediately, relatively unimportant signals may be discarded, and other information is passed to the memory region to be stored for future use. The brain and nervous system of the cat developed slowly through millions of years of evolution. Today's cat is a highly efficient carnivore, among the most perceptive and alert of all mammals.

Characteristics of very primitive brains can be found in the structure of the cat's brain, which consists of three clearly defined regions. The *forebrain* is concerned with the sense of smell, but also contains the *thalamus*, which responds to impulses travelling from the spinal cord, and the *hypothalamus*, which controls internal regulatory processes. The *midbrain* contains the *optic lobes* and is the area which deals with signals stimulated by light. In the *hind-brain* the *cerebellum* controls balance, and the enlarged end of the spinal cord forms the *medulla*, controlling the animal's respiratory and circulatory systems.

During the brain's evolution, new areas developed around the rudimentary core, each new structure adding to and modifying sections of the older brain. In the brain of today's domestic cat the original core may still be seen connected to the original brain centre, or limbic system. The core performs the same functions that it did in the earliest vertebrates, regulating endocrine gland production, controlling respiration and metabolism, and maintaining homeostasis. The maintenance of a constant internal environment is vital to all forms of mammalian life. The cat's heart rate, blood pressure and temperature are kept steady by the regulation of mechanisms within the hypothalamus which receive and process feedback from the animal's body.

Digestion is controlled by the limbic system, which is also responsible for all activities requiring a set pattern of sequential response. This part of the brain is vital for the survival of the cat. Hunting, eating, mating and escaping all require patterns of behaviour that must be carried out in the correct sequence in order to be totally effective.

The cerebral cortex is the most recently evolved structure in the brain of the cat. It is deeply wrinkled, or convoluted, giving a great surface area, without the necessity of increasing skull size. The two large and symmetrical hemispheres at the top are made up of many neurons, or nerve cells, and are separated by a deep groove which runs from the front to the back of the brain. The left hemisphere controls most of the functions of the right side of the body, while the right hemisphere controls those of the left side, and a network of nerves connects both hemispheres for the correlation of information. The animal's legs are controlled by an area at the front of the cerebral

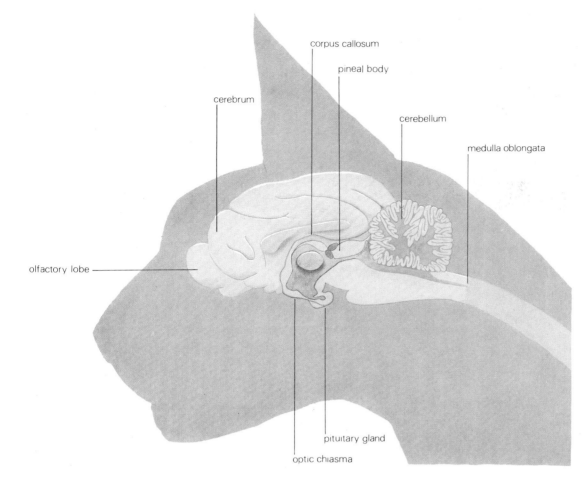

corpus callosum

pineal body

cerebrum

cerebellum

medulla oblongata

olfactory lobe

pituitary gland

optic chiasma

The brain of the cat.

cortex, the body is controlled by an area in the central region, and a section at the back of the cortex deals with the processing of visual stimuli. Auditory processing areas are situated at the sides of the cortex, and there are also many complex zones specifically concerned with activity, learning, memory and all conscious sensations.

Neurons are specialized cells which perform all mental functions. Each neuron has a nucleus and other parts as found in the normal, somatic cells of the body. Finger-like dendrites project from the neuron and receive signals from adjacent cells, and the neuron transmits its own messages to other neurons through a long fibre known as an axon.

The neurons are wired together rather like an electrical circuit, with the nervous impulses moving generally in one direction, from dendrite to cell body, then on through the axon to the dendrites of neighbouring cells, until they reach their destination at a muscle or gland. The cell wiring system is very complex, with axons from hundreds of neurons connecting on other individual neurons at junction points known as synapses. Neuronal transmissions are chemical in action and highly complicated in function. Dendrites and axons grouped together in bundles form nerves.

Nerves which are outside the central nervous system act upon the body muscles and form the peripheral nervous system. These nerves carry information to the spinal cord from the skin, whiskers, pads, muscles and joints. The spinal

cord transmits the messages to the brain, and then the motor region of the brain sends its return message back through the spinal cord, and along a separate set of nerves, informing the muscles of their necessary action.

Actions which continue during waking and sleeping are controlled by the autonomic nervous system, formed of sympathetic and parasympathetic nerves. Sympathetic nerves become activated when the cat is emotionally aroused, causing increase of the heart rate, dilation of the heart and muscle arteries, contraction of the skin and internal organ arteries, and the secretion of hormones into the blood-stream. When this sequence of events happens, the cat is prepared for any action, aggressive or defensive. The parasympathetic system affects one organ at a time, and controls and conserves and stores bodily resources. In the complete sex act of the male cat both divisions of the autonomic nervous system are employed, as the parasympathetic system produces the erection and the sympathetic system allows ejaculation.

As it is a solitary creature relying on its own powers of coordination for survival, the sophisticated development of its autonomic nervous system is very important to the cat. Domestication has done little or nothing to modify this system in the cat, which is possibly the reason why stray and feral animals are often able to survive successfully in seemingly hostile conditions.

The highly evolved brain ensuring the future of the species.

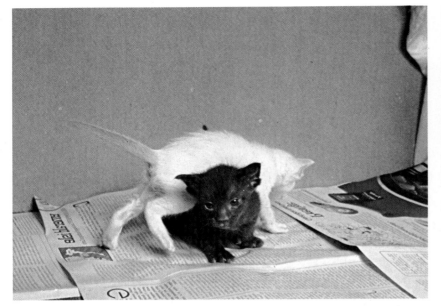

Above At about four weeks of age the young kittens toddle from the nesting box for the first time to explore their environment.

Above right Every new surface is tested by being licked thoroughly so it is essential to avoid possible toxic hazards, such as unsuitable disinfectants or floor polishes, at this time.

At birth the kitten is cleaned by its mother's rough tongue as she removes the amniotic fluid and traces of the sac from its fur. The licking also stimulates circulation and respiration in the tiny creature. As soon as it is breathing properly, guided only by a strongly developed sense of smell, the kitten crawls forward towards the mother's nipple. Blind and deaf at this stage, kittens will still stake claims on particular nipples, and fight off other kittens with strong scrabbling movements of their forepaws. For the first few days of life, the kittens merely sleep and suckle, being cleaned at intervals by their dam. While suckling, the kittens tread with their forepaws on either side of the nipple, which appears to stimulate the milk flow.

The unique smells of the birth process are important to the newborn kittens, giving them a sense of security for the first few days of life. The secretions of birth are sterile and there is no reason why the bedding of the nestbox should be replaced straight after parturition. Owners of breeding queens may do psychological harm to their litters if they insist on removing every scrap of soiled bedding from the box, replacing it with a freshly washed blanket. It may be better to leave the nestbox alone until the kittens' eyes are open, by which time they will not be so stressed by the sudden change in their environment.

During the first few days of life the kittens seem to prefer certain sections of the nestbox. They crawl by pushing themselves forward on their bellies, as the legs are too weak for support at this stage. As they crawl, their bodies leave scent trails which they can clearly recognize. If the kittens are cold, they cluster together, forming a little heap; if they are warm, they spread out.

The kittens generally open their eyes when they are 2–10 days old, and they may be sensitive to strong light at this time. The hearing gradually develops, too, and with the increased sensitivity the kittens begin to explore their limited environment and to show signs of play behaviour. At first the young kittens pat at each other in a clumsy manner, but as the eyes focus better and the sight

gets stronger, they can be seen to watch their mother entering and leaving the box. Even at birth, the blind and helpless kittens will hiss if picked up, and may continue to do this for two or three weeks. Once they recognize the smell, voice and possibly the sight of their handlers, this behaviour stops.

At the age of three weeks the kittens can stand quite well and toddle around on their short, unsteady legs. They keep their heads close to the floor at this stage and can be seen to rely greatly on the sense of smell, retracing their steps to the safety of their special corner of the nestbox. The kittens can roll over and right themselves, too, at this age, and play with their siblings with little pats of the paws, and bites.

By the end of the fourth week the kittens may decide to explore the world outside the nestbox. The legs are much stronger at this age, and sight and hearing are used as much as smell in testing the environment. During their first excursions, the kittens rush back to the safety of the box whenever they are frightened by loud noises or sudden movements. It is at this age that kittens test new surfaces by licking and chewing, so it is vitally important that no toxic disinfectants, detergents or polishes are used where they play and explore.

At birth kittens have in their brains all the neurons that will be present for life, for the brain cells are never renewed. All mammals start life with millions of such cells, which gradually decay, slowing down the mental processes with increasing age.

Though the brain of the young kitten is functional at birth, its intelligence depends to a large extent on the number of synaptic junctions which form during the first few weeks of life. Proper stimuli and slight amounts of stress during the first critical weeks appear to help the development of the brain and so produce more clever cats.

Experiments have been conducted where litters were split, half being kept as a control, and left to lead a normal life in their nestbox until weaning time, the other half being consistently stressed by

Left At five to six weeks the kittens become more adventurous and begin to climb onto or over any small obstacles, keeping a wary eye out for danger at all times. If startled they fluff out their tails and try to run back to the safety of their box.

Left At three months of age the hunting instinct is well developed and each new possibility is examined and explored.

Right Hunting technique is learned through play and the kittens are seen to be particularly active at dusk. Given the opportunity, they will play-hunt together watching and learning from each other's behaviour. Here feral kittens hunt moths.

extra handling, and being subjected to sounds, smells and sights. In all cases the stressed kittens matured to surpass their litter-mates in intelligence, calm acceptance of handling by strangers and resistance to nervous disorders.

In normal rearing practice the kittens should be handled frequently between the ages of four and eight weeks. This period is roughly equivalent to the nest-changing age in the wild, and is the time for young kittens to recognize the difference between safety and danger. It is important to start gentle grooming at this age, especially in the longhaired breeds, with particular emphasis on inspection of ears and mouths. Training carried out at this stage is invaluable and lasts for life.

At five weeks of age the kittens' brains are almost mature, with the synaptic junctions formed and fully operational. Motor development, however, including the coordination of the limbs and muscles, takes longer and so the small animals should be protected from possible injury at this stage. The kittens are adventurous, and need space to play with each other, and with their toys. Ping-pong balls, golf balls, feathers and paper bags make excellent toys for the kittens, and they enjoy diving into and out of large paper bags and cardboard boxes. A variety of foods should be given at this age so that the kittens do not become conservative in their feeding habits later in life, and after meals each kitten should be placed gently but firmly on the toilet tray.

The kittens must be taught acceptance of strangers, children and dogs, and should be accustomed to household noises such as washing machines, vacuum cleaners and door-bells. Kittens destined for a show career should be picked up and stroked by visitors to the house so that they enjoy being handled by everyone they meet. This socializing period should not be underestimated. Kittens that do not receive the proper stimuli and treatment during the period may be difficult to handle later in life, every time they are removed from their own environment, or with strangers. Most veterinary surgeons and boarding

cattery proprietors have to bear the brunt of 'difficult' cats, and in many cases these animals are perfectly tractable in their own homes. Anywhere else, however, they are nervous, irritable and may well bite and scratch if handled. Their owners often confirm that such cats were once stray or farm kittens, taken in and tamed after the critical period.

Play is very important in the development of the kittens, and the role of the mother cat should never be underestimated. Even when the litter is very young she will be seen to entice them to play with the end of her tail. The queen teaches the youngsters when to run for cover by growling when danger threatens. She also teaches them to be independent by refusing to allow them to suckle somewhere around the eighth week. With a large litter she may show reluctance to allow them to nurse from about the sixth week, while the queen with one or two kittens may be prepared to feed them until they are really well grown. As the kittens get older, their needle sharp teeth hurt the queen as they suckle, and if she is allowed to roam

freely, she may well bring in some prey for the litter.

Confined cats often carry pieces of food to their kittens, uttering a distinctive cry. After the kittens have examined the meat, the queen eats it in front of them.

The play behaviour of kittens follows a fairly constant pattern. Some varieties are a little more forward than others, but basically all kittens, pedigree or pet, follow the same routines.

3 weeks Rolling
Kittens play by rolling on their backs, all four paws waving towards other kittens or their mother. (This position is held while mother cat cleans the kittens' genital region.)

3–4 weeks Standing
Kittens face each other, patting or biting at each others' faces and necks. Either may roll over and pull the other down with outstretched paws, then both kick at the other's belly with the hind-feet.

4–5 weeks Arching
Kittens learn to threaten by arching their backs and turning sideways on to present a larger image. They approach each other in a series of small sideways steps.

5 weeks Pouncing
Kittens crouch, head on forepaws on the floor, before pouncing forwards in a running spring.

5–6 weeks Boxing
Kittens stand up and pat at each other, patting with paws and neck-biting before rolling over.

6 weeks Chasing
Kittens chase each other.

6–7 weeks Leaping
Kittens jump right up in the air to avoid each other during the chasing games. This is usually done from a sideways stance.

7 weeks onwards Hide and seek
Kittens lie in wait before pouncing and chasing.

From the age of about eight weeks play patterns become more sophisticated, and hunting and killing actions are apparent in the games. The kittens practise using their forepaws to grasp while they administer neck bites to their litter-mates. The hind-legs are used for raking at the body of another kitten while the forepaws grasp it firmly around the neck. The kittens jump on their mother's tail, simultaneously biting at the part just in front of their grasping paws. Small toys are dribbled expertly across the floor before being passed through to the hind-legs, which perform kicking and treading movements. Kittens learn to carry small toys in their jaws, and may growl when another kitten approaches. When offered strips of raw meat, each kitten takes a piece and growls ferociously at the approach of a littermate. If touched at this time, the kitten will strike out, accurately and fast, towards the teasing hand.

At about twelve weeks the young kitten is independent enough to go to its new home. It is still developing physically and mentally, however, but it should have learned that it is a cat, and how to behave itself as a pet animal. If it is to be kept without other pets, the kitten should be given lots of toys, fuss and attention so that it grows into a well-balanced, happy cat.

The Self Correcting Reflex. This is not apparent in the very young kitten but develops early in life. When falling, the cat performs a series of quite definite, rapid movements turning its body in a spiral through $180°$ to land on its feet.

When the female becomes receptive and adopts the mating position, the male cat straddles her body, grasping the loose skin of her scruff in his jaws.

While most cats breed in the spring, the female cat, unlike the bitch, does not have set periods of oestrus (estrus). Climate and weather seem to play an important part in the sexual cycles of female cats, especially those living normal lives with access to the outside. Cats kept indoors, in heated accommodation and subjected to long hours of light conditions, certainly seem to breed at any season of the year. Feral and farm cats keep to a more natural pattern of reproduction, geared to the survival of their kittens, having one litter in early spring and another in early summer.

Having reached sexual maturity, both male and female cats continue to breed throughout their lives. The peak years of fertility in the male cat are between the ages of two and seven years, and in the female, between two and eight years. Old queens may still continue to produce kittens at the rate of one or two each year until they die. Old entire male cats continue to roam in search of calling queens, but take care to avoid fights with other males. Pedigree stud males seem to live longer, possibly owing to the fact that they do not have to fight and that they enjoy a better standard of living than free-ranging males.

Oestrus (estrus) in the female cat is easy to recognize (see Having Kittens), and may start when the kitten is about six months of age. It is not usual to mate pedigree cats until they are well-grown, but free-ranging females may become pregnant long before this. During her period of heat the queen becomes increasingly restless and tries to get out of the house. She pays particular attention to her toilet, washing around her vulva, and may start to call softly. As oestrus begins, she will call strongly and adopt a typical mating stance, and may be very difficult to handle.

Male cats do not have periods of heat, and are in mating condition at any time once fully developed. The male is attracted to the female by her calling, and by her evocative and subtle smell, which is thought to carry a considerable distance. Notes in her call, probably too high-pitched for human ears, may also attract and excite the male.

Under natural conditions several male cats may pay court to the calling female. The queen rolls and postures but may be unwilling to mate at first. The males square up to each other and the characteristic caterwauling begins as they decide the order of supremacy. The actual battles are bitter, bloody and fought in comparative silence, while the queen appears to enjoy the attention. She may be mated by a subordinate male while two dominant males fight it out, but it is more usual for the strongest male of the group to mount and mate her first. The queen may be mated many times during the period of oestrus and probably by more than one of the males.

Entire male cats, with their freedom, are motivated mainly by their sexual urges most of the time. They spend their days in marking out their large territories, mating and fighting. When there are no queens on heat, they rest and recuperate. If they have homes, these are merely places of convenience where they can get a meal and rest in peace. Toms fight fiercely and their long canine teeth inflict severe wounds on each other. The teeth go in deep, leaving bites which seal over on the surface, trapping bacteria inside the tissues which form abscesses.

A fight starts when two toms meet and square up to each other, hunching their shoulders and puffing out their thick jowls. By erecting the coat and tail, each cat tries to present a large, formidable appearance to the other. If there are no females in heat, one or other of the toms may back off and slink away. Otherwise the threat display might well develop into a serious battle. The second stage of the threat display starts with deep growls emitted from both cats. They may start salivating and lip-smacking while circling around each other. The attack is usually silent and sudden, when one cat lunges at its opponent's throat, biting hard and raking at his body with both hind feet. Locked together, the two cats roll over and over on the ground, biting and raking away great lumps of fur. When they break, one cat may run

off, or they may dive at each other's throats again. Occasionally the victor bites the defeated cat at the base of the tail, near the testes, as a final gesture.

In mating, the male cat seizes the female's scruff in his jaws, usually approaching her from the side as she postures and calls. If she remains in the mating position, he straddles her body and kicks at her hindquarters with his hind-feet, encouraging her to raise her tail. Crouched over her body, the male tries to effect penetration, which may take some time as the queen wriggles and moves around. The cats often make crooning noises to each other at this time, and the male's eyes constantly search around for signs of possible danger from other cats. Eventually penetration occurs and the queen growls fiercely, moving forward. The male cat holds her scruff firmly in his teeth until he has ejaculated, then releases the queen and leaps away. The reason for this is apparent as the queen, usually growling fiercely, turns to attack him with teeth and claws. Then she rolls on her back on the ground before licking her genital areas thoroughly. As soon as the queen begins her toilet, the tom attends to his own, and washes his penis. He constantly glances towards the queen, and as soon as she relaxes and shows signs of regaining the mating posture, he is ready to mount and mate her again.

Keeping a watchful eye for possible danger from other cats, the male then kicks at the female's hindquarters to encourage her to elevate her hips.

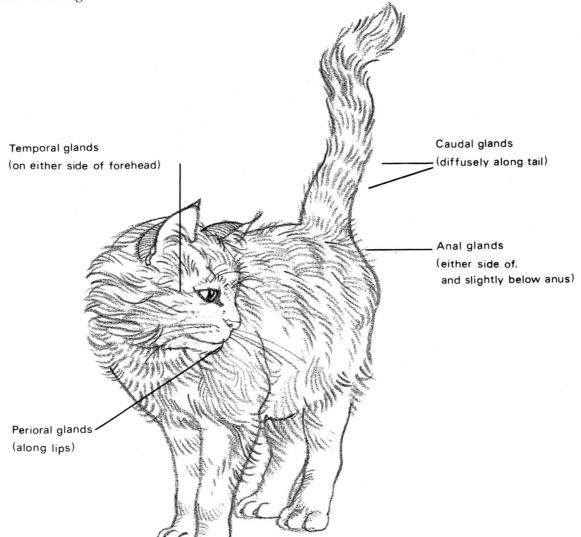

Temporal glands
(on either side of forehead)

Caudal glands
(diffusely along tail)

Anal glands
(either side of,
and slightly below anus)

Perioral glands
(along lips)

Areas of glands used for
scent marking.

Right An Abyssinian
queen, probably in the
early stages of oestrus,
using her perioral glands
for scent marking.

Cats have several methods of marking and identifying property and places. They are equipped with various scent glands on the head and body. On either side of the forehead, just above the eyes, the temporal glands are situated, while the lips have perioral glands. Both sets of glands are used in marking. The cat also has scent glands near the root of its tail. To use the head glands for marking, the cat rubs the areas vigorously against the chosen object, either a piece of furniture, another cat, a dog, or the arms, legs, shoulders or face of a human friend. In rubbing the glandular areas over the chosen site, the cat deposits minute smears of the scented secretions, thus marking it with its own distinctive odour.

Marking with the forehead and lips seems to give the cat pleasure, for it may knead with its forepaws and purr while carrying out the rubbing. If another friendly cat has marked the same spot, the animal may drool and salivate while carrying out its own lip-marking, rubbing its jaw and chin firmly on the object, sometimes even rearing up on its hind-legs in order to rub even harder. Having used the temporal glands for the initial marking, the cat may then turn around to complete the mark with the tail gland.

This type of marking is most easily observed

when the cat uses it to leave its signature on its owner, who is, perhaps, standing in the kitchen preparing a meal. The cat winds itself around its owner's legs, leaning inwards, and allows its forehead and the side of its jaw to rub the area first. As the animal moves forward, the body rubs over the same area, followed by the tail, which winds around and wipes the area with its entire length.

When male cats mark out their territories, they generally spray droplets of their strong-smelling urine onto every convenient object along the perimeters of their ranges. The tom examines a post or bush, turns his back on it, raises his tail, then, with two or three pedalling movements of his hind legs, urinates high and accurately. Sometimes he will turn again to examine his signature, or he may back up and rub his tail and hindquarters against the damp patch. Occasionally the cat turns and smells the mark, then strops his claws vigorously. Female cats sometimes develop the habit of spraying, either when their hormonal balance has been upset by doses of contraceptive pills or when they have become frustrated by frequent periods of heat. Such queens adopt the typical male position and direct their urine backwards in a fine jet.

An emotional disturbance may trigger off the spraying habit in the neutered cat, and this is particularly annoying if the cat persists in spraying indoors. Neither females nor neutered cats produce spray which smells anything like the pungent urine of the male cat; however, the urine is sticky and difficult to clean from household furnishings. In the neuter spraying generally occurs when the cat feels that its position in the household is threatened, by the arrival of a new baby, a new kitten or puppy, or in some cases by the arrival of a new piece of furniture or carpet.

When the cat feels particularly upset, it may defecate as well as spray, and may choose to do this where it will have the most devastating effect, in the middle of the carpet or on the best cushions. The spot chosen is always very conspicuous, and totally unlike the procedure normally carried out when emptying the bladder and bowels, when the cat tries to cover up and hide its signs.

In examining the smells left by other cats in marking out territories, the cat may show the characteristic flehmen reaction. Drawing back the lips and raising the head so that every vestige of the smell can reach the Jacobson's organ in the roof of the mouth, it savours, tests and identifies the odour.

Left, above The male cat marks out the perimeters of his territory with drops of urine ejected by spraying backwards at the chosen object.

Left, below Friendly cats often greet one another by rubbing or sniffing at the perioral region.

Above A cat savouring and examining a smell with the characteristic flehmen reaction.

Cats have a wide range of facial expressions and bodily postures with which they are able to communicate with other cats and humans. The alert cat has a very direct gaze, with forward-pointing ears and whiskers. If the alert cat is also slightly nervous, his nostrils may twitch slightly as he tries to identify and recognize by smell as well as by sight and sound. When the scent has been identified and recognized as friendly, the cat raises its tail and approaches, slightly stiff-legged, in greeting. If the visitor is another cat, then some mutual rubbing or grooming may follow the preliminary nose-touching. Adult cats may greet each other, then indulge in some play, either a mock battle or a game of tag.

A normal and non-aggressive cat in its own territory may receive a threat, perhaps from another cat or a strange dog. At first the cat will freeze and look at the intruder, then its tail will start to flick slowly from side to side. Its whiskers and ears point forward and its nose quivers as it attempts to identify the threat object. As the intruder approaches more closely, the cat changes its stance. The point of the lifted tail turns

Facial Expressions: *above* watchful but benign, *far left* defensive, apprehensive, *left* threatening to attack.

downwards, the chin is drawn in and the ears flatten as the cat begins to turn slowly to one side. Gradually the hairs on the cat's back and tail rise up until the animal has assumed its aggressive posture.

This typical display continues if the intruder comes forward, and is very menacing. The cat faces the enemy but with the body turned sideways to present as large and formidable an area as possible. The hind-legs are tensed and ready to spring forward in attack or away in flight, and the weight of the front of the body is poised on one foreleg while the other, claws unsheathed, is prepared to strike out. The cat's chin is drawn tightly in to protect its throat, the ears are laid flat to its head and the lips are drawn back, showing the teeth as the cat snarls fiercely.

If the unwelcome visitor backs away from the

threatening cat, the latter may move forward a little, smacking its lips and salivating, while continuing to growl. When the threat has disappeared entirely, the cat will sniff at the invaded ground and may spray, defecate or strop its claws before regaining its normal appearance and composure.

The signs of extreme agitation in the cat are easy to recognize. Its eyes open wide and glance rapidly from side to side while the body is crouched, chin held in and the ears held out at the side of the head. A cat showing these signs should be coaxed gently, and should not be touched until the eyes and ears regain their normal appearance, or the animal may well bite and scratch in defence.

Cats can communicate affection as well as fear and threat, by bodily posturing. The tail, in particular, is most expressive. Carried erect, it indicates a feeling of contentment, and if it is carried straight up, it can also be a gesture of welcome. Even when the tip of the erect tail waves slightly to and fro, the cat is contented; but when it lashes from side to side, it expresses extreme annoyance and may presage an attack. A cat that stands perfectly still with the tail held out in a straight line is almost certain to attack. With all the tail hairs erect, it looks like a bottle brush, and when this is also accompanied by the erection of all the body hairs, the cat appears to grow to twice its normal size.

Contented cats will often purr and start to knead with their forepaws, replicating the action of tiny kittens, kneading while suckling. Some cats seem to hypnotize themselves by this action and will knead on freshly washed linen, or perhaps a fur rug, as if making bread dough. A cat kneading in this way almost seems about to burst with affection.

The cat is also able to communicate by means of its voice. Although the exact nature of the vocal chords is not thoroughly understood, it is known that there are superior, or false, cords as well as inferior, or true, cords. It is likely that the various cries made by the cat are produced by the true cords, while the false cords may be responsible for the animal's purrs. All cats purr, although some do it so softly that the sound cannot be heard, and the vibrations are felt in the animal's throat. Cats usually purr with contentment, with affection or even when in pain. Purring can begin in the kitten at about one week of age, and is usually heard as the little creature contentedly suckles. Young cats purr in a monotone, while older ones purr with two or three resonant notes.

Cats' sounds are more varied than their purrs, with many different calls and cries being made to express different needs and emotions. A queen and her consort have a whole language of love-calls, and mother cats communicate with their kittens in a range of different cries, mews and chirrups. Growls are also variable, and range from the scream of fear to the guttural choke of anger. Cats can also hiss and spit. Whatever method the cat chooses to communicate, it leaves one in no doubt as to its feelings and intentions at that particular moment.

Left Wide-eyed, tense and slightly nervous with ears tending to flatten, body and chin being withdrawn from the possible danger.

Body Language: *above left* retreating, apprehensive, *above* backed up, defensive but prepared to attack. Note semi-raised paw and warning hiss, flattened ears and erect coat.

At the age of six weeks, kittens usually begin to show the first signs of predatory behaviour when the mother offers them prey or pieces of meat. She calls to the litter and pats the offering around before eating it in front of them. This is the time when the small creatures first start to practise hunting techniques, using their siblings as mock prey, crouching, pouncing, making mock attacks and head- and neck-biting movements.

Even the most docile of pet cats will occasionally go hunting, given the opportunity, unless it is very overweight. Well-fed but fit cats hunt whenever they can, rarely eating their prey but obviously regarding the pastime as an enjoyable sport. It has been found that farm cats kept for killing rats and mice were more efficient in their jobs if fed properly, and were less likely to be injured by bites from the vermin. Cats are excellent hunters and often upset their owners by bringing home feathered trophies.

Most cats prefer to hunt alone, but there have been recorded cases of cooperative hunting between cats from the same family. Cats usually hunt at twilight or dawn, when their ability to make the best use of poor light conditions stands them in good stead.

Acute hearing also helps in pinpointing prey, before making the final, death-dealing pounce. Cats generally prefer to hunt in their own carefully defined territory, and country cats usually have set

Above The hunting cat uses every available inch of cover when stalking its prey.

When hunting grasshoppers and crickets the cat pinpoints the insect by sound first, then having located its position it watches carefully before making its spring.

Right The farm cat waits patiently and virtually camouflaged in the tall grass for prospective prey to approach within attacking range.

beats through favourite copses, woods and hedgerows. Their safe passage through dense undergrowth and pathways is ensured by the use of sensitive whiskers, eyebrows and ear-tufts. Soft pads with retracted claws enable silent, swift movement, and the powerful muscles of the hindquarters produce the propulsion for the final attacking spring. Victims are grasped between the forepaws, with the claws fully extended to give the cat extra grip on the prey, and the killing bite is delivered to the neck region.

The hunting of birds in the open takes a lot of skill on the part of the cat. First the animal flattens the body to the ground and glides forward in long, fluid movements. The hips and shoulder-blades are kept level and low, and the cat's head is fully extended forward with flattened ears. When the cat is within springing distance, it pauses and swings its hips and tail rapidly from side to side, gathering impulsion for the forward leap. With a sudden release of the built-up energy, the cat catapults forward, often pinning the prey to the ground with its claws. It is quite common for the cat to injure its prey, but to defer death for a while in order to practise its hunting techniques. The hapless victim may try to escape, but may be tossed, patted, caught and bitten for some time before it dies. The cat may become highly aroused during such play and continue to toss the small body around long after it is dead. Some cats like to hide their victim's body under a rug or piece of furniture, then walk away as if they have forgotten about it. Then they turn, run and pounce, hooking it out of hiding with a sweeping forepaw in mock-serious play.

When a cat decides to eat its prey it often devours the entrails, and then it may or may not finish off the rest of the body. Larger animals, such as rabbits or hares, are usually eaten over a period of time, the cat returning to the carcase until it is finished. After that, it may not eat again for two or three days. Smaller prey such as mice and small birds are often eaten entirely within a few minutes, starting with the head. The less digestible portions such as the fur or feathers may be regurgitated later.

As hunting and killing are inborn features of the domestic cat, confined cats may need compensat-

ing in some measure for the lack of facilities for these natural pursuits. Caring owners provide toys and games for their pets as substitute prey. Paper balls on strings, feathers, and catnip stuffed mice all help to exercise the cat and stimulate it into a close simulation of a serious hunt, thus maintaining the link with its natural past.

It is the innate hunting instinct that enables the domestic cat to survive if left suddenly to its own devices. Many cats have been known to become lost during house removal, car and train accidents and abandonment. Some cats have travelled great distances in order to return to an old home. Cats have been recovered after months or even years of living rough, some may have obtained food from scavenging but it is obvious that they also had to hunt in order to survive.

Even cats which have led closeted, cosseted lives seem able to revert to nature when necessary, and their first clumsy attempts at catching prey, spoiled by over-enthusiastic rushes, soon become more sophisticated and result in kills as their innate skills reassert themselves.

Right The cat is content to watch the exit holes of small rodents for long periods of time, probably kept alert by subtle sounds of activity in the burrow detected by its sharp ears.

Far right Farmyard cats thrive on wild rabbits and hares and one kill may sustain a cat for several days.

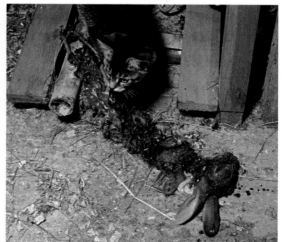

Cats' sleeping patterns were carefully studied during research into the sleeping habits of humans, and it was established that cats have two distinct sorts of sleep. A very light sleeping state occurs during the odd cat-naps of the day, during which the blood pressure remains normal and the temperature drops slightly, while the muscles are slightly tensed. In deep or paradoxical sleep, however, the temperature rises, the blood pressure falls and the muscles relax. Electroencephalograph recordings taken during light sleep show a typically slow wave pattern, while recordings made during paradoxical sleep show short, sharp patterns. A defence mechanism exists in the sleeping cat, whose hearing becomes even more acute than when it is awake.

During paradoxical sleep cats can be seen to dream, sometimes purring, twitching, fluttering the paws or making running and jumping movements of the limbs. Sucking movements of the lips may occur or the tail may switch and the ears twitch. Why cats dream or what they dream about there is no way of knowing, but it is possible that, during dreaming, the events recently learned during the waking hours are being sorted and important information is stored away in the memory bank.

One-third of the cat's sleeping time is spent in this deep paradoxical sleep, and cats deprived of enough of it can become quite ill. In experiments cats were kept without deep sleep for several weeks, and were found to have accelerated heart rates. After the experiment the cats spent a great deal of time sleeping, as if trying to catch up on the lost sleep, but it took several weeks before the heart rates returned to normal.

Newborn kittens spend the first week of their lives in paradoxical sleep, broken only by short periods of wakefulness in which they suckle. From the age of 1–4 weeks they spend longer periods awake, but slip straight back into paradoxical sleep without any transitory light sleep phase. From the age of four weeks onwards kittens start experiencing light sleep phases, too, which coincide with the completion of the development of the synaptic junctions in their brains.

Cats can sleep at any time, day or night, and seemingly in any position. Although they prefer warm cosy beds, cats can relax on any surface no matter how uncomfortable it seems to humans. A cat may sleep curled up in a tight ball, or stretched on a ledge, with its head hanging over the edge. Some cats seem to sleep all day long; others are much more active and only seem to take cat-naps. Some cats put their forepaws over their eyes before going to sleep; some sleep on their stomachs and others on their sides. Occasionally a cat may be seen sleeping flat on its back. Kittens play hard and sleep hard – in fact, they often stop right in the middle of an exciting game and collapse in a heap of gently undulating, sleeping bodies.

When waking up from sleep, the cat usually goes through a routine of stretching and flexing exercises, particularly of the spine and limbs. If it has slept for a very long time, it may be reluctant to exercise much for a while and may decide to have a drink and a wash before going about its business.

A Foreign Lilac queen takes her cat-nap in the warm, spring sunshine.

The action of light and warmth on the coat of the cat usually stimulates the washing reflex. To wash, the cat employs both tongue and paws. It is able to clean most of its head and body. The tongue of the cat is covered with tiny projections called papillae which can be used to wash and comb the coat. After feeding or sleeping, the cat sits up and licks its mouth and lips; then, licking a paw until it is damp, the cat passes this over its head, into and around the ears, over the eyes and down the side of the nose. The paw is licked again

groom each other as a sign of great affection, usually after a meal and before settling down together to sleep.

The mother cat washes her kittens a great deal. At birth she licks away the amniotic fluid from their coats and eats the membranes of the birth sac. She stimulates them to excrete urine and faeces by licking them in the genital area several times a day, swallowing all the waste products to prevent any soiling of the nestbox. The mother cat continues to carry out this function until the kittens start eating solid food, when the faeces change considerably. As well as washing the tiny kittens so hard that she often lifts them off the floor, she pays great attention to her own toilet, and spends a great deal of time licking, washing and grooming her coat, vulva and nipples.

Young kittens begin to wash themselves in a rather ineffectual way at about three weeks of age. When they are eating solids, however, at about six weeks of age, they are able to wash their paws and faces quite well, and clean up their tail-ends every time they use the toilet tray.

There is an old saying that a cat that is bathed will never again wash itself. This is quite untrue, and any cat that becomes excessively soiled or contaminated in any way can be bathed with a specially formulated shampoo. The water must be comfortably warm, and the shampoo applied carefully and rinsed out thoroughly before the cat is dried off. A cat that has been bathed in this way will usually help the drying process by licking its coat back into shape. It is much more inclined to lick a clean coat than a heavily soiled one.

Cats that refuse to wash may have trouble in the mouth, and the first thing to check is for the presence of tartar. Queens that stop washing their genital areas could have a distasteful discharge, and, again, this needs checking out. Full males that appear to have a greasy patch on the tail probably have 'stud tail'. This must be treated with soap and water to remove the grease and the tail then kept scrupulously clean.

Above Adopting the yoga position, the cat is able to reach its hindquarters and tail region which is kept clean by licking with the rough tongue.

Right Apart from the area at the back of the neck, the cat seems able to wash its entire body, the head being cleaned by means of a well-licked paw.

and again, and the washing motion is continued until the cat feels clean; then the other paw is licked in order to wash the other side of the head and face. Each shoulder and foreleg is licked in turn; then the sides and flanks, the hind-legs and the genital area, and the tail.

Tangles and burrs in the coat or between the toes are bitten out, and mud on the pads is removed with great care. Cats often mutually

Older cats expect a little indulgence and this dignified ginger gentleman has adopted his owner's sewing bag as an ideal bed.

The company of an aging cat in good health is delightful and soothing, and to play with him is as rewarding as playing with a tiny kitten. The old cat's reactions are sharp, his movements are subtle, and he may deign to chase string and pat feathers, as long as he is not made to look foolish.

Old age in the cat can be anything from nine to nineteen years, but the cat can be considered old when it starts to take things easy and spends even more time than usual in sleeping. The cat then needs feeding a good light diet and grooming every day, as he might not spend enough time in caring for his own coat and toilet. The old cat should not be allowed to get overweight, as this puts an undue strain on the heart. It is a good idea to have his mouth and teeth checked over at regular intervals, and to have his general condition checked to ensure that there is no sign of kidney disease.

If the old cat's teeth deteriorate, a soft diet can be given, and if the kidneys do begin to fail, a low-protein diet padded out with rice and pasta can be given. The fresh clean drinking-water which should be readily available to all cats is particularly important to the cat in old age.

Old cats need a great deal of love and affection, and should not be ignored, just because they sit around the house, undemanding and quiet. It is common practice to obtain a new kitten when one cat is getting old, and this can be a good thing or a bad thing, depending on the temperament and nature of the old cat. If the established cat likes the new kitten, its presence could bring him a new lease of life as he watches the youngster romp and play. The kitten's keen appetite may stimulate the old cat to eat better and take a renewed interest in life generally. On the other hand, a cantankerous older cat, perhaps with general discomfort from

his kidneys or stiff joints, may really resent the playful antics of a kitten. The kitten's attempts to get him involved in his games could be met with hostility, and the old cat may be so resentful that he goes off his food, and becomes depressed, ill and incontinent. If the old cat is the only one in the household and has always been a loner, it would be better to postpone the acquisition of a new kitten. If, however, the old cat is one of several family pets, he probably would not have any objection to a newcomer.

As the cat ages, so a certain amount of tissue degeneration occurs. This is inevitable and cannot be prevented, although, with care, the effects can be eased. Regular visits to the veterinary surgeon are important; every six months should be sufficient unless courses of treatment are required. Disturbed behaviour patterns may be the result of chronic illness in the old cat. For example, a previously clean cat may begin to have slight accidents, making little puddles on chairs, cushions and carpets. Treatment might remedy the problem, but it is better to confine the old cat to areas of the house where the occasional lapse of manners will not matter. It is cruel and unfair to chastise the old cat or to ban him from the house for something that is beyond his control.

Eventually the old cat sleeps more and more, and is increasingly reluctant to exercise. It may drink lots of fluids but take very little food. While it is able to function normally, if only in this modified way, it is probably quite happy and contented. If its bladder and bowels begin to fail and the cat is unable to eat, veterinary advice must be sought, for the only humane thing to do in these circumstances is to have the old cat put down, allowing him to die in dignity.

Above, right and left As the cat ages it spends more time than ever resting and sleeping. In cold months a cushioned chair is chosen, while on sunny days a shaded spot in the garden provides the perfect spot.

Left With increasing age the cat may develop bladder weakness and ask to go out several times daily. It is kind to provide a cat flap so that he can come and go as he pleases, or an indoor toilet tray.

Cats often acquire strange and unusual tastes, and this Burmese has become addicted to photographic emulsion.

When we take a cat as a pet, we take away its need to hunt by providing it with food, and neuter it so that it does not breed. Alternatively, we may breed from the cat by artificial selection, and under artificial conditions. We cosset the cat, protecting it from stresses, extremes of temperatures, hazards and disease. We should remember that the tolerant cat which lives in such harmony with humans is still very independent at heart, with built-in abilities to survive in the wild. It also has very powerful sexual drives and is a very perceptive creature with highly tuned reflexes. Above all, it is basically a solitary animal.

When we think thus about the cat, and realize what should be construed as usual behaviour, it seems hardly surprising after all that a few cats, on occasion, revolt against all this domestication and exhibit strange, abnormal or unusual behaviour patterns.

Shock and trauma can produce behaviour disorders in cats. In countries at war cats are badly affected by shelling and gunfire, and may be seen crawling into cellars and dark corners to die. Rough, unkind handling can result in a totally unbalanced and unpredictable cat, and any form of severe shock may result in reactions which induce a vasovagal attack, collapse and death. It is usually overhumanized cats on which care and love have been lavished that are affected in this way, and the attack is a direct result of the overstimulation of the nervous system.

Road accidents can produce severe shock in the cat, as can a fight with another cat or a dog. A cat suffering from shock is listless and depressed. It will not eat or drink and its pulse rate is high. The cat tries to hide its head and its pupils dilate. It may shiver, and the pads of the feet perspire. In some cases the cat may be too hypersensitive to be touched, and will bite and scratch severely if handled. The cat in shock should be rolled over in a thick towel, put in a safe carrier and placed in a dark warm situation until it is calm enough to be professionally examined.

A very frightened cat may become catatonic and assume an attitude of death. Other animals perform this trick in order to escape being eaten by predators, and it is sometimes called 'playing possum'. It is a rare occurrence in the cat, however, and a catatonic cat must be treated for shock – complete rest, in a dark, warm place.

Pet cats rarely become aggressive unless they are being teased or ill-treated. Sometimes cats react violently to being touched when they are reacting to another threat. For example, a cat may be watching a threatening dog or a noisy vacuum cleaner when its owner tries to pick it up. The cat thinks that it is being attacked by the cause of its fear and retaliates by biting its owner severely.

Above When access to the garden is restricted, the cat may try to find a substitute for grass.

Above right Wool-sucking is possibly inherited behaviour. The cat first relaxes and kneads at the woollen object, then licks and sucks at the fabric, often ingesting large quantities of the material.

This behaviour is quite normal and understandable, being part of the cat's complex and highly developed defence mechanism.

Drugs and food additives can cause unusual behaviour in cats. Benzoic acid, a food preservative quite safely used in the preparation of dog food, causes a nervous condition in cats. The affected animals become wild, hysterical and very sensitive to light, finally developing severe muscular spasms.

Some drugs have been known to have far-reaching effects on the physiology as well as the psychology of cats, one often having a bearing on the other. An example of this effect is brain damage caused by antibiotics, which, in turn, caused deafness. Deaf cats are especially vulnerable, being unaware of approaching danger.

Introducing a new kitten, puppy or human baby to the household can cause behaviour upsets in the cat. Antisocial ways of showing displeasure are quite common, and include urinating in strange places such as on the hearth-rug and the top of the stove. Some cats just refuse all food for several days until they become quite ill. Others methodically break every small ornament that can be tipped off mantels and shelves. Some cats start to strop every soft furnishing in the house. Occasionally the disturbed cat will indulge in self-mutilation, licking at paws, flanks or tail until the area chosen is raw and bleeding. Others sit and pluck out the fur on their chest or flanks. One Siamese, jealous and unhappy, was placed in a boarding cattery, while his fate was decided, and, in five days, chewed half his tail away.

Cats which are extremely bored, or badly reared, may indulge in excessive self-grooming. This may happen during long confinement in kennels where there is a total lack of stimuli. Such cats lick and groom their bodies until some areas are raw. They may suck at their paws, tail or rear nipple, purring and kneading, regressing mentally into kittenhood.

Wool-eating seems to be related to self-sucking and seems to be an inherited trait, especially in some strains of Siamese. It is virtually impossible to live with a wool-eating cat, for as soon as it is relaxed, its eyes glaze, its paws knead and it licks at the nearest woollen object. The cat tugs at the wool, sucking and chewing simultaneously. Some cats only go this far, others chew all manner of material and will also suck and chew human hair. Some wool-eating cats swallow large amounts of man-made woollen-type fibres, which become impacted in the stomach and intestines and need surgical removal.

Sexual disorders sometimes manifest themselves in pet cats when they are kept entire and become frustrated. Neutering usually brings about a marked improvement in behaviour and general health.

Some cats like to play with water; some even like to swim. Some cats play with dripping taps; some are clever enough to use the lavatory pan. There are cats that like snow and ice, others that will not go outside in the rain. Cats like to roll on cold concrete, they paw at window panes, they make rude covering-up gestures around food not quite to their liking and they sulk, backs to their owners when they have been teased.

On the whole, considering the way in which we expect them to live, domestic cats are well-adjusted creatures who should be excused the occasional lapse in their usual behaviour.

Right **Oxus Mountain Ringlet** Brown Tabby longhaired neuter showing the typical 'M' marking on his forehead.

Far right **Suki**, an exotically ticked silver shorthair, is the result of an accidental mating between a Siamese and a Chinchilla.

Tabby Patterns
Left to right Ticked; Mackerel; Spotted; Classic or Blotched.

Coat colour and pattern in the domestic cat depend on the presence of pigment granules in the cells of the animal's epidermis. The granules consist of melanin, which is found as two compounds: *eumelanin*, giving rise to black and brown pigmentation, and *phaenomelanin*, which produces red or yellow. Eumelanin is converted in a series of slow stages from the amino acid *tyrosine*, by the action of an enzyme containing copper. Cats with a deficiency of copper in their diet may, therefore, be unable to develop their true coat colour. Phaenomelanin is derived from another amino acid, *trytophan*.

The melanin is produced by *melanocytes*, specialized cells which form the pigment, then pass it to the skin, hair and eyes of the cat. The number and distribution of the melanocytes in the individual is genetically determined, and the cells form in the embryonic kitten, spreading through its body to their designated positions in the early stages of its development.

It is the variety of ways in which this distribution and clumping together of the melanocytes occurs that produces the range of colours and patterns that can be seen in the domestic cat of today.

Agouti is the name given to the original wild-type coat in which the basic black hairs are banded or tipped with yellow. This fundamental coat pattern, with its ticked effect, is caused by the action of both types of melanin being present in the hair, and is commonly seen in wild mice and rabbits, as well as in cats.

In the wild state the ancestors of pet cats were shorthaired, with black pigmented areas creating patterns of spots and stripes against the paler, ticked background hairs. The designs produced by these areas of solid pigment are called *tabby patterns* and are very variable in the domestic cat.

There are four basic tabby patterns, however: the *ticked* type, as found in the Abyssinian breed, the longitudinally striped *mackerel*, the clearly defined *spotted* and the intricately marked *classic* or *blotched*.

It would seem likely that the first mutation to occur in the cat was a simple non-agouti gene which gave rise to black cats (see Genetics). The same mutation also occurred in other species of cat, too, and melanistic, or black, specimens are fairly common in wild populations.

Another mutant gene occurred which has the effect of reducing the normal black pigmentation

to brown, or chocolate. It is the effect of this gene which can be seen in the Self-Chocolate Long-haired cat, and the Havana, or Oriental Chestnut. The effect of this gene on yellow pigment produces the auburn effect seen in the cinnamon tabby.

A dilution of black to blue was brought about by a simple mutant gene, inherited as a recessive. The pigment granules within the hair-shafts are arranged in such a way that the animal appears to be slate-grey in colour. This dilution gene also works on yellow pigmentation, changing it to cream, and on chocolate, changing it to lilac.

The mutation which gave rise to orange or red colouring in the cat is particularly interesting, as the gene is linked to the X chromosome and the coloration it produces is therefore sex-linked. The orange gene is independent of other colour and pattern genes, and so can be inherited along with them, giving rise to many beautiful and variable coat patterns, particularly in the female.

Some of the most popular pedigree cats have coat patterns produced by a related group of alleles known as the *albino series*, responsible for silver, Burmese, Siamese and albino cats. Each mutant allele in this series removes more of the pigment from the coat. The gene for silver takes

out most of the yellow, especially in any agouti areas, but leaves the black. The gene for Burmese takes out even more yellow and modifies the black areas to dark brown. The Siamese gene has the effect of removing the colour from the body, leaving it only in the regions known as the 'points', and reducing the intensity of colour here from black to dark seal-brown. Finally, the albino gene produces a cat without any pigmentation, so that the coat is white.

Whiteness of a different sort is caused by another gene. This is known as dominant white, and the effect of the gene is to prevent the migration of the melanocytes throughout the body of the embryo kitten. Without these cells there is no pigmentation, and therefore the animal is white. It is thought that a similar gene produces cats with white markings. The clumping of the melanocytes and their uneven distribution give a coloured cat with a white belly, throat or paws.

Eye colour in the cat is very variable and is also due to the distribution of melanin. Some genes which influence coat colour also affect the colour of the eyes – all Siamese or Himalayan patterned cats, for example, have blue eyes, whatever the colour of their points.

Far left **Rababar Lilac Solitaire** combines the elusive lilac colouring with the spotted tabby pattern and is a lilac Oriental Tabby.

Left **Grand Champion Edelstein Mr. So-So** presents a perfect example of the effect of the Himalayan gene which restricts the intense colour to the points and produces blue eyes.

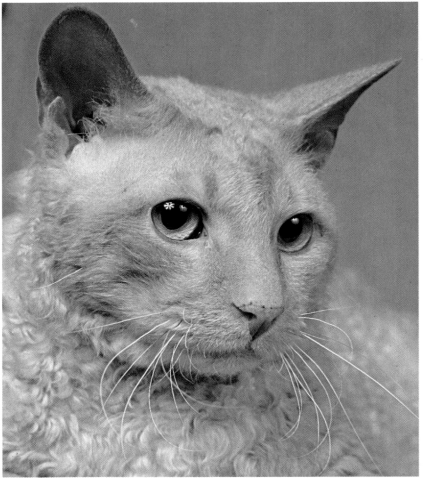

Above **Grand Champion Senty-Twix Jaspar** a typical curly Cornish Rex male.

Above right **Blue Betty Boop** a blue female Devon Rex, has a softer waved coat and different bone structure.

From the cat breeder's point of view one of the most significant mutations that occurred in the development of the domestic cat was the gene for long hair. Pedigree longhaired cats have full and silky coats produced by careful selection over many years, while mongrel longhairs have coarser, slightly shorter and less silky fur. Selective breeding for any trait brings about the manipulation of many *polygenes*. These are genes which individually exert very small effects on characteristics and phenotype. Differences in length and texture of the cat's coat are due to the multiple effect of polygenes, as are differences in intensity of eye colour. While the basic genes or monogenes make the cat longhaired, with blue eyes, for example, it is the quantitative effect of the polygenes that determines how long the hair will be and how blue the eyes.

The coat of the cat is generally made up of three types of hairs. *Guard* hairs are straight and taper to a fine point, while *bristle* or *awn* hairs are thinner than guard hairs, also tapering to a point, but with a characteristic swelling just below the tip. Guard and awn hairs are known collectively as the *overhairs*. The *underfur* is made up of *down* or *wool* hairs. These are the thinnest of the three types of hairs and are of even diameter throughout their length and characteristically curved or crimped. The underfur keeps the cat warm, while the overhairs act as a protective, insulatory covering.

In 1950 a cat with tightly curled hair was

discovered in Cornwall, England, and founded the breed now known as the Cornish Rex. The unusual coat was caused by a mutant gene which inhibited the production of normal guard hairs, and in some cases awn hairs also. Ten years later, in the neighbouring county of Devon, another curly cat was found, but breeding tests soon proved that this animal's coat was due to the effect of a different gene mutation. This Devon Rex coat is also devoid of guard hairs, and there is a tendency for these cats to lose their soft down hair in patches during moulting (shedding), which results in bare patches, especially under the body. In 1951 a rex cat was identified in East Berlin, Germany, with typically soft and smooth waved fur, devoid of coarse guard hairs, which appears to be similar to the Cornish Rex.

New mutations of cats have been reported from time to time in the United States. One, the Oregon Rex, appears to be due to a quite distinctive rex gene, as crosses between such cats and both Cornish and Devon Rex produced only normal-coated offspring. Another mutation in the United States has occurred which resulted in the American Wirehaired cat. The coat of this animal feels coarse and looks untidy. All three types of hairs are present in the coat, but the guard hairs are abnormally curved and much thinner than is usual. The awn hairs are very undulated and often curved right over towards the tips, while the down hairs are irregularly bent. While the rex-coated

effects in cats are due to recessive genes, the wirehaired effect appears to be due to a dominant gene.

Taillessness is the main feature of the cat known as the Manx. The mutant gene which causes this effect may also affect the entire spinal column, producing varying degrees of spina bifida in kittens. It is possible that the dominant Manx gene is a semi-lethal one, and that kittens homozygous for the gene usually die in embryo (see Genetics).

A similar effect can be seen in the Scottish Fold cat. Instead of being held in the normal, upright position, the ears in this breed are bent forwards and downwards. This condition is due to a simple dominant gene, also, it would appear, sometimes combined with defects of the cat's skeletal formation.

Above **Champion Viking**, male, and *centre* **Champion Calliope Rosey Dawn**, female, are two fine examples of the tailless Manx breed.

Right **Denisla Morag** shows the typically curved ears of the Scottish Fold.

Right An elusive gene appeared in recent years. This has the effect of lightening the already diluted colours and is exhibited here by **Solitaire Cariji**, a cinnamon Egyptian Mau.

For the cat breeder whose ambition is to perfect the overall quality of his stock, a basic working knowledge of the science of genetics is essential. Combined with adequate facilities, time and patience, this will enable him to fix good points such as conformation, temperament and stamina, to introduce desired features and colours and to eliminate hereditary faults. While it is a fact that some top show cats are bred without any genetic knowledge having been applied to their production, the breeder who works carefully and methodically towards his goal, using planned breeding programmes, will achieve consistently good, sound stock.

Genetic literature can be quite baffling to those without any scientific knowledge, the technical terms and symbols making the subject completely incomprehensible, so it is intended to give here a simple outline of heredity as applied to the cat.

The science of genetics deals with all matters of reproduction and the functions of every part of the mechanisms of living. A basic understanding of the subject will help the cat breeder to know how breeds or varieties can be changed, how patterns and colours can be modified, and how, despite the fact that no two individuals are ever identical, a strain can be produced by selective breeding, closely resembling one another in all desired features.

The concept of heredity as an exact science was formulated by a nineteenth century monk named Gregor Johann Mendel, who later became Abbot of the monastery at Brno in Czechoslovakia. A keen gardener, he experimented by crossing varieties of garden pea and produced results which were later acclaimed for their accurate simplicity. In 1865 Mendel published a paper which caused little interest at the time. In 1900 it was rediscovered simultaneously by three scientists working quite independently, and the importance of Mendel's work was at last recognized. The definite hereditary units which he called Mendelian factors are the genes of present-day terminology.

The life of an individual cat starts with the union of the sperm from the male and the ovum of the female, which joins to form one new cell called the *zygote*. The sperm and ova are known collectively as the *gametes*.

Each microscopic cell is formed of a jelly-like mass called cytoplasm contained within a thin membrane, and every cell has a denser ovoid or spherical body called the nucleus, which plays a controlling part in the life of the cell. Each nucleus carries the material that transmits hereditary characteristics from the parent, and when two gametes join in sexual reproduction, the two nuclei fuse and become one. The new zygote divides by the process called *mitosis* first into two cells, then four and so on, until at maturity a cat has about ten thousand million cells.

The division of the cell is always preceded by the division of the nucleus, within which are found the most important genetic structures – the *chromosomes*. These rod-like bodies carry the genes. The cat has nineteen pairs of chromosomes in every cell

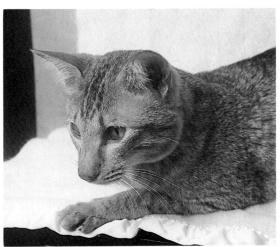

in its body, each duplicated like prints from a negative from the original cell formed by the fusion of the gametes. Chromosomes differ from one another in size and shape, but, with certain exceptions, occur in identical or *homologous* pairs.

Each chromosome has an attached set of genes arranged in fixed order along its length, and each gene on the chromosome has a partner at the same position on the other chromosome of the pair. Genes related in this way are called *alleles* or *allelomorphs*. During the process of mitosis each chromosome is split lengthways into identical halves which travel to opposite ends of the cell to form two new nuclei. Both daughter cells have sets of chromosomes identical with the parent set, and in this way chromosome identity is maintained throughout all the body cells.

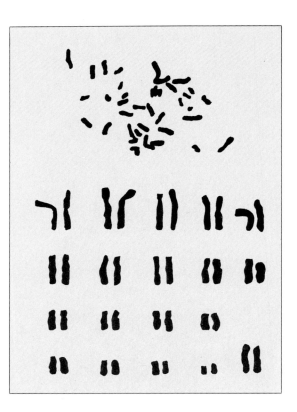

Above A white female
with tabby and
tortoiseshell markings,
mated with a plain black
male, is capable of
producing sons in
several combinations of
colours – orange, black,
tabby, orange and white,
black and white, tabby
and white. Her
daughters may be black,
tabby or tortoiseshell,
coloured all over, or
with white.

Left The cat's 19 pairs
of chromosomes within
the cell (above) and
organized into pairs for
microscopic examination
(below).

Right This little cat from
Singapore has the
strangely bobbed and
knotted tail that was
often seen in imported
Siamese at the end of the
nineteenth century.

Right The blue of this Blue Persian kitten is produced by the action of a simple recessive gene diluting black, and is often called the Maltese Factor.

Centre **Champion Midsummer Raffles** a cream and white longhaired Bicolour. Cream is a simple dilute of red, known genetically as orange.

Below **Yesso Genevieve**, a blue tortie-and-white longhaired queen, is the dilute form of the usual dark tortie-and-white. Black is diluted to blue, and red (orange) to cream.

A kitten that receives identical genes from both its sire and dam for a particular characteristic is said to be *homozygous* for that particular feature. On the other hand, a kitten may receive one gene from its sire and an alternative allele from its dam; it is then said to be *heterozygous* for that feature.

A cat that is homozygous for any feature will express that feature irrespective of its dominance or recessivity. The appearance of the heterozygous cat, however, does depend upon the dominance or recessivity features.

Hereditary characteristics are sometimes linked with sex, an example in the cat being the red factor, called yellow by most geneticists, and symbolized as O, for orange. To understand sex-linkage, it is essential to know how the sex of a kitten is determined. While the female cat has nineteen pairs of homologous chromosomes, the male cat has only eighteen such pairs. The remaining chromosome pair do not match, one being of medium size and known as the X chromosome, the other, much smaller, called the Y chromosome. Male cats therefore are characterized by having XY chromosomes, while female cats have XX chromosomes. Every ovum carries an X chromosome, while a sperm may carry either X or Y chromosomes. When an ovum is fertilized, it may fuse with an X-bearing sperm; the result will be XX and the sex of the kitten will be female. If the ovum fuses with the Y-bearing sperm, then the result will be XY and the kitten will be male.

The red colour in the cat can only be carried on the X chromosome, and as the male cat has but one X he can either be O (orange) or o (non-orange).

The female cat, having two X chromosomes, can be OO (orange), Oo (tortoiseshell) or oo (non-orange). The unique tortoiseshell is the heterozygote, and her coat shows the influence of both the O and o, the orange areas corresponding with O and the non-orange areas with o. Some results of matings may make this clearer:

Example a.

Black Male x Orange Female

Orange Males x Tortie Females

Black Males | Tortie Females
Orange Males | Orange Females

Example b.

Orange Males x Black Female

Black Males x Tortie Females

Black Females | Tortie Females
Orange Males | Black Males

An orange female can only be produced when both sire and dam show that colour, and these results apply to any breed of cat carrying the orange gene, be it Persian, Shorthair or Siamese.

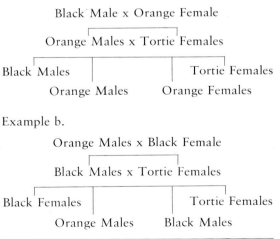

Breeders and fanciers are mainly concerned with coat colour, length and pattern, so it is important to know which factors are dominant or recessive to others. For example:

White is dominant to all other colours. Black is dominant to blue. Tabby (agouti) is dominant to non-tabby. Shorthair is dominant to longhair. Full coat is dominant to rex coat. Manx is dominant to normal tail.

Following Mendel's experiments, it is possible to predict the way in which the two alleles of any gene pair will segregate and their subsequent behaviour. This is most simple when one studies the effect of single gene differences. First of all we will see what happened in the first crosses between mutant cats when the agouti (symbol AA) mated with the non-agouti or black (symbol aa).

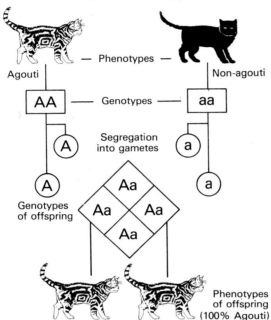

Then when the heterozygous agouti cats (Aa) are mated together:

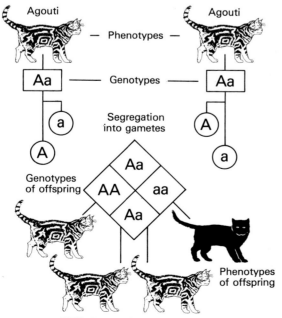

And then what happens when a backcross occurs between a heterozygous agouti (Aa) and a homozygous non-agouti (aa):

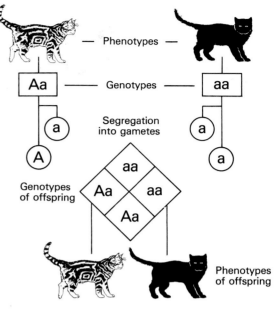

(50% Agouti; 50% non-agouti)

There are six possible crosses between one gene pair and any dominant gene symbol can be substituted for A, while the corresponding recessive one can be substituted for a.

Cross	Parent 1	Parent 2	Kittens
1	AA	AA	AA
2	aa	aa	aa
3	AA	aa	Aa
4	Aa	AA	1 × AA; 1 × Aa
5	Aa	aa	1 × Aa; 1 × aa
6	Aa	Aa	1 × AA; 2 × Aa; 1 × aa

Note: AA and Aa are agouti in phenotype or appearance, while aa are non-agouti. AA are 'pure' agouti in genotype, while Aa are agouti 'carrying' non-agouti, and only when the genotype is aa can the animal show the non-agouti appearance.

Far right This modern Abyssinian queen shows a perfect example of the agouti or ticked effect of the wild-type coat in the domestic cat.

Cat Care

Kittens look so helpless and prettily appealing that they are often bought or adopted on impulse. Sometimes this works successfully; sometimes it proves to be disastrous, especially if the kitten is frail or sickly owing to incorrect or thoughtless rearing. A badly reared kitten, particularly one starved of essential proteins, vitamins and minerals in the first few weeks of life, may never develop properly. The very best of food and care fail to right the damage already done. It can cost a small fortune in veterinary fees to bring such a youngster through the transitory phase of kittenhood, when teething, worming and vaccination programmes all add to the stresses on its system. In extreme cases kittens have died of gastritis or nonspecific enteritis soon after settling in their new homes, to the distress of their caring owners.

Before taking on a kitten, which has a life expectancy of fourteen years or so, it is advisable to decide just what sort of cat would best suit the household. Cats come in all shapes and styles, although, as adults, they are all roughly the same size. They can be pedigreed or pet, male or female, and can be bought in a wide range of colours and designs. Cats can be short and dumpy or long and lithe, and their coats either long- or short-haired.

Temperament is an important factor in the

busy household with young children and other pets is not the place for a timid and sensitive kitten, and an outgoing, mischievous kitten might prove a little too lively for a quiet and peaceful home.

If it is possible to see the litter with their mother, the kittens can be observed for a while, and their characters can be assessed. It is much better to obtain a pet kitten from a neighbour or friend than to buy one from a pet shop or store, where it may have contracted infection. Farms and animal sanctuaries often have a surplus of kittens each year, and if they are not homed, they are usually humanely destroyed. Such kittens should not be accepted out of pity, however.

Pedigree kittens should always be bought directly from the breeder and never through a store or agency. Bona fide breeders want to meet the new owners of their precious, carefully reared kittens, to ensure that the new home will be up to standard and that the kitten will be properly treated and fed in the future.

The best place to see lots of pedigree cats and kittens is at a large Championship Cat Show. Most major cities have at least one such show each year, and they are widely advertised. At the cat show the cats and kittens are in numbered cages, and their details listed against the corresponding number in the official catalogue. Exhibitors are usually delighted to explain the virtues of their specialist breeds, but it must

selection of the right kitten, for some cats are quiet and staid in their habits, while others are extroverted clowns. It is even possible to recognize kittens of both types in the same litter. A noisy,

also be remembered that they might be slightly biased.

Kittens can be booked at a cat show, but should not be taken to their new home straight from the show hall. Shows take a lot out of a small kitten, and its lowered resistance might make it liable to develop a minor infection. It is better to pay a deposit and collect the kitten a few weeks later.

Some breeds need companionship in order to thrive, and kittens usually seem to do better in pairs, so this is well worth thinking about. Two kittens growing up together play endlessly – delightful, amusing games, before falling asleep in a heap, paws around each other's necks. The friendly competition for food ensures that they eat well, and they are never lonely if left indoors for long periods or boarded in a cattery.

Plain or fancy, the points to look for in selecting a healthy, sound kitten are the same.

It is important that the kitten is properly weaned. To be certain, it should have been separated from its mother for at least a week before it goes to a new home; two weeks would be even better. Many people think a kitten is weaned when they see it tucking in to solid food, but it is surprising how much milk it is still drawing from its mother at that stage. If it is taken away suddenly at this age, it may be incapable of eating sufficient solid food and will suffer a severe setback in its growth rate and development.

The new kitten should look clean and healthy, with a firm, lithe body. The backbone and hips should be well covered, but there should not be any sign of the pot-belly which could denote the presence of worms. The eyes should be clear and bright, with no sign of any discharge, and the third eyelid or haw should not protrude at the inner corner. The ears should be spotlessly clean inside, without any black grits, which could indicate canker. The coat should be soft, with clean separated hairs, and when parted behind the ears and at the root of the tail, must be free from the tiny round black grains which are excreted by fleas. There should be no discharge from the nostrils of the new kitten, and the teeth and gums

must be fresh and healthy. The last thing to check is under the tail, for any yellow staining here might mean that the kitten is suffering from diarrhoea.

If the kitten passes all these tests, it should be safe to take it home. If not, it should be left in the environment it knows until it is treated.

A pedigree kitten will have a written record of its ancestry, and registration papers. Depending on its age, it may also have been vaccinated before sale and have the relevant certificates. Naturally all this is reflected in the price paid, but a sheaf of

Above The Abyssinian is generally faithful, quiet and rather retiring.

Left If possible, it is wise to have two kittens for they will be perfect companions and play together all their lives.

Far left Bright eyes and general cleanliness of the coat and skin denote a healthy kitten.

paperwork does not necessarily mean a better kitten.

Pedigree or pet, the kitten chosen must be the right kitten, for young animals should not be exchanged or passed from home to home. The transition from one home to another must be made as quietly and as comfortably as possible to avoid any unnecessary stress to the young cat.

Right To sex kittens they are turned over to lie comfortably on their backs. The exposed genitals are then clearly seen. In the female the two orifices are close together, the elongated vaginal opening and the circular anus forming a small question mark. In the male, both openings are circular and farther apart, separated by the small swellings of the testes.

When one goes to collect the new kitten, a safe carrier should be taken along. Kittens should never be carried unconfined in cars or on public transport. Carriers are available in several sizes, and are made of mesh, cardboard, basketwork, glass fibre, wood and Perspex. A good carrier is a worthwhile investment, for it should last for years, and should be large enough to carry one or two adult cats. It is very tempting to buy a small carrier for a tiny kitten, but this will soon become obsolete. The carrier should be lined with layers of newspaper topped with an old sweater or piece of warm blanket. If it is a cold day, a rubber hot-water bottle filled with water of a comfortably warm temperature can be wrapped well and tucked inside also. The kitten may protest at being shut inside the carrier during the journey home, but the lid should not be opened under any circumstances despite the wails.

The kitten should be greatly fussed over and petted on its arrival in its new home. It should be confined to one fairly small room at first so that it can get its bearings. There should be no hazards in the room, such as electric flex (wires), unguarded fires, open windows, uncovered fish tanks and impregnated fly-strips. All these things can be dangerous to a tiny kitten exploring a new environment.

At first the new kitten will miss its mother and litter mates and must be compensated by a great deal of tender loving care and play sessions. The first essential is a warm bed in which the kitten can rest and sleep. A solid cardboard box is better than a wicker basket at this stage. It can be disposed of when soiled and replaced with another box, and the firm sides prevent any draughts entering the

kitten's bed, causing chills. The bed makes a safe refuge also, from which the small animal can explore, retreating every time it feels nervous or threatened. The box should be thickly lined with newspaper, with a blanket on top. The blanket should be pulled up around the sides of the box, forming a nestlike depression in the centre into which the kitten can curl and sleep. Later on, as the kitten grows, a smart sleeping-basket and cushion can be bought.

Another similar cardboard box makes an excellent play cave. Kittens love to climb into boxes to play. Just cut some small, kitten-sized holes in every side of the box, place the open end on the floor and toss the kitten's toys inside. It will dive in and out of the opening with great enjoyment. The box may be covered with washable wallpaper or kitchen paper, so that it can be sponged over now and again to keep it clean and fresh.

There are many ingenious toys on the market designed expressly for cats and kittens. They vary considerably in price and suitability. Some are excellent, and provide hours of fun and excitement for both kittens and their owners. Others are potentially dangerous. The ones to avoid are those with long pieces of cord or elastic attached, or with stitched or wired glass eyes, tiny bells or any other object that can be chewed off and swallowed by a kitten. Some synthetic rubber or plastic toys are also dangerous. The soft material is easily chewed by the teething kitten and may be swallowed, with fatal results.

Simple toys are perfectly acceptable to cats and kittens, and even a small ball of crumpled paper provides hours of fun. Small mice can be stitched from scraps of thick material, stuffed with dried

Above left A kitten needs lots of sleep so a comfortable bed is important. Baskets of various shapes and sizes are available and may be lined with soft paper, blanket material or a cushion.

Above Some cats choose their own bed and like to curl up in seemingly unsuitable small places.

Far left Some baskets are designed for use as carriers or beds.

Left Small kittens love to play in old cartons which may be discarded when soiled.

catnip from the pet shop, and have a short, thick piece of string firmly attached as a tail. A spider, made of four pipe-cleaners, laid across each other and bound firmly and tightly around the middle, forming eight legs, is a favourite toy, which a kitten will carry around and take to bed with it. Table tennis balls, cotton reels and hen feathers all make perfect toys for kittens and encourage play, which helps to build up muscle and sharpen the reflexes.

A shallow toilet tray must be provided for the new kitten, and can have proprietary cat litter, wood shavings or chippings, peat moss or torn kitchen paper towels spread inside. The kitten will look for its toilet tray soon after its first meal in the new home and should be gently placed on the litter. There will be no familiar smell to reassure the kitten, so it may need placing on the tray several times before it decides to use it. Having used the tray once, the kitten will be confident that this is the correct place to go, if praised and petted. The tray should be kept in the same place, not moved around the room, or the young kitten might make a mistake and use the floor in the place where the tray had been. The litter must be changed frequently, and the tray washed when necessary with a mild solution of household bleach, or other safe disinfectant recommended by your veterinary surgeon. The tray may be sterilized with scalding water.

The breeder's diet sheet should be followed rigorously until the kitten has settled down, but even then, changes in the diet should be made very

gradually if gastric upsets are to be avoided. Food must be fed at room temperature and in shallow, spotlessly clean dishes, reserved for the kitten's exclusive use. Fresh drinking-water must be available to the kitten at all times.

The only other requirement in providing a perfect home for the kitten is a piece of timber on which it can strop its claws. All cats do this, and if they are not given a proper scratching post, they will use the furniture. Special scratching posts are made for cats and can be purchased at the pet shop. Some of these are excellent and are made of a log set upright on a firm wooden base. Others are attractively covered in carpet, but a cat encouraged to use such a post might well decide that all carpets may be used for stropping. Any piece of rough timber can be used as a scratching post or block, but the kitten or cat will be more inclined to use an upright piece than one laid flat on the floor. In a garden a cat will strop on a tree trunk, stretching up and scratching with delight. If the scratching post is made to simulate a tree trunk, it stands to reason that the animal will be more likely to use that than the best armchair.

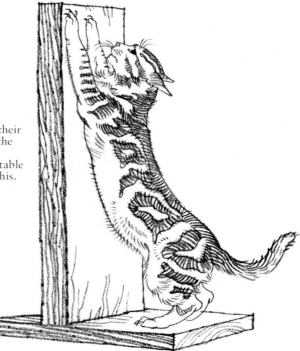

Cats need to strop their claws and will use the upholstery unless provided with a suitable scratch board like this.

Cats are generally thought of as being solitary creatures, preferring to be left alone to lead their own isolated and totally independent lives. Anyone who has had the opportunity to observe cats left to live in this way, and compared them with others, soon realizes that cats are better with companionship of some sort. Some cats get along well with other felines, some live in perfect harmony with dogs, and others crave human company at all times.

The best time to introduce a kitten to a new companion is while it is still at its most adaptable age, which seems to be between six and twelve weeks. Even in the following weeks a kitten will accept new friends, but as it grows older so the acceptance time increases. At six weeks of age it is possible to place kittens from several litters in the same pen, and although they will spit at each other at first, within a few minutes they will all play happily together. At twelve weeks it may take several hours before the kittens will accept each other, and at five or six months of age it could take at least five days.

When a new kitten is introduced to a pet dog already established in the home, it is important that the dog is not jealous and feels no resentment towards the kitten. If it does, it may attack the tiny creature. The two animals must be introduced in stages, and should not be left alone together until they have become obvious friends. At meal times a dog and cat must be fed quite separately. Firstly, they have different food requirements, and secondly, the dog will probably eat at high speed, quickly finishing its own meal before demolishing that of the cat. The animals should either be shut away in different rooms with their food bowls or fed at different levels, the dog on the floor and the cat on a high shelf.

Introducing a new kitten to an older cat is a similar situation, as the established animal might feel resentment towards the youngster. Patience and thoughtfulness must prevail, both animals being fussed over and petted, fed separately and only allowed to stay together unattended when the spitting and hissing has stopped. It may take a week or more for an older cat to accept a new kitten, although the kitten is obviously willing to be friendly. It is very rare for the cat to fail to accept the kitten in the end, no matter how strong its initial reactions are.

Contrary to popular belief, many cats get on very well with young children, provided that both have been properly brought up to show mutual respect. Even tiny human babies can be taught to stroke cats. The little hands are gently held with flat palms and passed along the cat's fur. The cat likes it, and it is quite evident from the gurgles of the child and the excitement in its eyes that it enjoys the sensation too. When the baby is old enough to sit up, the family cat may spend hours sitting close at hand, watching intently as the child plays. At the toddling stage the baby may be inclined to grasp the cat too tightly, and must be trained in gentleness. Some cats object to this firm handling and may scratch; others seem to thrive on the extra attention and keep coming back for more. Occasionally a cat becomes very possessive over a small child, and spends every spare moment by the cot or high chair, growling fiercely whenever strangers enter the room. Cats must be taught not to try to eat the baby's meals, and crawling babies should be kept away from the cat's dishes. Cats kept with children must be carefully and regularly wormed, and their toilet facilities should be kept out of the house if possible, with the provision of a cat-flap in the outside door so that the cat can come and go as necessary. Failing this, the litter tray should be positioned safely out of the baby's reach.

Above left A small child soon learns to enjoy stroking the family cat using a flat, not grasping hand.

Above Introduced with care and understanding, cats and dogs often become loving inseparable companions.

 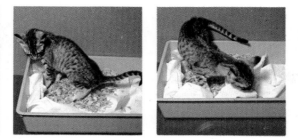

Sufficient litter must be provided for the kitten to perform its instinctive digging behaviour.

The kitten uses the tray, appears to check its progress, then covers up carefully.

A cat-flap is an ingenious device which is let into an outside door. It can be opened from either side unless a special locking section is fitted, which enables the cat to be kept either in or out. The cat may have to be trained to use the flap, and the best age to start this is at about three to four months. Lightweight cat-flaps are easily pushed open even by quite small kittens. The training should commence at feeding time when the cat or kitten is hungry and has seen the meal being prepared. The animal is placed outside the door and the cat-flap is slightly opened from inside so that the cat is conscious of the food. It will quickly push its way through the hinged opening, and should be allowed its meal. At the next meal repeat this procedure, and do so at every meal until the cat is used to coming in through the flap. Some cats learn to push the flap after only one lesson, others take a little longer. Once the cat is used to coming in through the flap, the same procedure is used to teach it to get out. On some flaps the door is kept closed by a magnetized strip, and this offers a little more resistance when opened from indoors. Because of this it may take the cat a little longer to learn to push through the opening from the inside. The locking device is useful. It enables the flap to be secured at night, keeping your cat safely in and other unwelcome cats safely out.

Cats can be trained to behave in an acceptable manner so that they fit into the family routine. It is possible, but very difficult, to teach them to perform various movements on command, too, but few people think the results justify the effort involved. The first thing that any cat should be taught is its name. If several cats are kept, each should have a distinctive name so that the required animal can be called at any time. This does not necessarily mean that the right cat will come, of course, but it makes sound sense to try. Some breeders with lots of house cats perform this exercise as a party piece. They wait until all the cats are asleep together, then quietly call one cat's name, when that cat looks up, they call the next name, and so on, until each animal has been individually aroused and responds.

Short sharp words of command can also be taught to the cat – 'get down' seems to be the most effective, and used most often when cats are thieving from the kitchen worktops. It is taught by using a firm sharp voice and clapping the hands together at the same time. Cats do very much as they please most of the time, and training really consists of observing their behaviour, ignoring them when this is totally acceptable, and scolding them when it is not. A cat that starts to strop the carpet, for instance, should have a sharp 'no', and

be put firmly by its scratching post.

The same procedure is followed for any cat that makes a mess or wets in the wrong place – a sharp reprimand, and then it is put on its toilet tray. If the cat is to be taught that toilet facilities are out of doors, it must be trained gradually. The toilet tray is moved near the door; then, over a period of a few days, it is put outside for a few hours. Eventually some soiled litter in the required place in the garden should encourage the cat to use that spot. If possible, however, the cat should be allowed to use a clean toilet tray whenever it requires to do so. In this way a careful check can be kept on its motions for signs of constipation, diarrhoea or worms. Any kidney or bladder trouble will also be noticed, and the cat is less likely to pick up infection if it has indoor toilet facilities. Many cats spend their entire lives indoors in these days of heavy traffic and other hazards. They are quite contented and healthy, if they have not been used to an outdoor life. If a cat is to be kept permanently indoors, it should be started off as a young kitten, so that it knows of no other form of existence. The indoor cat must be given plenty to occupy its time and another pet as a companion. Pots of grass and scratching posts help to compensate for the facilities of the garden, and some form of climbing frame is appreciated.

A cat flap can prove to be a boon for the owner whose pet spends much time in the garden. Constant use can, however, remove considerable hair from the animal's back.

It is important to train a kitten to enjoy being put in its carrier, for there are many times during a cat's life when this is a necessary procedure. There will be excursions to the veterinary surgery and to the boarding cattery, and sometimes perhaps the kitten may be taken on holiday, or to a cat show.

The kitten can have its carrier as a component of its play area. In this way the basket or box will soon have a familiar smell to the sensitive feline nose. A blanket can be placed inside the carrier, and the kitten may well use it as a bed. It is a good idea to put some paper in the carrier and to feed the cat its favourite meal inside. The door or lid can be left open the first time this is done, but later meals can be given with the carrier closed. When released, the cat should be greatly fussed over and petted, and eventually the carrier will be associated with good things. A carrier should always be used to transport cats and kittens, for if they escape in strange surroundings, they may be so frightened that they run off and are never seen again.

Carriers should be well-made and have secure fastenings that cannot be opened by a clever cat. A frightened cat may eat through a cardboard or wicker carrier, and should never be sent unaccompanied in such a container.

If for some reason a carrier is not available, a cat can be restrained and controlled to a certain extent by the use of a harness or collar and lead. Special harnesses are made for cats. They are of very soft leather or nylon material and are designed to fit comfortably and well without rubbing. They are made so that there is no way that the cat can wriggle free, and a sturdy ring is fitted to which a matching lead may be attached. Cat collars are also specially manufactured, but these are not really satisfactory for use with leads because they have an elastic piece inset in the collar. The object of this is to allow the cat to free itself from the

Above left Car training commences by confining the cat to the car for periods, perhaps feeding it there and providing a litter tray for its comfort.

Above right Most cats readily accept a light harness to which is attached a lead for added security while travelling.

Right Many types of carrier are available. A good carrier must be escape proof, large enough to enable the cat to stand up and with safe fastenings.

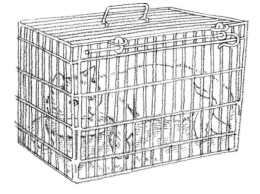

Above Cats soon accept conditions in good boarding catteries, where they are safely confined within wired runs.

Above right Although they are, in effect, cages, properly planned cattery runs provide comfortable conditions.

collar if it gets caught up on a branch or twig while hunting. Obviously the cat could soon get free if held on a lead. In an emergency, if a cat has to be transported and there is no carrier of any sort available, put the animal inside a pillow case and secure the open end with a stout elastic band. The cat can be reassured and carried comfortably. Plenty of air can penetrate the material and the cat, although it may object, will be perfectly safe. As a last resort, a stout, zipped-up shopping-bag may be used.

If a cat is going to have to accompany its owners on journeys quite regularly, it must be trained to accept this from as early an age as possible. The young kitten can be popped in its carrier with its favourite toys and a titbit, and taken in the car every time its owners go out for short journeys. The kitten will soon get used to the noise and motion of the car and will realize that it will only be in the carrier for a short while. Some owners train their cats to lie along the parcel seat in the back of the car. This seems all right in theory, but in the event of an accident, the cat might get lost. If startled, it could jump into the front of the car and get under the brake pedal at a critical moment. The proper way for a cat to travel is in its carrier.

Carriers are necessary, too, for travelling with a cat on trains, buses and planes. Sometimes it is possible to take the animal into the passenger section and have the box or basket on the seat. Sometimes regulations insist that the carrier be placed in the luggage section. Various airlines have different regulations regarding transportation of cats. If they are accompanied, they may occasionally travel in the cabin with their owner. More often, though, they must travel as cargo and must be packed in specially constructed, crush-proof wooden crates.

Strict regulations apply to the transportation of

cats between various countries of the world, and these should be carefully studied before one attempts to take a cat from one country to another. The animal may need to have specific injections and certificates for entry into some countries. It may need to be confined in quarantine kennels for several months on entry into others.

There are boarding catteries near most towns at which cats and kittens can be accommodated during their owners' holidays. These establishments vary a great deal in the facilities that they offer. Some are built and run exclusively for cats and some are annexed to dog boarding kennels. The construction and licensing of catteries is controlled by local authorities and varies a great deal. The basic requirements for boarding a cat are shelter, warmth, food, cleanliness, attention and affection. That the shelter must also be escape-proof goes without saying.

The best boarding catteries have a small building for each cat, in which there is room for its bed and belongings, food and water, plus space for it to exercise itself. Joined on to this is an outdoor run, securely wired in to prevent the escape of a nervous or frightened cat. The run is of easily cleaned concrete, and has a covered or indoor toilet tray and a sunning log or shelf. The sleeping compartment will be lined with easily cleaned material, and be light, warm and well ventilated, with access to the outdoor run.

Indoor boarding catteries are not wholly satisfactory, owing to the high risk of infectious disease spreading from cat to cat unless there is an adequate airflow. In areas of suitable climate, outdoor catteries equipped with heating units and run by experts are ideal. Healthy, vaccinated cats can be left with the proprietors in the sure knowledge that they will be contented and cared for until the owners return from holiday.

The coat of the longhaired kitten before grooming.

Cats are fastidious creatures and care for their own toilet very well, but because they have been domesticated and do not lead natural lives, a little extra care and attention may be required from time to time. The responsible cat owner should have a set routine of cat care, apart from the daily food preparation, feeding and changing of the toilet tray. Grooming (page 104) may be carried out daily, weekly or at other regular intervals, depending on the requirements of the cat's coat, but the ears, teeth and claws should be checked, without fail, once a week.

Ears: Inside, the cat's ears should be spotlessly clean with a very slightly moist appearance. If there is any sign of greyish wax, this can be wiped out with a dry cotton bud. Some cats have a lot of hair inside the ears and the wax may clog around this. A piece of cotton-wool (see Glossary) lightly moistened with warm water and baby soap is then used to wipe the wax away. Water must not be allowed to trickle down inside the ears, and the cotton buds must not be used to poke around inside the ear canal itself.

Black or dark brown gritty material in the ears usually indicates the presence of ear mites (see Common Parasites). The cat should be examined by the veterinary surgeon, who will prescribe the drops necessary to treat these parasites. Ear drops are sucked into the dropper provided, which is then placed in a dish of hot water for a few moments. The cat will not mind warm drops in the ear; cold drops will make it struggle violently. The oily liquid must be allowed to run right down to the base of the ear, where the mites live and breed. The cheek should be massaged at the point of the jaw to help the liquid penetrate every crevice at the base of the ear. When it is released, after a moment or so, the cat will shake its head violently to remove the liquid, but must be restrained as long as possible so that the drops can do their work. The drops are usually administered over a period of about three weeks, depending on their formulation, and it is important to carry out the instructions exactly. Any debris that floats out of the ear can be wiped away with dry cotton-wool.

Kittens' ears may get very dusty, and need wiping out constantly. It is important to teach the kitten to enjoy having its ears cleaned by making it a part of petting, before feeding time.

Teeth: Every cat should be accustomed to having its mouth examined without fuss. Kittens need regular checking to ensure that the teeth are erupting properly, and that the milk teeth are being shed. Many breeders receive frantic telephone calls from owners whose new kittens refuse all food. In most cases it is because new teeth are coming through, the milk teeth are still present, and the poor little creature has a very sore mouth indeed. Kittens accustomed to having a small strip of raw meat each day rarely have teething problems. The meat helps to remove the first teeth quite naturally as the new teeth come through. Soft foods help to encourage the build-up of layers of tartar along the gum margins of cats. Regular weekly checking ensures that this never becomes a serious problem. Some people clean their cats' teeth using children's soft toothbrushes or soft wooden dental sticks impregnated with an oral antiseptic. The cats seem to enjoy the procedure. Feeding raw meat and a few hard pellets of crunchy cat food is a more natural way of keeping the cat's teeth and gums healthy. If a cat salivates excessively but is otherwise well, it may be due to an extreme build-up of tartar and this must be removed by the veterinary surgeon without delay. If it is neglected, the cat may need to have teeth extracted under a general anaesthetic.

Claws: It is a good idea to examine each of the cat's feet once a week, checking the pads for thorns, cuts or abrasions, and at the same time the claws can be extended by gently squeezing each foot in turn. If a claw is broken off, it can become infected and a swelling may be found right up in the claw bed. The whole foot can be bathed to give relief (see First Aid). Sometimes the area around each claw bed becomes neglected and dirty. If this is so, each foot should be carefully and thoroughly washed with warm water and baby soap, rinsed and dried. Each claw is then carefully examined to make sure that there is no sign of infection, for this is the site most commonly attacked by a fungal disease such as ringworm. If the claws are very long and catch in the carpet or furnishings, it is advisable to cut them back a little, and to blunt them off. No cat should be declawed or have the claws cut so that they would be useless in an emergency. Cats need their claws to climb out of trouble at times, and to fight back if attacked by a dog or another cat. To shorten the claws, a pair of nail clippers with a spring handle is necessary. Scissors must not be used, for they will splinter the claw and make it sore. If the claw is examined, the sensitive quick is easily seen as the pigmented part within the paler keratin. The tip of the claw is clipped off smartly with the clippers safely below the quick and, if necessary, the edge can be rubbed down with a fine emery board until it feels smooth.

The Old Cat: Old cats need especially careful attention to their ears, teeth and claws. Everything should be done to keep them feeling as well as possible. If the old cat has trouble walking, its pads may be cracked and it should be confined to

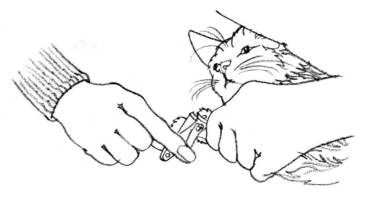

Left The old cat may need a little help with its toilet, and any dirty areas around the nostrils, eyes or lips should be wiped clean with a damp cloth or sponge.

Right Claws are shortened with nail clippers, taking care to avoid the sensitive quick.

the house for a few days while vegetable oil is worked into the fissured skin. A little oil added to the cat's diet might also help the condition. The old cat's health is often dramatically improved by having bad teeth extracted. Its strength should be kept up while the mouth heals by feeding a light liquid diet for a few days. Old cats often neglect their coat and tail area in the process of self-grooming, so extra attention may be necessary, particularly in the anal region, which may be sponged with warm water and then dried. Talcum powder can be used in the coat, if necessary, to keep it sweet and soft (see Grooming).

The Shampoo: Cats may also be given wet baths if necessary, and if the water is at the correct temperature, some cats actually appear to enjoy the operation. It is preferable to have access to a double sink; failing this, two large polythene bowls are used. The water must be comfortably hand-hot, and the cat is placed gently but firmly in a sink or bowl a quarter filled with the water, which is ladled over the coat until it is evenly saturated. Many cats' coats repel water, and a

little shampoo may be added, if necessary, to help the water to penetrate the hair. When the coat is thoroughly wet, a shampoo specially formulated for cats only should be worked well into the hair with a massaging motion, all over the body but avoiding the face. It is necessary to have an assistant to hold the cat's scruff while this is done, as two hands are needed to shampoo properly.

The second bowl of hot water is used to rinse out the shampoo and is poured gently over the cat until every bit of foam is removed. It may be necessary to change the water in which the cat is sitting, if bowls are used. If the cat can sit in a sink or bath while being rinsed, the whole operation is much easier. The important thing is to leave the coat rinsed clear; then the cat can be dried as thoroughly as possible with a thick towel. Some cats will allow themselves to be finished off with a hair-dryer or fan heater, others must be placed in a very warm spot inside a mesh carrier until the coat is completely dry. Most cats aid the drying process by licking the fur vigorously. It is important to dry the coat as quickly as possible, so that the hair can be groomed into place.

In bathing the cat the coat is thoroughly wetted (a), before the shampoo is worked well in (b), then after rinsing carefully the cat is towelled as dry as possible (c).

A well-groomed cat glows with health.

Grooming is carried out for two main purposes. Firstly, it keeps the coat in good condition by removing all dead hairs and flakes of dead skin; it cleans and separates the growing hairs, and so improves the cat's appearance. Secondly, it stimulates the circulation and tones up the muscles of the body, thus promoting a sense of well-being in the cat.

Different grooming techniques are employed for grooming longhaired and shorthaired cats, and for exhibition purposes even more sophisticated routines are used. Owners also have individual methods of grooming their cats, but here we will examine the basic routines only.

Grooming the Shorthair: Shorthaired cats only need grooming once each week unless they are shedding a quantity of hair or are to be entered in a show. The basic routine is very simple. The cat is brushed lightly but thoroughly from head to tail to remove loose hair and to stimulate the circulation. A moderately stiff bristle brush is best and will not damage the growing hair. Particular attention should be paid to the throat, armpits and inner thighs, and the coat should be checked for signs of the black grits which show the presence of fleas (see Common Parasites).

If necessary, a pesticide suitable for cats, or a correctly formulated coat dressing may be applied

Grooming the Shorthair
Above The coat is thoroughly brushed to remove dust and dead hairs.

Above centre Coat dressing or pest powder may be sprayed over the body, avoiding the eyes and genitals.

Far right A fine-toothed comb removes parasites and dead hair as well as flakes of dandruff.

Right Buffing with a soft cloth or hand buffing brings up a healthy sheen on the coat and promotes muscle tone.

Grooming the Longhair
Far left Powder is sprinkled into the coat and *centre* rubbed well in. After brushing the powder out again, *right and below*, a coarse comb is used to separate all the hairs.

and worked into the coat. Next a fine-toothed comb is used all over the cat from head to tail, to remove loose hairs, scurf and parasites or grit. A pad of soft cloth or a chamois leather can be used fairly firmly along the muscular areas to raise a sheen on the coat; then the hands are used all over the cat, smoothly and firmly, to promote muscle tone. Finally, the ears, eyes, anal region and claw beds are examined and cleaned if necessary.

Grooming the Longhair: Longhaired cats usually require daily grooming from kittenhood, with an extra-special session once a week in which the ears, claws and teeth are checked and cleaned if necessary. Some longhaired cats need powdering every day if their coats are especially soft and mat together easily. Others only need powdering once a week or so. Specially formulated grooming powder is best, but baby powder may be used. It is sprinkled lightly into the coat and then worked in with the fingertips, as the hairs are gently separated. While the powder is absorbing grease from the coat, a wire rake or special mitten may be used to tease out any knots or tangles.

The rake or mitten must be used carefully so that the skin is not scratched or damaged in any way. When any tangles have been cleared, the powder is brushed out of the coat, and the cat is combed with a coarse, blunt metal comb all over the body, finishing off by working up from the tail to the head against the lie of the coat. If the long-

haired coat is neglected, it becomes clumped together as the hairs form thick matted lumps. These prove impossible to tease out in the usual way, and they must be cut off at the roots of the hair. A seriously neglected coat might need complete clipping or de-matting, and this frequently has to be carried out under a general anaesthetic by a veterinary surgeon. As the new hair grows, it must receive daily attention so that it never mats again, but in such soft-coated cats it is a good idea to keep the underneath of the body clipped fairly closely, unless the cat is going to be competing at shows.

The Bran Bath: A very soiled or oily coat may be best cleaned by giving the cat a bran bath. A quarter pound or so of bran is spread evenly on a baking pan and heated through in a warm oven until it feels comfortably hot to the touch. It is then tipped onto a large sheet of newspaper, on which the cat is placed while the bran is worked well into its coat. The bran is massaged in, right to the roots, and the cat is wrapped in a large, hot towel and petted soothingly for about ten minutes. When the towel is removed, the cat stands on the newspaper while the bran is brushed and combed from the coat, bringing with it dust, scurf, dirt and loose hairs. The next day the cat must be thoroughly groomed again to remove the last traces of bran from the coat, which will look greatly improved, with a good sheen.

Unless a cat is to be used specifically for breeding purposes, it is sensible to have it neutered. Full males allowed their freedom soon develop unsocial habits, such as the spraying of urine all around their territories, straying and fighting all the other male cats in the neighbourhood and wailing through the night. Entire females, on maturity, come into season with great regularity, and if allowed their freedom, will easily get into a regular cycle of kitten production. If confined, they may become frustrated, possibly develop dirty habits in the house, and may even become difficult for their owners to handle. Neutering takes care of all these problems, and neutered cats make clean, affectionate and easily cared for pets.

The Male: Male cats are neutered by castration. This is carried out under a general anaesthetic. A small incision is made in the scrotum through which the testes are removed. It is not necessary for any stitches to be inserted unless there are complications, and the operation is very quick. Male cats are usually neutered at about six months of age (see Showing), but they can be operated on at any age from four months. Even quite old, battle-scarred tom-cats come through the operation without any apparent ill-effects.

The Female: The female cat is neutered by an operation commonly known as spaying. She is given a general anaesthetic and the site of the operation is shaved and cleaned to prevent infection entering the wound. In the USA it is usual to make an incision mid-line, i.e. along the middle of the abdomen from the navel towards the hind legs. In European countries and Australasia it is more common to operate through a small incision in the flank. The ovaries and uterus are removed and the incision is closed with two or three stitches which may require removal about a week later. In some instances the vet may decide to spay the female cat by the stab method, in which neither sutures nor stitches are necessary. The female may be neutered at any age from about four months, but the operation may be postponed if the cat is in advanced pregnancy or has just kittened. The neutering of pedigree or show cats is often delayed to allow their full physical development.

Both males and females are kept without solid food and fluids for twelve hours before the operation so that they do not suffer any dangerous effects from the anaesthetic. Males usually recover more quickly than females as their operation is generally more simple, but both males and females are usually playing, eating and drinking within a few hours of their operations, although females with mid-line incisions may take about 48 hours to recover.

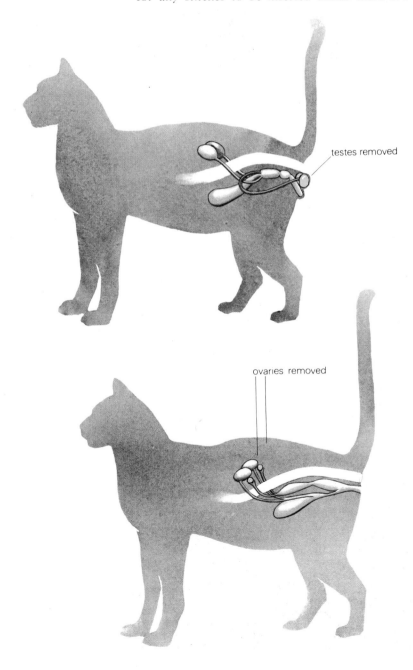

testes removed

ovaries removed

Left Neutering of the male *above*, cat involves the external operation of removing the testes while *below*, spaying the female requires an abdominal incision to facilitate the removal of the ovaries.

Above A spayed female just recovering from general anaesthesia. Note the small shaved area in the flank and the neatly closed incision. Raised third eyelids are common until the anaesthetic wears off completely.

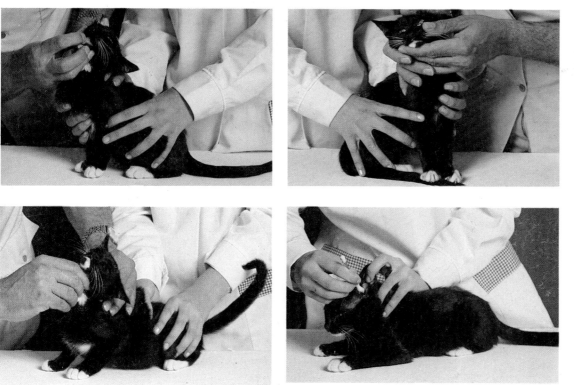

Far left Checking mouth as routine.

Left Checking eyes for inflammation.

Far left Checking glands of the throat.

Left Checking and cleaning the ears.

The responsible cat owner ensures that the pet cat is protected against disease as far as possible by keeping up to date with vaccinations and avoiding contact with sick animals. It is common practice to vaccinate 9–12 week old kittens against the dreadful disease feline infectious enteritis, or panleucopenia (page 130). Having been correctly vaccinated as a kitten, the cat is given booster doses of the same vaccine every year or two years (depending on the type of vaccine used) to maintain the level of protection. The cat may also be vaccinated annually against cat flu by injection, or by a vaccine applied in drop form up the nostrils. It is vital that cats at risk be regularly vaccinated. Brood queens are particularly vulnerable, and so are stud cats receiving visiting queens. Cats being shown regularly are also in danger from infection, and any cat that is to be placed in a boarding cattery must have a current certificate of vaccination. All good catteries refuse to take boarders unless this documentation is produced.

During the general grooming routine, the skin should be checked for lesions. A lesion is any change in a tissue or an organ. Therefore any scratch, scab or patch of bare skin can be classed as a lesion, and cats are banned from entering a cat show if any such suspect places are present on the skin. The veterinary surgeon may diagnose the cause of skin lesions by routine examination. He may dismiss the scratch or scab as the result of a fight or minor accident, or he may feel that further investigation is needed. A skin scraping can be performed, when a tiny sliver of skin is removed from the affected area with a scalpel blade. The skin is examined microscopically, and if any mites are present, they can be identified. Fungal infec-

tions are more difficult to recognize, but the lesions may fluoresce when exposed to the light of an ultra-violet (Wood's) lamp (see Diseases of the Skin).

Parasites such as fleas may bite the cat, which then shows an allergic reaction to the flea bite. After getting rid of the fleas, the owner may be horrified to find scabs all down the spine and flanks of the pet cat. Some foods also may give rise to skin allergies, and these can be very difficult to track down.

To keep a cat healthy, then, it must be fed well, and groomed regularly. The vaccination programmes must be followed carefully, and attention must be given to the control of parasites. The cat should be wormed at regular intervals, and checked over by the veterinary surgeon whenever problems arise. Above all, the cat should not be put at risk unless it is really necessary. If there are any epidemics in the area, keep your cat safely indoors and discourage visitors who have sick cats at home.

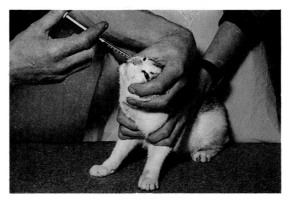

Giving an intra-nasal vaccine against upper respiratory disease.

It is essential to provide your cat with plenty of fresh drinking water each day, served in a clean bowl.

In determining the correct diet for the domestic cat, scientists continue to carry out extensive tests. One of the first of these was an exhaustive study of the animal's natural diet. A small rat or mouse is the normal prey of the cat, who eats the entire carcass. A cat that lives on a diet of small rodents stays very fit and looks to be in perfect health. The mouse consists of about 70 per cent water, 15 per cent protein, 10 per cent fat and 1 per cent carbohydrates. It also yields minerals and vitamins, and it would seem logical that any diet we devise for our pet cat should correspond as closely as possible to the make-up of the natural food.

When the cat evolved and adapted to a strictly carnivorous diet, it virtually lost the capacity to digest and utilize plant foods. The cat just cannot exist on a low protein diet. It requires large amounts of meat daily, in relation to its size. The only way in which the cat can digest carbohydrate is in the cooked state, such as in baked biscuits, bread products and boiled root vegetables. The cat needs a relatively high level of vitamin A to keep its body cells working properly, but far less vitamin D in relation to A than needed by dogs or humans. Vitamins of the B group are important for the maintenance, in particular, of the central nervous system.

Natural food yields a high level of calcium and phosphorus, which the cat requires for the growth of its bones. These elements may be lacking in the meals fed to the domestic cat. The signs of deficiency show as fractured or deformed bones, especially in the four to six month kitten. Cats are often seen to chew grass, which supplies folic acid, necessary for their well-being but lacking in cooked meat diets.

When the cat has eaten, and following digestion, the food undergoes the process of oxidation within the body, and energy is released. The energy is measured by scientists in units of heat called calories. In a healthy cat the number of calories it requires balances the number of calories that its body uses each day. If this balance is maintained, then the cat stays fit and well and its weight remains constant. A cat that is underfed gradually loses weight and condition as the body draws on the reserves of fat or protein to make up the deficiencies.

Depending on its pattern of activity, the normal female cat requires 200–250 calories per day, while the male needs 250–300 calories. Kittens need more calories in relation to their body weight, because they are growing rapidly, their smaller bodies are subject to more heat loss and their energy requirements are higher.

It is convenient to know the relative calorie values of various meats fed to the cat. It must be remembered, however, that meat varies in quality, and that with a high fat content will have a higher yield of calories than a lean cut.

Approximate Calorie Values of Some Foods

Food:	Calories:
Rabbit	600 per lb
Chicken	500 per lb
Heart	550 per lb
Liver	600 per lb
Melts (spleen)	450 per lb
Lights (lungs)	500 per lb
Lean minced beef	750 per lb
White fish	500 per lb
Oily fish	750 per lb
Milk	400 per pint
Canned cat food	200 per small can
Dried diet	1,600 per lb

These figures are an approximate guide, but show how an average cat's diet can be conveniently broken down and varied. For example, a cat with a weekly calorie requirement of 1,400 to 1,800 units could have, during the week, seven cans of cat food and a pint of milk, OR 1 lb of dried diet and half a pint of milk, OR 2 lb of rabbit, $\frac{1}{2}$ lb of liver, $\frac{3}{4}$ pint of milk, OR 1 lb of beef, 1 lb melts, $\frac{1}{2}$ lb oily fish, $\frac{1}{2}$ pint of milk, OR 4 cans of food, $\frac{1}{4}$ lb dried diet, $\frac{1}{2}$ lb of white fish, $\frac{3}{4}$ pint of milk.

Some cats enjoy cooked rice added to their meat, and this is an excellent way of adding calories to the diets of thin or finicky eaters.

The pet food industry is vast and spends enormous amounts of money in research and in the testing of foodstuffs for animals. Canned food for cats can vary in quality, but the canned diets put up for cats by the leading manufacturers are guaranteed to be correctly balanced. Vitamins lost in the cooking process are replaced, and the ingredients are carefully selected before being prepared under conditions of hygiene and efficiency. Complete dried foods are available, carefully formulated to contain everything a cat needs to stay healthy. Cats fed on dried diets must be given plenty of water, and they should be watched to ensure that they drink well. Kittens weaned onto dried foods usually drink adequate amounts of water and do well; older cats, taking to the dried diet later in life, may be too lazy to drink enough, and health problems may occur. Some cats become so addicted to the flavoursome crunchy dried cat foods that they refuse everything but their favourite brand. Most cat owners, however, prefer their pets to enjoy a very varied diet, including some of the dried food to keep the cat's teeth healthy.

Water, in a clean bowl, should be put down every day so that it is always available to the cat. Some foods contain much more water than others, and dried foods contain a much higher percentage of solids than fresh foods. Therefore it is obvious that only approximately one-third the amount of dried food is fed by weight, compared with fresh food.

A pinch of table salt added to the food is helpful in encouraging the cat to drink plenty of water.

Composition of Cat Food:

Food	Moisture(%)	Dry solids(%)
Fresh meat	70	30
Fresh fish	80	20
Canned cat food	75	25
Dried diet	10	90

This kitten has recently recovered from a debilitating illness and has lost weight as can be seen from the flanks, shoulders and haunches. Condition and muscle tone is restored by an intelligent combination of correct feeding and exercise.

In the wild state the cat hunts and kills, feeds off the prey, then rests. It may gorge itself on a whole rabbit one day, then go without food for the next two or three days. Pet cats are different and are usually fed once or twice each day. Adult cats do quite well if fed only one meal daily. Those kept in catteries, however, seem to enjoy two smaller meals; possibly the routine of feeding helps alleviate boredom. Pregnant and lactating queens can have their food requirements split into three or even four meals, and kittens need tiny meals at fairly frequent intervals.

Cats that are addicted to one type of food may suffer disastrous consequences if they refuse to eat anything else. For example, carcass meat is low in calcium, vitamin A and iodine. If a cat will only accept carcass meat, a condition known as osteoporosis may develop, in which the bones lose much of their mineral matter and become fragile or deformed. The cat may well become infertile. Of course, the missing components may be added to the food, but it is easier to feed a varied diet in the first instance, to prevent the development of a finicky feeder.

The cat addicted to liver, on the other hand, risks building up an excess of vitamin A. This results in bony outgrowths forming around the joints and spine and makes the movements of the cat stiff and obviously very painful. Adding too much cod liver oil to the cat's food can produce the same results.

Meat can be fed either cooked, canned or raw. Cooking at home destroys many vitamins, unless the meat is sealed in foil and baked in the oven before being fed complete with all the escaped juices. It should be cooked for the minimum time possible, cooled rapidly and fed fresh. Canned food, if of high quality, is reliable and correctly balanced.

Raw meat may be fed to the cat if it comes from a reliable source and is not contaminated with the micro-organisms which turn foodstuffs bad. Infected raw meat causes severe gastric upsets, and may even lead to death. All raw meat fed to cats should be fit for human consumption. It can be dangerous to handle any other raw meat, which could contaminate utensils and other food, during its preparation.

Milk is an acceptable food for some cats and is rich in valuable proteins. Unfortunately, some cats are unable to digest the lactose present in milk and the result is a persistent and severe diarrhoea. Other cats may show an allergic reaction to the protein in cow's milk. Sometimes these cats can take goat's milk as a substitute; otherwise milk must be banned from their diets. Many breeders find it best to use canned evaporated milk for rearing their kittens and for giving extra calcium to pregnant and lactating queens. It is usually diluted with an equal quantity of hot water and is then readily acceptable to most cats. If there is any diarrhoea as a result, however, the milk should be withdrawn. Calcium can easily be added to the diet by means of specially formulated tablets, or by feeding sterilized bonemeal as a supplement.

There are several vitamin and mineral supplements prepared for cats. Most of these are quite harmless and some of those in tablet form are regarded as treats by many cats. Unfortunately, some owners believe that giving these tablets every

Neutered cats tend to over-eat and gain weight unless the diet is restricted. Overweight puts an added strain on the heart and may shorten the cat's life.

Right Chopped heart may be fed cooked or raw.

Centre right Fillets of white fish are cooked lightly, then skinned before feeding.

Below left Approximately 2 ozs of complete dried diet is equivalent to 8 ozs of fresh raw beef, or *below centre and right* 6 ozs of steak, complete with fat, and kidney.

Feeding Guide

Age	Body weight (lb)	Daily food requirements (oz)	No. of feeds
Newborn	0.25	1.0	10
5 weeks	1.0	3.0	6
10 weeks	2.0	5.0	5
20 weeks	4.5	6.0	4
30 weeks	6.5	7.0	3
Adult male	10.0	8.5	1
Pregnant female	7.5	8.5	2/3
Lactating female	5.5	14.0	4
Neuter	9.0	6.5	1

day acts in some magical way to prevent illness and infection. If a cat is fed on a varied and well-balanced diet, vitamin and mineral supplements are not necessarily good things. By adding them certain elements could be increased to danger level. There are no hard and fast rules for feeding cats; each must be individually assessed. The veterinary surgeon is the best person to advise on the feeding of the adult cat proving to be a problem. If the animal is overweight or under-weight, losing its coat, has foul breath, flaking skin or shredded claws, the diet could be at fault. Infertility, uncertain movements, neurotic be-haviour and sensitivity to light can all be the results of inadequate or incorrect feeding. A thorough check-up and an accurate list of the cat's diet will help the veterinary surgeon to pinpoint the problem area. A course of vitamin injections and some special supplement may be prescribed, but the revised diet sheet must be carefully followed.

A cat that is fit and well, is glowing with health, is lively and happy, and lives a normal life is obviously getting the correct nourishment from the food it eats, and there is no need to change its diet in any way.

A Sample Diet for a Young Adult Cat

Morning: An optional meal of 2–3 oz of milk – cow, goat, dried, or diluted evaporated. 5 ml of cod liver oil may be added twice a week.

Evening: 6–9 oz canned or fresh food, depending on the size and activity of the cat. Vary as much as possible.

An entire, adult female cat is known as a queen. Depending on her breed, her physical state and the prevailing climate, she may be in breeding condition for most of the year. Definite peaks in sexual activity do occur in the queen, however, usually in spring and again in late summer. Queens kept indoors, where they are at a constant temperature and are subjected to long hours of white light, have been noted to breed more regularly than those kept more naturally. There would appear to be a correlation between day length and fecundity in the female cat. In nature kittens born during the warmer months stand a better chance of survival, and this is reflected in controlled litters. Spring and summer kittens do tend to be more robust and disease-resistant than

Typical stance of a queen in oestrus – the mating position.

winter-born kittens from the same parents.

Puberty can vary in the female cat from as early as four months in some precocious kittens to about fifteen months in others. As any experienced stud owner will confirm, most young females seem to come into breeding season early in their first spring, regardless of their age. The telephone rings constantly over a period of several days, as distraught owners seek advice about their frantically rolling and calling female kittens.

The signs of oestrus in the cat are easy to recognize and consist of four definite stages in a cycle. A queen in oestrus is often said to be 'on heat', 'in season' or 'calling'. *Pro-oestrus* is the preparatory stage, when the reproductive organs undergo changes in readiness for mating, fertilization and pregnancy. The queen becomes extra-affectionate and restless. If confined, she will pace the floor and spend some time looking out of the window. She will rub the scent glands of her lips against the furniture and floor, and may roll from time to time. At this stage she may be interested in the male cat but is not ready for mating. Pro-oestrus lasts from one to five days and is followed by *oestrus*. This is the period when mating will take place readily, and has a duration of about seven days. The queen becomes increasingly agitated. She rolls vigorously on the floor and cries, often quite fiercely, with a distinct cry known as the call. She will try to escape from every door and window, if confined; her cries become deeper and more urgent; and she may reject all food. If stroked along the back, the queen in this condition immediately takes up the mating position and may be touchy if lifted or handled. An extremely frustrated queen in oestrus may behave unsocially in the house by neglecting to use her toilet tray and

spraying the furniture and walls instead.

Metoestrus is the third stage in the cycle and takes place if the queen has not been mated and fertilized during oestrus. The whole reproductive system relaxes. Metoestrus lasts about twenty-four hours. During this stage the queen may still accept the advances of the male but will be reluctant to allow actual mating. The final stage of the cycle is *anoestrus*, the resting period, and a time of peace for the cat and owner, when the female is quite relaxed, is disinterested in males and lives a normal life. Anoestrus can last for any length of time from about ten days to several months. The duration varies considerably with individual queens, but each queen will be seen to have a fairly consistent cycle of her own if carefully observed. Oriental and Siamese queens seem to call with a very much greater regularity than those of the longhaired and shorthaired varieties.

In Europe pedigree queens, if fully grown and well-developed, are usually allowed to mate with a selected male cat, on their second period of heat. In the USA cats are often mated on their first heat if this occurs after the queen has attained the age of 10 months. The responsible owner will have arrangements made with the veterinary surgeon for a pre-mating check-up before taking the cat to the stud. The queen will be checked for general health and to ascertain that there is no sign or symptom of any infectious disease.

At the pre-mating check-up, a sample of the queen's motion should be handed over for checking. The motion should be taken from the toilet tray that morning and placed in a clean glass jar. It will be analysed under the microscope, and any worm eggs present will be identified. The veterinary surgeon makes a careful check for other parasites, such as fleas and ear mites, for no queen should be taken to stud harbouring either of these pests. The vaccinations given as a kitten may need an additional booster dose well before the queen is mated, as a precautionary measure. The queen will be checked to ensure that she is adequately built to give birth and that there are no apparent problems in the pelvic region or the mammary area which might cause difficulties.

If she passes her check-up with a clean bill of health, the queen is cared for in the normal way until her next period of oestrus proper, when she may be taken to stud. She should be given an adequate and well-balanced diet, as varied as possible, with some raw meat to keep her teeth healthy. She should be groomed daily to keep her muscles well toned and her coat free from loose hairs and scurf, and her ears and claws should be immaculate. While waiting for the oestrus period to begin, the queen should be fairly confined to ensure that she does not come into contact with any diseased or infectious cats.

A secure and comfortable carrier is necessary in which to take the queen to stud, and this should be purchased well before the event so that she can become accustomed to it. Oestrus is a time of great stress for the queen, and everything should be done to make the stud visit as calm and ordered as

sexually active during the spring months, being stimulated by the subtle scent of females in oestrus and attracted by their strident calls. Puberty usually occurs between eight and twelve months in the male cat, although younger kittens have been known to impregnate females. Kittens occasionally indulge in sexual play, mounting, neckbiting and treading other kittens of either sex. Sexual maturity varies from breed to breed and also in individuals of the same variety. As in the females, males of the Oriental and Siamese varieties appear to be more precocious than those of the long-haired and shorthaired breeds. Adolescent males may be kept together until they are about 15 months of age, and rarely fight or spray unless a calling queen is in the vicinity. After this they should be separated and given individual living quarters before they are introduced to stud work.

Although well in season and in breeding condition the queen is aggressive towards the male who takes up a typically defensive, though interested attitude.

Below The stud male is usually friendly and affectionate at all times, and spends much of his leisure time marking the objects in his run with the scent glands of his lips and tail.

possible. Having a familiar carrier, full of the odours of home, can be a factor in ensuring a successful mating.

A male cat used for stud purposes must be an exceptional specimen of his breed or variety, for during his working life he will sire hundreds of kittens to many different queens. The stud male is generally selected after winning consistently on the show bench, but his true quality will only show by the standard of his progeny. An experienced breeder can recognize show and stud potential in a kitten and will often retain a promising youngster. After showing him and watching his growth and development, the breeder may either keep the young male on to perpetuate his line, or sell him, for stud purposes, to another cattery.

The male cat must have other qualities besides conforming to his breed standard and being very handsome. He must be bred for stamina and disease-resistance, for he will come into contact with a steady flow of low-grade infections throughout his busy stud career. Visiting queens bring slight bacterial infections of all kinds when they come to stud, and cats on the show bench are also at risk from the more serious feline diseases. The stud cat must possess an equable temperament, too, for he will certainly have to cope with very difficult and spoiled queens, and he must be able to treat their tantrums with the nonchalance they deserve. He must trust and love his handler, who may have to pick him up immediately after mating, to protect him from the queen's fiercely attacking claws.

Male cats do not have periods of heat, but are in breeding condition at all times. They are more

The stud cat must have his own exclusive accommodation, in effect a large and well-appointed cage, with living and exercising areas. There must be a pen of some sort, comfortable and easily cleaned, into which the visiting queen can be securely placed on her arrival. It can take several hours before a queen, no matter how furiously on heat, settles down and is willing to mate.

Experienced male cats can cope with virtually any queen in season, but the young male should only have older, steadier and good-tempered queens in his first working season. The young stud will mark his house and run with droplets of powerfully scented urine, by the procedure known as spraying. He will be inclined to spray more when he has a newly painted or scrubbed house than when he has occupied it for some time. He may well attempt to spray on the queen's carrier and blankets, so these should be stored out of his way.

After the visiting queen has had time to settle, she is offered a meal when the stud is fed. In most

The stud and visiting queen gradually get to know one another and after a tentative approach, each sniffs at the other's face and neck.

Gestation chart

for cats mated between January 1 and June 30

Mated **January**	1	2	3	4	5	6	7	8	9	10	11	12	13	14	15	16	17	18	19	20	21	22	23	24	25	26	27	28	29	30	31
Due **March** / **April**	7	8	9	10	11	12	13	14	15	16	17	18	19	20	21	22	23	24	25	26	27	28	29	30	31	1	2	3	4	5	6

Mated **February**	1	2	3	4	5	6	7	8	9	10	11	12	13	14	15	16	17	18	19	20	21	22	23	24	25	26	27	28
Due **April** / **May**	7	8	9	10	11	12	13	14	15	16	17	18	19	20	21	22	23	24	25	26	27	28	29	30	1	2	3	4

Mated **March**	1	2	3	4	5	6	7	8	9	10	11	12	13	14	15	16	17	18	19	20	21	22	23	24	25	26	27	28	29	30	31
Due **May** / **June**	5	6	7	8	9	10	11	12	13	14	15	16	17	18	19	20	21	22	23	24	25	26	27	28	29	30	31	1	2	3	4

Mated **April**	1	2	3	4	5	6	7	8	9	10	11	12	13	14	15	16	17	18	19	20	21	22	23	24	25	26	27	28	29	30
Due **June** / **July**	5	6	7	8	9	10	11	12	13	14	15	16	17	18	19	20	21	22	23	24	25	26	27	28	29	30	1	2	3	4

Mated **May**	1	2	3	4	5	6	7	8	9	10	11	12	13	14	15	16	17	18	19	20	21	22	23	24	25	26	27	28	29	30	31
Due **July** / **August**	5	6	7	8	9	10	11	12	13	14	15	16	17	18	19	20	21	22	23	24	25	26	27	28	29	30	31	1	2	3	4

Mated **June**	1	2	3	4	5	6	7	8	9	10	11	12	13	14	15	16	17	18	19	20	21	22	23	24	25	26	27	28	29	30
Due **August** / **September**	5	6	7	8	9	10	11	12	13	14	15	16	17	18	19	20	21	22	23	24	25	26	27	28	29	30	31	1	2	3

for cats mated between July 1 and December 31

Mated **July**	1	2	3	4	5	6	7	8	9	10	11	12	13	14	15	16	17	18	19	20	21	22	23	24	25	26	27	28	29	30	31
Due **September** / **October**	4	5	6	7	8	9	10	11	12	13	14	15	16	17	18	19	20	21	22	23	24	25	26	27	28	29	30	1	2	3	4

Mated **August**	1	2	3	4	5	6	7	8	9	10	11	12	13	14	15	16	17	18	19	20	21	22	23	24	25	26	27	28	29	30	31
Due **October** / **November**	5	6	7	8	9	10	11	12	13	14	15	16	17	18	19	20	21	22	23	24	25	26	27	28	29	30	31	1	2	3	4

Mated **September**	1	2	3	4	5	6	7	8	9	10	11	12	13	14	15	16	17	18	19	20	21	22	23	24	25	26	27	28	29	30
Due **November** / **December**	5	6	7	8	9	10	11	12	13	14	15	16	17	18	19	20	21	22	23	24	25	26	27	28	29	30	1	2	3	4

Mated **October**	1	2	3	4	5	6	7	8	9	10	11	12	13	14	15	16	17	18	19	20	21	22	23	24	25	26	27	28	29	30	31
Due **December** / **January**	5	6	7	8	9	10	11	12	13	14	15	16	17	18	19	20	21	22	23	24	25	26	27	28	29	30	31	1	2	3	4

Mated **November**	1	2	3	4	5	6	7	8	9	10	11	12	13	14	15	16	17	18	19	20	21	22	23	24	25	26	27	28	29	30
Due **January** / **February**	5	6	7	8	9	10	11	12	13	14	15	16	17	18	19	20	21	22	23	24	25	26	27	28	29	30	31	1	2	3

Mated **December**	1	2	3	4	5	6	7	8	9	10	11	12	13	14	15	16	17	18	19	20	21	22	23	24	25	26	27	28	29	30	31
Due **February** / **March**	4	5	6	7	8	9	10	11	12	13	14	15	16	17	18	19	20	21	22	23	24	25	26	27	28	1	2	3	4	5	6

Left The stud and visiting queen making preliminary advances before mating.

Right The queen rolls and gestures provocatively while the interested male watches and waits.

cases neither cat will eat at this stage. If the queen takes a very long time to settle in, or seems to have gone off call, she must be taken away from the stud house, so that the male can rest and feed. Most queens settle in fairly quickly and within twelve hours of their arrival they are posturing and crooning. When this happens, mating will take place, so the queen can be released from her pen. The stud owner should stay, keeping perfectly quiet and still and not interfering with the procedure. After mating, the queen turns and attacks the male, sometimes quite fiercely, and the owner must ensure that he is not injured in any way.

Both cats will be ready to mate again within a few minutes, and will continue to mate, if allowed, for several hours. It is usual to shut the stud away in the queen's pen for a while, before letting them mate again. It is easier to shut the stud away than to try to pick up the rolling queen, who might bite and scratch at this time. Most stud owners allow the cats to mate four or five times daily for two days before the queen is returned home.

Keeping a stud male is not a job for the novice, for a sound knowledge of husbandry, plus a smattering of cat psychology, is essential in order to establish the necessary relationship between the working male and his owner. Entire males are very loving and affectionate. They crave for attention and love to be petted and groomed. Unfortunately, their natural inclination to spray on everything means that they have to be confined to their own accommodation and cannot be kept as house pets. The stud house should be situated so that the cat can be given lots of attention and company, and is not allowed to become bored and frustrated.

Daily grooming builds a good relationship between stud male and owner. Even the Oriental breeds, which only need a daily buffing with a chamois leather, appreciate the attention. The stud male must have a routine for feeding, grooming and exercise. He should be fed really well on a varied and well-balanced diet, high in protein. He must have a large bowl of fresh drinking water provided at all times. He must be meticulously groomed, as advised for his breed and coat, and his ears, teeth and claws must be checked weekly. Sunning shelves and logs in his run will encourage him to jump and climb, and to strop his claws when necessary. Pots of coarse grass are appreciated by all cats, as chewing grass aids digestion. Above all, thorough cleaning of the house and run every day keeps it wholesome, despite the stud's pungent spray.

A pregnant queen, obviously nearing parturition, relaxes in the spring sunshine.

After mating, a queen will settle down but must not be given her freedom for a few days, until all signs of oestrus have passed. It is difficult to tell whether or not a queen is pregnant in the first few weeks after mating, and she should be treated quite normally, and fed her usual diet. Three weeks after conception, a careful inspection of the cat's nipples may show them to be distinctly pink and very slightly enlarged. This is easier to observe in a maiden queen and usually indicates the fact that she is in kitten, although it is by no means an infallible test. A female that has already produced several litters has permanently enlarged nipples in any case, and these often appear pink-toned towards evening, whether she is pregnant or resting between litters.

During the fourth week of pregnancy, the veterinary surgeon can palpate the queen and feel the tiny embryos within the uterus. Inexperienced breeders should not attempt this test themselves for the probing of inexpert fingers can cause internal damage to the queen. At five weeks, the pregnant cat will become slightly pear-shaped as her abdomen begins to swell, and in all queens the nipples show a definite degree of enlargement.

The time from conception to birth is known as the gestation period. In the cat this averages 65 days. Most experienced breeders count nine weeks from the date of the first mating, and watch the queen carefully from that day for signs of labour. Kittens have been successfully reared after only 59 days' gestation, but this is extremely rare. Some queens habitually carry their litters until the due date is well past, and kittens born after 67 or 68 days' gestation are fairly common.

Cats are spontaneous ovulators, which means that the ripe eggs are only shed from the ovaries when stimulated by the act of mating. Fertilization then occurs. When the queen has been mated over a period of several days, it is impossible to correctly pinpoint the date of conception. If the queen is eating well and behaving normally, she should have her litter on time and there is no need to get alarmed when day 65 comes and goes without the emergence of the kittens. Should the queen seem lethargic and hot to touch, or have a

vaginal discharge and loss of appetite, she should be examined by the veterinary surgeon.

During pregnancy the queen must be treated quite normally. She must not be fussed over or coddled, for she is performing a perfectly natural function which should not be overstated or sentimentalized. Queens treated as invalids or children tend to be extremely bad mothers and often refuse to nurse or attend to their kittens' needs unless their owners sit with them at all times. These queens often resent interest in the kittens and carry them in and out of the nestbox, marking their necks badly in the process and sometimes injuring the kittens quite severely.

Half-way through her pregnancy, the queen begins to notice the increase in her weight and the differences in its distribution. She can be seen to take more care in jumping and in passing through narrow openings. She spends more time on grooming and pays great attention to her flanks and stomach. At this stage her appetite may increase, and the breeder should add a midday meal to her usual breakfast and supper. This is better than increasing the size of the existing meals, for the enlargement of the uterine horns may press on the stomach, restricting the amount of food that the queen can cope with at one meal.

At six weeks' gestation, the cat appears obviously pregnant and is less inclined to exercise herself. She must not be allowed to gain too much surplus weight at this time, and should be encouraged to exercise to keep her muscles well toned. The kittens are growing rapidly at this time, and it may be necessary to add some calcium to her diet of high protein foods. Some cats like milk and get their calcium requirements from this. Others, especially the Oriental varieties, find milk products intolerable, but the veterinary surgeon can advise in such instances.

From six weeks' gestation until the litter is due, the queen's abdomen gradually increases in size and her coat blooms with health. She spends her time quietly grooming herself, resting and prowling in the garden, if allowed to do so. Her diet and bowel movements must be watched carefully to ensure that all is well. If she appears to be slightly constipated, oily foods such as pilchards or sardines can be given. As the kittens move within her, the queen rolls and stretches her body sinuously along the floor, then washes her enlarging nipples vigorously. In the seventh week the nesting instinct becomes apparent as the queen paces the house, looking into cupboards and dark corners, trying to find a suitable place for the birth of her litter.

It is at this time that a large dark box should be provided and filled with several newspapers. During the last fortnight of her pregnancy, the cat should be encouraged to spend some time in her box, and she may tear the newspapers to shreds with her teeth and claws until they form a soft bed. Other pets and small children should be kept well away from the kittening box, or the queen may become disturbed and decide to have her kittens elsewhere.

In the last ten days of the pregnancy, the queen

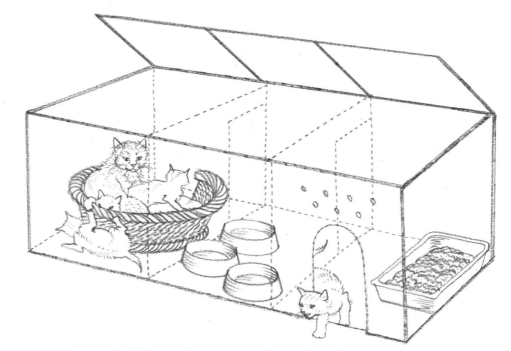

Above An ideal kitten-rearing unit constructed to provide separate sleeping, feeding and toilet areas, and with hinged lids to facilitate cleaning and servicing. This type of unit is ideal in homes where the queen might be harassed or distressed by children, dogs or other pets.

Below A queen who has had her litter delivered by Caesarian section must be encouraged to rest and to suckle her kittens. The stitches are generally removed from the small incision after a period of 7–10 days.

rear their kittens, but most prefer to have the litters delivered and raised in the house so that their progress can be carefully monitored. Many breeders have special kittening boxes constructed, complete with heating units and so on. It would seem preferable to use disposable materials for parturition, so that there can be no build-up of infection.

A sturdy cardboard carton, with sides about twenty inches long, is ideal for kittening. A neat round hole about eight inches in diameter is cut, with a serrated knife, in one side, about six inches from the floor. The hole enables the queen to get in and out of the box without undue strain, and keeps the interior of the box draught-free. The box itself should be placed in a convenient corner of the room, on several thick layers of newspaper to insulate the bottom. A roll of kitchen paper towels can be torn into sheets and spread inside the box to form a soft, absorbent and disposable mattress for the birth. If the weather is cold and the room rather chilly, an infra-red heating unit can be suspended over the open top of the box. If the room is warm enough without additional heating, a sheet of cardboard can be used as a removable lid for the box. Such a box is greatly appreciated by the queen, for it provides a safe, dark and secluded nest. It is convenient for the breeder, too, as the queen can be attended by simply removing the lid. When the litter starts to leave the nest at about four or five weeks of age, a new box can be provided for them, and the kittening box, and all its soiled contents, can be burned.

Once the queen has accepted her kittening box, she will go into it from time to time and shred some of the paper. She should be left in peace to settle down. As her time draws near, she will become increasingly restless and find it impossible to sit in one position for very long. Her appetite should remain good to the end of the pregnancy, but about three days before kittening her coat may look rather loose and full of dandruff.

should be gently groomed to remove all dead hair and to tone up her muscles. If she is carrying a large litter, she may be unable to clean her anal area and this should be sponged twice daily with cotton-wool and warm water. Her nipples should be examined, and if they appear dry or scaly, a little vegetable oil may be rubbed in gently. The queen's coat must be kept free from all parasites by combing through the hair with a very fine-toothed comb. Pesticide powders should never be used on a pregnant or nursing queen. Her ears should be kept spotlessly clean. If necessary, overlong claws can be clipped back carefully, avoiding the quick, and smoothed with an emery board. some queens seem to be unable to retract their claws fully during the last few days of pregnancy, and they may catch in carpets and blankets. Longhaired queens may have the long hairs neatly clipped from around the birth canal and also the nipples to facilitate the kittens' suckling.

Some breeders have special outdoor accommodation in which the queens can produce and

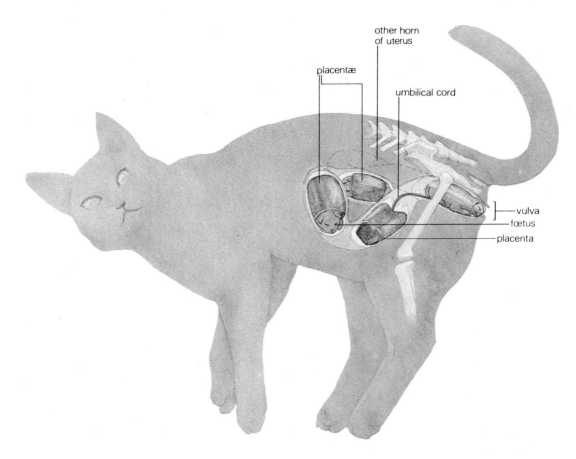

other horn
of uterus

placentæ

umbilical cord

vulva

fœtus

placenta

During birth the kitten moves down the birth canal and is squeezed from the placenta to be expelled encased within an amniotic sac. It is attached to the placenta by the umbilical cord through which it receives oxygen and it is important that the kitten's face is cleared and it starts to breathe before the cord is severed.

When the queen first feels the pangs of labour, she may go to her toilet tray and strain, looking behind herself from time to time in an agitated and puzzled manner. She may pace around the room growling softly, or she may utter cries similar to those emitted when she called. She usually refuses all food for several hours before the birth, in fact, the refusal of a favourite meal is taken by most experienced breeders as a sign that the birth is fairly imminent. The first signs of labour might continue for several hours in the maiden queen, but be barely perceptible in an older queen. Eventually second-stage labour begins and the female must be persuaded to go into the kittening box if she has not already done so. Fierce contractions soon ripple down the queen's flanks as the first kitten moves into the birth canal. The queen may lie on her side and push her hindlegs against the side of the box. When the head or tail of the first kitten is presented, she may sit up, pushing downwards until it is expelled. The kitten may be presented either head first or tail first. Only when a tail first kitten is presented with its legs turned forwards instead of extended does the cat seem to have any problems in delivery. Just prior to the expulsion of the first kitten, an empty sac of fluid may be passed and often causes concern to the novice breeder. This sac is quite normal and prepares the birth canal for the passage of the first kitten.

After the delivery of the first kitten, the mother

usually licks the membranes of the amniotic sac away from the tiny creature's head and body. She licks hard with her rough tongue and in doing this stimulates the kitten into taking its first breath of air, expanding its lungs. As the queen licks the kitten, she lifts it forward and the placenta, still attached to the kitten by the umbilical cord, passes from the vagina. Most queens then attend to the placenta, eating it quickly, and then chewing along the cord to a point about one inch from the kitten's body. As the rest of the litter is born, the queen usually deals with them in the same methodical manner. The whole litter may be born in a matter of an hour or so, or may be spread over twenty-four hours, with the queen taking long rest periods between kittens. Unless the queen is distressed in any way or labours long and hard without producing a kitten, there is no need to be alarmed by long delays.

When the litter is safely delivered, clean and dry, the queen cleans her legs, flanks and vaginal area before settling down to nurse the kittens. She will appreciate a bowl of beaten egg, hot milk and glucose at this time, even if she would normally refuse such a meal. Then, gathering all the babies to her, she will curl around them and rest for about twelve hours.

Occasionally things go wrong with the birth and human intervention is necessary. A kittening kit can be prepared before the birth and may prove very useful in an emergency. The kit consists of an

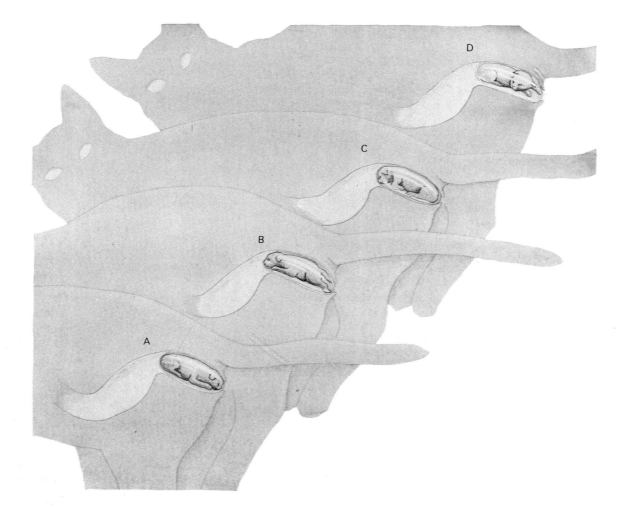

Various presentation positions of the kitten:
(a) head first and normal – usually presents no difficulty;
(b) tail first and normal – usually presents no difficulty;
(c) butt-end first – often causes delay in birth;
(d) head turned position – often requires veterinary intervention to correct the position before birth proceeds.

old terry towel, cut into small squares, which are washed, boiled to sterilize them, then stored in a polythene bag; a pair of blunt-ended scissors; a bottle of astringent antiseptic lotion obtained from the veterinary surgeon; a roll of cotton-wool; a rubber hot water bottle and the veterinary surgeon's emergency telephone number.

The birth of a maiden queen's first litter can be a long and frustrating business. There is no need to call out the veterinary surgeon unless the cat has strained without results for two hours or shows signs of exhaustion or anxiety. Sometimes a kitten is half presented and, despite strenuous pushing by the queen, appears to be stuck. A small square of towelling placed over the part of the kitten protruding from the birth canal enables it to be gripped firmly, and gently. As the queen strains again, the kitten can be eased slowly and steadily downwards and between the queen's legs, until it is free. The kitten must not be pulled, only eased forward, and if it is a breech presentation, the body may need to be very slightly rotated in order to free the head.

Sometimes the queen is so busy producing the next in line that she does not have time to attend to the last-born kitten and prompt human assistance is necessary. The kitten's head must be freed from the sac without delay, and the mucus cleared from the face and nostrils. After the membranes have been wiped away, the kitten is placed on the palm of the hand, head downwards, and is rubbed with

a square of towel from tail to head, firmly but gently. This action clears the fluid from the lungs and nostrils and encourages the kitten to breathe. While this is going on, it is possible that the placenta is still inside the queen and attached to the kitten by the cord. If this is so, the cord can be pulled gently as the queen strains, until the placenta is delivered.

The cleaned kitten should be placed near the mother cat's head and she may eat the placenta and sever the cord. If she is disinterested, then the cord can be severed by hand. It can be cut with blunt, sterilized scissors, about one inch from the kitten's body. The blunt blades crush the cord as it is cut, preventing bleeding. The astringent antiseptic is then applied to the cut end of the cord, with cotton-wool. Experienced breeders prefer to sever the cord by pulling it gently apart with well-scrubbed fingers and thumbs, having been instructed in the art by the veterinary surgeon. This method breaks the cord at its natural place of severance, and no bleeding takes place, but it should not be tried by the novice.

If the mother ignores a kitten completely, it should be rubbed with a towelling square until dry, then placed on a hot water bottle until the queen is ready to nurse it. Bouts of labour pains might make her temporarily unwilling to care for one or all of the kittens, and they must be cleaned and kept warm until she completes her kittening and accepts them.

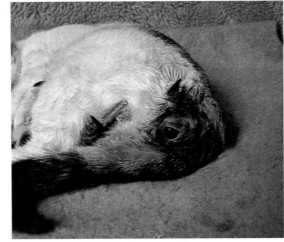

A Normal Birth (Tail-first presentation)
Right and centre top As the queen strains, the bubble of the amniotic sac enclosing the kitten may be seen emerging from the vaginal opening. Further contractions push the kitten's tail end into the world and, *far right*, the queen sits up in order to exert more pressure into her efforts.

Below left Still attached to the placenta by the umbilical cord, the kitten takes its first breaths of air, stimulated by the rough tongue of the queen as she licks him vigorously to remove the amniotic sac membranes from his coat. Finally *below right*, the queen rests until further contractions occur which will expel the placenta.

Most feline births go according to plan, and cats make excellent natural mothers. There are times, however, when things do go wrong, and the cat breeder must be prepared for the occasional emergency situation. When a queen has laboured hard, with strong contractions, for two hours without any signs of the kitten's head or tail appearing, it is essential to telephone the veterinary surgeon. A kitten delayed for too long in the birth canal may die, for there is a limit to the length of time that a kitten can survive in such a situation, after the placenta has become detached from the uterus. The movements of a live kitten seem to help the queen to bear down naturally, but a dead kitten usually presents problems at parturition.

Occasionally a kitten is wrongly presented and needs gentle manipulation before it can be passed normally. The veterinary surgeon will gently examine the queen internally, and determine just where the problem is. The most troublesome presentation is one in which the kitten has turned, with the head trapped near the cervix, so that the back of its neck and shoulders block the entrance to the vagina. To disengage the head from its trapped position within such a confined space takes expert skill, but the kitten can be delicately turned and should eventually slide into the world, alive.

The veterinary surgeon will also help in cases where the queen has entered a state of uterine inertia. She just stops contracting, and sits listlessly in her box, ignoring the kittens already born, and looking most dejected and unhappy. A substance is injected which works rapidly, inducing contractions which expel the next kitten. Sometimes, when a kitten firmly blocks the birth passage, or is just too large to be born in the normal way, there is no alternative but to perform a Caesarean section operation. This is only done as a last resort, for veterinary surgeons are fully aware of the fact that many queens rest for very long periods between kittens, finally producing fine sturdy litters, with no ill-effects.

A Caesarean section is carried out with great care under a carefully selected general anaesthetic. It is particularly important in this operation that the kittens be affected as little as possible. An incision is usually made along the midline of the cat's stomach and the kittens are removed to be cleaned, revived and dried by a nurse while the incision is being sutured. The queen may take some time to recover from the anaesthetic, and may not want to be bothered with her kittens. They must be kept warm, but do not need any nourishment for some hours.

When the queen has completely recovered from the effects of the anaesthetic, she may be glad of a milk, egg and glucose. The kittens can be put in with her, but she must be carefully watched for she may take time to accept them. Some post-operative queens accept the kittens immediately, some sniff at them in a disinterested way at first, before accepting them, and some are so disorientated by the operation that they refuse to have anything to do with the kittens. In this case the kittens must be treated as orphans (see Orphan Kittens), and raised by hand unless a foster mother can be found.

Abnormal Kittens

Now and again cats produce abnormal kittens. Sometimes this is due to genetic factors, or incompatibility between the tom and the queen. It may be caused by an accident to the mother during pregnancy, or by the administration of vaccines, drugs or pesticides. Whatever the cause, it is unfair

passed on to future generations.

There are many minor bone deformities to be found in cats which cause no harm or discomfort. Polydactyls have extra toes. Sometimes the affected cat has one extra toe on each forefoot, but the condition varies so much that cats have been known to have four completely double feet. Kinked or reduced tails are also common, and harmless.

Kittens born with open eyes should be kept in dim light for a few days. The eyes may close again, but whether they do or not, the kitten should have perfectly normal sight. Those with serious deformities of the eyelids usually have additional internal defects and die soon after birth.

Perhaps the most distressing deformity in the new-born kitten is that of a pronounced umbilical hernia, when the whole of the kitten's intestines are enclosed in a pouch of skin, right outside the body cavity. Such kittens are usually active and vigorously crawl to the queen's nipple to suckle. There is nothing that can be done for this condition and the kitten should be put down without delay.

Left A cleft palate – a serious deformity in the new-born kitten.

Left below A projecting sternum, fairly common in some breeds, but not serious.

to attempt to raise a seriously deformed kitten and the unfortunate little creature should be painlessly destroyed as soon after birth as possible.

The most common deformity found in some strains of pedigree cats is known as *cleft palate*. The kitten seems normal at birth, but after some hours it becomes restless and noisy, moving from nipple to nipple, searching for nourishment. When it attempts to suck, some milk may be seen to drip from its nose and the kitten makes a slight wheezing noise. When examined, it will be found to have a cleft palate where the bones in the roof of the mouth have failed to join together. If the cleft is only partial, the kitten may survive with careful feeding, but must spend its adult life as a neutered pet, not used for breeding. If the cleft runs halfway or more across the palate, the kitten must be humanely destroyed without delay.

Kittens are sometimes born with the hindlegs twisted, so that they appear to have been put on back to front. Such kittens should be examined by the veterinary surgeon to determine whether or not the legs have the correct number of bones, and to check the hips for deformities or dislocations. If there is normal bone structure, exercise and careful manipulation can correct this condition. In this case it is only the muscle that is causing the deformity, and physiotherapy can enable the kitten to walk quite normally. On maturity, neutering is advised so that the condition is not

Kitten Development
Typical shorthaired kittens at birth, *right*, 10 days old, *far right*, 21 days old, *left, opposite page*, 6 weeks old, *right, opposite page*. Finally 8 weeks old and feeling independent, *below left, opposite page*.

As soon as kittens are cleaned and dried after birth, they crawl towards their mother's nipples, nuzzling blindly into her soft fur. Eventually the whole family settles down to rest for several hours.

Excessively soiled paper can be quietly removed from the nest box, and fresh, torn kitchen paper towels added. It is a mistake to change every shred of bedding at this time. The secretions of birth are quite sterile, and have a sweet, distinctive smell which the new-born, blind kittens can recognize.

The queen must have fresh water available at all times. She may be a little fussy about food in the days following the birth, but if she has eaten the rich placentas, these will sustain her for some time. She may be very reluctant to leave the kittens at first, but should be encouraged to stretch her legs and to pass water. Sometimes, placing the queen on a fresh litter tray effects the desired results. The kittens should be examined daily to ensure that no infection has entered through the severed end of the umbilical cord. An infected navel looks very sore and often has a raised pale-green rim where the cord enters the body. This is usually treated by the veterinary surgeon by administering an antibiotic to the queen, which is then passed through the milk, to the kitten.

To ensure that the milk is flowing properly, the queen's breasts should be examined gently the day after the kittens are born. Sometimes one or more blocked nipples may be discovered. These must be bathed with warm water, then olive oil used to massage them gently until the milk flows through freely. If neglected, the milk gland behind a blocked nipple becomes hard and inflamed and the queen needs veterinary attention. Occasionally a queen may have one or more blind teats. These are nipples with non-functioning milk glands. They rarely cause any trouble, but with a large litter there may not be enough teats to go around.

The birth weight of kittens is very variable, with the longhaired and shorthaired breeds weighing in at about four ounces, while Siamese kittens may weigh as little as two ounces. A lot seems to depend on the make-up of the parents and litter size, although there can also be some variability within the litter itself. Kittens gain weight steadily from birth onwards if they are receiving adequate nourishment. The birth weight should be added each week if the kitten is thriving. Dedicated cat breeders make it a routine to weigh each kitten once a week and to check its progress on a small chart. If a kitten falls below its expected rate of growth, it should be thoroughly checked for signs of disease or deformity. If all the kittens show poor rates, the queen's diet and milk glands should be checked.

For the first few days after birth, the kittens only sleep and feed. They are kept spotlessly clean by the mother cat, who grooms them constantly. She stimulates the evacuation of each kitten's bladder and bowel by licking its tail end, and ingests the excreted material, keeping the nest free from soiling and odours. It is easiest to sex the kittens immediately after birth while the soft hair in the genital area is still damp and the organs are clearly defined. In the female two round openings are found quite close together, while in the male kitten the small round anus is separated from the tiny dot of the penis by the two small swellings indicating the testes. It is easier to sex kittens if both males and females are present for comparison. Once the kittens have dried off, it becomes harder to decide on their sex, but they can be checked again at about four weeks, when the difference between the males and females is much more obvious.

If all is well, the kittens will open their eyes at from three to ten days after birth. Siamese kittens often open their eyes on the second or third day; domestic cats wait as long as twelve days in some instances. There is no need to worry about late opening of the eyelids unless there is any apparent swelling or the lids are discharging pus or fluid.

Normal rate of kitten growth

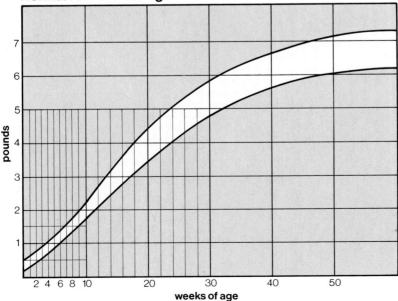

pounds / weeks of age

Any stickiness of the eyes should be bathed away with cotton-wool (cotton-ball) and a saline solution.

The lactating queen should be given four good meals daily, and plenty to drink. It is important that the meals be small, well-balanced and fed fresh. The queen should not be given cold food straight from the refrigerator, or she may get diarrhoea. All food should be fed at room temperature, and meat, which takes several hours to digest, should be fed at midday and last thing at night. Other meals can consist of fish, cheese, eggs or milk products.

At four weeks the kittens play well and start nest-leaving activities. It is at this stage that they first begin to show an interest in their mother's food. As they eat more and more solids, their excreta change, and the mother cat stops cleaning up after them. The kittens should be provided with their own toilet tray at this age, and placed on it after every meal. They will eat a little more solid food each day but continue to take milk from the queen for several more weeks if allowed to do so.

Orphan Kittens

If a mother cat dies in giving birth, or is unable to rear her kittens for any reason, it is best to try to find another cat as a foster mother for the babies. Failing this, it is possible to hand-rear kittens, but it is a long, tedious business and should not be undertaken lightly.

The kittens must be kept at a constant temperature, 90°F for the first few hours, 85°F for the first week, then about 75°F from then on. A dull emitter infra-red heater is best, suspended over their box. A thermometer should be kept in the box, level with the kittens' heads. The kittens must be fed every two hours day and night with a syringe or special feeding bottle and milk formula designed for kittens. Each kitten should take about 5 ml of the milk at first, increasing to about 10 ml by the end of the first week. In the second week the feeds can be three-hourly, and in the third week night feeding can be discontinued, the last feed being given at midnight and the next at 06.00. The freshly made-up formula must be fed slowly and should be warmed to blood heat.

After each feed the kitten must have its mouth thoroughly cleaned with damp cotton-wool; then it is turned on its back and the mother's washing action around the genital area is simulated, with a pad of cotton-wool, until the kitten urinates or passes a solid motion. Hand-reared kittens need extra vitamin A, which will be provided in the correct strength by the veterinary surgeon. They will not have had immunity against disease from their mother's colostrum, and may be prone to minor infections, so they should be kept away from visitors until they are vaccinated, and well grown.

Orphan kittens can be reared with constant care and attention. They must be fed from a syringe or special feeding bottle and encouraged to urinate and defecate by the stimulation of a warm, damp sponge simulating the effect of the mother cat's tongue.

At weaning, kittens should be healthy and alert with bright eyes and shining coats.

Below Prior to the weaning stage a mother cat may feel the need to move her litter, usually to protect them from something that she considers to be a potential danger. She moves them singly and transports them by carrying each kitten in turn, holding it around the neck in carefully controlled jaws.

At six weeks the kitten, though still suckling, takes a lot of solid food and should be encouraged to try a variety of things. Kittens that are reluctant to eat should have food rubbed on their lips until, in licking it off, they get to enjoy the taste. Some breeders wean kittens by giving milk mixed with baby cereal, and many kittens naturally prefer their mother's milk to this. Other breeders prefer to provide meat to simulate prey: raw meat cut in long narrow strips for the kittens to growl over and chew. At first kittens must be watched while they eat solids, for their lack of technique may result in lumps of food becoming wedged across the palate. If this happens, a match-stick or plastic spoon handle can be used to prise the food gently away from the roof of the mouth.

Kittens should always be fed fresh food at every meal. Any that is not cleared up in ten minutes should be taken away. In this way the kittens will become used to feeding at regularly spaced intervals, and they will be less likely to suffer from gastric upsets and diarrhoea. The meals should be as varied as possible, for it is at this age that kittens learn what they will or will not eat. A wide variety of food at this stage prevents a kitten from developing into a finicky cat.

The stomach of a young kitten is very small, only about the size of a walnut, so it must be given only small meals at fairly frequent intervals if gastric upsets are to be avoided. Kittens can be reluctant to drink, and often become slightly constipated. If this happens, a little water can be stirred into meat meals. A touch of table salt added to the food will also increase the thirst and help to train the kitten to drink more liquid. Kittens like warm liquid, and warm water or milk is accepted more readily than freshly drawn water or milk from the refrigerator. With the increasing use of dried complete foods for cats, it is important that kittens be trained to drink plenty of liquids from a very early age. Problems can occur in adult cats fed on dried foods when they do not drink enough.

As the kittens take more solid food, they will naturally train themselves to the litter tray. This must be changed frequently – two or three times daily should be enough – and any type of litter may be used. Those who live in town houses can use a proprietary brand of fuller's earth or litter, which can be close wrapped after use and put in the waste bin for disposal. Those who live in country areas can dispose of their litter by burning, and may use torn paper, wood chippings or shavings, or peat moss.

By the age of six weeks or so, the kittens will be trained to the toilet tray. At this age they can get

digestive upsets from all manner of things. They spend a great deal of time trying and testing various objects by smelling and tasting. They may be seen to lick the floor from time to time. It is very important that cleaning materials and disinfectants used around their living area be non-toxic and safe for cats. Perhaps the best method of cleaning around the kittens' play area is to wash the surfaces with soap and water, and then wipe over with a sponge dipped in a correctly prepared solution of household bleach. Food dishes and toilet trays should also be cleaned in this way: washed thoroughly, then sterilized in a bleach solution. All dishes, trays and play areas treated with the solution can be dried with kitchen paper towels before re-use. Household bleach is prepared from sodium hypochlorite; it kills most germs and is non-toxic to cats and kittens if correctly diluted. Many famous brands of disinfectants advertised for household and medical use, and for cleaning around human babies, are quite unsuitable for use with felines. If ingested, they cause gastric disturbances, muscular spasms and even death in some cases.

At eight weeks the kittens may be completely weaned from their mother if desired. The kindest way of doing this is to remove the litter for long periods at the seventh week, then take half the litter, usually the largest of the kittens, right away during the eighth or ninth week. The following week the remaining kittens are also removed. If the mother still has milk, her water bowl should be taken away for a few hours, and her food cut right down, so that any milk that she produces can be resorbed by her body. If the milk glands are still swollen veterinary advice should be sought.

If the kittens are fed six small and well-spaced meals, they will quickly forget the queen's milk. They are quite capable of eating enough food at this time to satisfy their bodily requirements. They may need a calcium supplement, especially if they are of Oriental or Siamese blood lines, and a course of gentle worming tablets may be commenced.

After two clear weeks have elapsed from the final feed of any of their mother's milk, the kittens may receive their first vaccination against feline infectious enteritis. If possible, it may be better to wait a further two or three weeks, for after twelve weeks of age they can be given a combined vaccination against enteritis and cat flu. All kittens should be professionally immunized in this way before they go to new homes.

There is just a little more to rearing a litter of kittens than feeding them, training them to use their toilet tray and keeping them healthy. Kittens grow into pet cats, and it is very important that they be humanized and that they enjoy being handled. If they are destined to be show cats, this is even more important. To this end the kittens must be handled, petted and groomed as often as possible during the weaning period. They must learn to come when called and must be given a reward, either a meal or a petting. They must be taught to have their mouths opened and their ears cleaned without fuss, and should learn that being brushed is a most pleasurable experience. Gentle handling produces happy, gentle cats.

Appearance: The signs of good health in the cat are quite unmistakable to the intelligent owner. The fit animal has bright shining eyes, with clear luminous pupils that respond rapidly to every change in light intensity. The coloured iris is clear and free from any cloudiness, and the nictitating membrane (haw), or third eyelid, remains tucked away at the inner angle of the eye. The eyelids themselves are healthy, and there is no sign of discharge at the inner corners of the eyes. On inspection the mouth is wholesome, with clean white teeth and healthy pink gums. The rough tongue flexes and is free from any sign of soreness or ulceration. The healthy cat has spotlessly clean ears, looking very slightly moist at the entrance to the ear canal, but without any dark discharge or sore scratch marks which could point to infestation with ear mites.

A fit cat is firm to hold and lithe in appearance, without any ribs or vertebrae showing through the coat. It should not carry any excess weight. A sensible combination of correct diet and adequate exercise keeps pet cats in good physical shape.

The coat of the cat generally reflects the animal's condition, and in the fit cat it looks clean and glossy. The hair lies smooth and close in the shorthaired varieties and is softly fluffed out in the longhaired. The healthy cat has very elastic skin which can be lifted and moved easily with the hands where it lies over the powerful muscles of the shoulders, back and hips. The coat should be free from loose hairs, flaking skin, lesions and the tell-tale grits excreted by the flea.

Behaviour: A cat in good physical condition, receiving proper exercise, will have a consistent appetite and eat its regular meals with obvious enjoyment. The healthy cat is supremely alert, the ears showing constant tiny movements as they are directioned to pick up every new or sudden sound. The eyes catch the minutest movement and the nostrils constantly monitor the air for subtle scents. Interest in minor disturbances is indicated by the twitching of the tail tip, while annoying stimuli may cause the tail to lash from side to side.

The well cat purrs readily with an even cadence,

A healthy coat with bright clear eyes, a shiny close-lying coat and an alert expression.

and when stroked firmly from head to tail, arches its back upwards against the pressure of the hand. When it is particularly pleased, it may also rhythmically extend and contract the claws of its forepaws. Enthusiastic claw stropping is a sure sign of good health in the cat, and experienced breeders regard this action as being the first true indication of a return to health after a serious feline illness.

Every normal healthy cat spends a great deal of time each day in washing and grooming, especially after meals and periods of exercise. The grooming follows particular patterns in most cats, and they resent distractions during this important function. The head and neck are washed with the aid of a well-licked forepaw, and the rest of the body, tail and limbs are groomed with the animal's rough tongue. Particular attention is paid to the genital region and the paws, and any dried mud or matted hair is bitten out with the teeth.

Far left The healthy cat constantly grooms and cleans its coat.

Left Eating grass and herbage is an essential part of cat behaviour. Grass provides folic acid, one of the vitamins of the B-complex.

The onset of many feline diseases can be very sudden, and the intelligent, observant owner may well save his pet's life by noticing a change in behaviour or appearance early enough to solicit prompt veterinary advice. During the incubation period of some diseases there is a sudden loss of appetite, perhaps combined with increased thirst. The cat may have either a raised or lowered temperature, in which case the coat will stand up away from the skin and the cat may sit with hunched shoulders and extended head, looking thoroughly miserable. In some diseases the cat experiences pain on being handled and may cry out, growl or bite. Other diseases start with mild vomiting, and the first indication of trouble is the discovery of a small ring of clear, frothy vomit. Diarrhoea can be the result of unwise eating, or it can herald serious illness in the cat, so should never be neglected. Quite often the first sign of trouble is noticed when the cat refuses a favourite meal and, on closer examination, it is found to be hot to the touch and has the third eyelids showing at the inner corners of the eyes. If the owner then takes a look inside the cat's mouth, there may be ulcers on the tongue and the throat may look very

sore. It is time to contact the veterinary surgeon.

In the early stages of viral respiratory diseases the cat may be seen to gulp and swallow several times on the first day. On the following day it may sneeze, or may have discharging eyes and nostrils, or it may have thin trickles of saliva coming from the sides of the mouth.

The sick or sickening cat stops washing and grooming itself, and it stops stropping its claws. And although even dying cats may still purr, the sick cat is unlikely to push itself against the stroking hand of its owner. During illness the skin of the cat loses its elasticity and feels tough and tight when the animal is handled.

In some diseases the cat may cry out when passing water, or its abdomen may look very distended. It may be seen to spend a great deal of time licking the genital region and to return to its toilet tray several times in an agitated manner. All these signs are signals of danger which should be noted carefully and passed on to the veterinary surgeon while he makes his examination of the cat thus helping diagnosis of the trouble.

Any cat or kitten that shows an abrupt or gradual change in appearance or behaviour should be watched carefully. The cause could be teething, oestrus (estrus) or seasonal moulting (shedding), or it could be something serious.

Do not watch your cat all day and then decide to call the veterinary surgeon at midnight. If you are worried, call for advice during the daytime, follow the instructions to the letter, and call with a progress report and for further instructions the following morning. The veterinary surgeon would far rather help with advice during a false alarm than be presented with a cat in an advanced stage of infectious illness. Always arrange a firm appointment for the examination of a cat you suspect has an infectious disease, for it is very unfair to take such an animal into a crowded waiting-room where other cats are at risk. In some countries the veterinarian is prepared to make house calls, in others, cats have to be taken for examination and probable hospitalization. In all cases early diagnosis and the administration of prompt treatment are important for the well-being of the cat.

Examining the Sick Cat
The veterinary surgeon uses his stethoscope to listen to the heart of this ailing Siamese (note the raised haws or third eyelids), *right*.

Next the eyes are carefully examined to check for any infection, *below left*, then the mouth and throat are checked for signs of ulceration, *below right*.

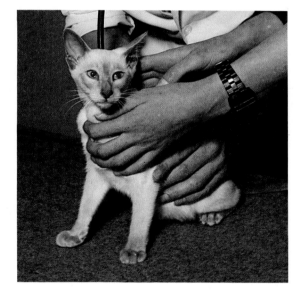

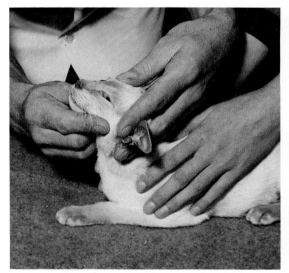

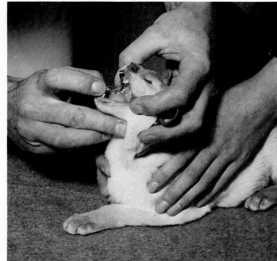

Legend: ● Main symptom ◐ Frequently found sympton ○ Possible symptom

Category	Disease	Dehydration	Weight loss	Coughing/sneezing/nasal discharge	Difficulty in eating	Loss of appetite	Vomiting	Blood in urine/Difficulty in passing urine	Dullness/fever	Increased thirst
Major feline viral diseases	FPL/FIE	●				◐	◐		◐	
	Leukaemia		●			○	○		◐	○
	Respiratory disease			●	○	◐			◐	
Diseases of the digestive system	Dental disease		○		●	◐	○			
	Gastritis		○			●	◐		○	○
	Enteritis (Non-specific)					●	◐		○	○
	Obstructed bowel					◐	●		◐	
Diseases of the uro-genital system	Cystitis	○				○	○	●		○
	Metritis	◐	○			◐			●	◐
	Nephritis	○				◐	◐	○	◐	●
	Urolithiasis					○	○	●	◐	○
Diseases of the nervous system	Rabies		◐		◐	◐			◐	
	Stroke				◐	◐	○			
Diseases of the skin	Eczema		◐							
	Ringworm									
	Ear mites								○	
	Fleas/Lice/etc.									
Injuries and accidents	Fracture/dislocation				◐	◐		◐	◐	
	Poisoning	◐			◐	◐	◐	◐	◐	◐
Miscellaneous	Abcess					◐	◐		◐	
	Faulty diet					◐	◐	◐	○	
	Foreign body			○	◐	◐	◐	○		
	Fur ball			○		◐	●		○	
	Internal parasites		○	○		○	◐	○		

Marked change in behaviour	Scratching/licking	Signs of acute pain	Diarrhoea	Constipation	Haws showing	Difficulty in breathing	Ulceration of mouth	Pallor of lip and gums	Swollen abdomen	Stiff or unsteady gait	Lameness	Fur loss	Failure to wash or self groom
●		●	●	●	●								●
			●		●	●		●	●				●
			●		●	●	●						●
	●	●					●						●
		●	●		●								
		●	●							●			
		●		●	●	●	●	●	●	●	●		
		●								●			
		●					●			●			
								●			●		
	●	●				●		●	●	●			
●		●				●	●	●		●			
●				●	●	●				●	●		
●	●											●	
●	●	●										●	
●	●	●	●							●		●	
●	●	●	●									●	
●		●		●		●		●		●	●		
●		●	●	●		●	●	●		●		●	●
	●	●									●		
			●	●	●		●	●	●		●	●	
●			●	●	●						●		●
				●	●	●			●				
	●		●		●			●		●			

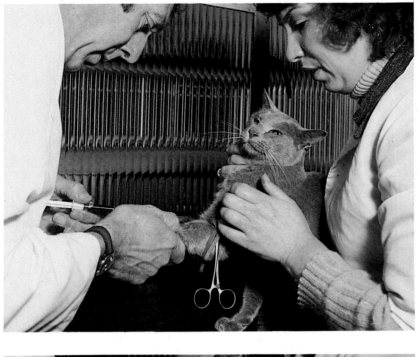

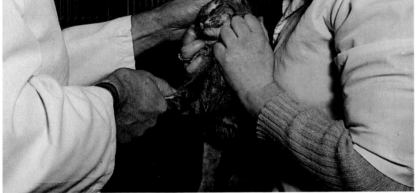

Above To test for the presence of FeLV, the veterinary surgeon takes a small blood sample from a vein in the cat's foreleg. This is quite simple and painless and it is rare for a cat to object if held firmly and sympathetically by an experienced nurse.

Below After the blood is drawn off, the veterinary surgeon applies pressure to seal the tiny puncture wound and reassures the cat.

Viruses: Of the many infectious feline diseases there are four of viral origin which are considered by veterinary surgeons to be of major clinical importance. These viruses are widely distributed and have been carefully studied. The first and perhaps best understood of the four viruses is the one that causes Feline Panleucopenia (FPL) otherwise known as Feline Infectious Enteritis (FIE). The second virus is probably the most important cause of fatal disease in the cat, and is known as Feline Leukaemia Virus (FeLV). The third and fourth of the viruses are often found together, giving rise to the syndrome known as 'cat 'flu'. The fragile herpes virus causes Feline Viral Rhinotracheitis (FVR) and a series of Calcivirus strains cause Feline Calicivirus (FCV).

Feline Panleucopenia (FPL): This disease is highly contagious, with an incubation period of 2–9 days, but usually less than 6 days. It is characterized by its very sudden onset, so sudden, in fact, that young cats have been found dead on occasion, without the owner having noticed any symptoms of illness. More typically, however, there is profound depression in the cat, which refuses all food, and starts vomiting usually in a few hours.

The animal's temperature may be as high as 105°F in the early stages of FPL, but then quickly reduces until it is subnormal. Dehydration of the body tissues is very rapid and the cat appears to shrink quite visibly. The affected cat usually sits hunched up with its coat erect and staring, and its head drooping over its water bowl. Now and again it may look as though it intends to drink, but instead may gulp, or lick its lips. When touched or lifted, the cat may cry with a despairing note of pain, and its body feels cold and rigid in contrast with its normal warmth and suppleness.

The FPL virus invades the rapidly dividing cells in the bone marrow and gut lining of the young kitten, and also attacks the liver, spleen and lymph nodes of the older animal. Having found a perfect environment, the virus multiplies fast, decimating the host cells. If the animal lives for more than a few days, diarrhoea may develop and this may well be bloodstained.

During the course of FPL the cat must be carefully nursed under veterinary supervision. It will constantly try to crawl away from its bed to sit on a cold surface, so it is best confined within a mesh carrier or a suitable pen sited away from draughts, in which it can be kept comfortably warm until recovered.

It is important to ensure that everything used in caring for the sick animal's needs is dispensable, for all items should be finally incinerated if possible. Metal pens can eventually be sterilized by heat, or by being immersed in a formalin solution (see Glossary). It is best to have dishes, feeding syringes and bedding of disposable materials. The nurse should wear disposable or easily sterilized clothing when handling the sick cat and should avoid contact with all other felines during the course of the illness and the subsequent period of quarantine.

Although the veterinary surgeon will try all possible treatment for cats which contract FPL, the mortality rate is very high indeed. Animals that do recover may shed viruses for some time and therefore must be isolated from any chance of contact with other felines. Recovery is usually a long slow process while the cat's body repairs the damaged tissue and organs, and extra vitamins and minerals are generally prescribed, along with substances which help to restore the delicate water balance of the cat's system.

FPL is spread by direct and indirect contact between cats or their handlers. The virus is the smallest of all the known animal viruses and consists of a single-stranded molecule of deoxyribonucleic acid, or DNA, packed within a stable protein coat. This coat is so tough that it enables the virus to survive away from a host for a considerable time, and also makes it impervious to most disinfectants. It has been found, however, that a 0.5 per cent solution of formalin inactivates the virus in twenty-four hours. The usual period of quarantine for catteries after an outbreak of feline panleucopenia is six calendar months after the final recovery date. It is not known for certain whether or not recovered animals can become carriers of FPL.

Prevention: There are effective vaccines available for protecting cats against FPL. The first injections are usually given to kittens, and booster doses are administered annually or biannually to maintain the levels of antibody in the bloodstream. In the weanling kitten the timing of the initial vaccination is important, for antibodies from the mother cat's blood will have been passed to the kitten through the first milk, or colostrum. These maternal antibodies protect the kitten from disease during the first few weeks of its life, but their presence prevents the kitten from manufacturing antibodies of its own. Queens vary considerably in the levels of antibody present at the time of parturition, so it is difficult to assess the length of time for which individual kittens might expect to be protected. As vaccination in the presence of the maternal antibody is non-effective, the veterinary surgeon's expert advice must be sought as to the best time for kittens to have their first injections.

Leukaemia in the Cat: In 1964 the feline leukaemia virus (FeLV) was isolated, and was found to thrive in the lymphoid tissue and bone marrow of the feline species. These are the areas of the body system which produce blood corpuscles, and the main diseases caused by FeLV are forms of leukaemia and anaemia. When present in very young kittens, FeLV, having attacked parts of the developing immune system, leaves them vulnerable to infections with other bacteria and viruses.

Leukaemia is a malignant disease of the white blood cells. The most common symptom of the disease in the cat is a slow and gradual loss of weight, and by the time the diagnosis is confirmed, the cat is probably nearing death. Various treatments have been tried for feline leukaemia, without success, and research into the development of a vaccine is in progress.

The virus is transmitted vertically from the pregnant queen to the fetus, or horizontally by contact between cats. The virus can be excreted into the air from the mouth of an infected animal and is inhaled by susceptible cats into their nostrils, to travel through the system to the bone marrow in which the blood cells are formed.

If a susceptible cat is subjected to minute doses of FeLV at widely spaced intervals, it seems that it is unlikely to become infected but may well build up an immunity to further doses. In this way feral cats and pets allowed comparative freedom are more likely to develop a natural immunity to FeLV than cats kept in catteries, or in small breeding colonies in the home.

If an infected cat, excreting virus, is introduced into a breeding colony, most of the cats will become infected with the virus. Some may well develop immunity to the virus, but the rest will remain infected for life, with the virus constantly present in the mouth and in the bloodstream. Cats with virus present in the blood are said to be *viraemic*, and such cats may develop a special immunity, not to the FeLV itself, but to FeLV-associated disease. These cats are apparently quite healthy, but they constantly excrete viruses, and

are therefore a danger to other cats. Other cats infected with FeLV have no immunity against associated diseases and are seriously at risk. Kittens born to infected queens have no immunity and may be infected and infectious.

The incubation periods depend on the type of disease, and may vary from a very few weeks to several years. This variation was a prime reason why the importance of the virus was not fully appreciated when it was first isolated.

Prevention: The feline leukaemia virus is transmitted by direct contact in most instances, so a degree of control is possible. Many dedicated cat breeders and catteries follow a fairly rigid system, first to eliminate any chance of FeLV infection in their stock, and then to insure as far as is possible that it is not introduced at any stage in the future.

The first stage is to have all cats in the colony tested. The veterinary surgeon takes a small blood sample from each cat – a comparatively simple and quite painless procedure. The samples are sent in sterile containers to a specialist laboratory for analysis. When the results are known, FeLV-positive cats must be removed from the colony. They can be homed as pets in households where they can be kept indoors as the only cat, or, alternatively, humanely destroyed. After the removal of the positive animals, the premises and all equipment must be thoroughly cleaned and disinfected. Three months later a repeat sampling is carried out to pick out any cats that might have been merely incubating infection at the initial testing. If all the cats show negative results, the colony can be considered free of FeLV.

If any new stock is introduced it should be tested and confirmed FeLV-free, or must be tested and kept in strict isolation until the second test at three months proves that it is clear. FeLV-tested stud males should only receive queens with a current certificate confirming that they also showed a negative test result.

The responsible cat owner and breeder can eliminate FeLV infections in his own stock, and so help to generally suppress such diseases in cats until such time as an effective vaccine is available.

Other Diseases Involving FeLV: In the treatment of other diseases, FeLV has been discovered in the systems of affected cats. It would seem feasible, therefore, to suspect the presence of the virus, and to test any cats that become gradually and progressively thin or listless, are infertile or abort litters, exhibit symptoms similar to those of FPL or have trouble with the kidneys.

Anaemia: Some types of anaemia appear to be linked by FeLV. *Aplastic anaemia* is the more serious and is usually fatal, for the cells necessary for the production of red blood corpuscles are destroyed. In *haemolytic anaemia* the red blood corpuscles are destroyed but the parent cells are unaffected, and they respond to the challenge by producing more red blood cells. The cat, though pale, lethargic and depressed, may overcome the disease, but will still be infected with FeLV.

Weeping eyes in this Longhaired cat could be due to blocked tear ducts, or, more seriously, herald the onslaught of an attack of respiratory disease.

Diseases of the upper respiratory tract in the cat are troublesome to breeders, boarding cattery proprietors and veterinary surgeons alike. As in the common cold of humans, these diseases are caused by viruses and are highly transmissible. The diseases are generally known under the one name *cat 'flu* in some countries, and as *pneumonitis* in others. 'Cat 'flu' is mainly caused by two viruses – Feline Viral Rhinotracheitis virus (FVR) and Feline Calicivirus (FCV) both thought to be of equal importance in causing the disease.

FVR is the most common and severe of feline respiratory diseases, highly infectious and with an incubation period of about 2–10 days. The first symptoms are general lassitude, loss of appetite and sneezing. The cat's temperature rises and the eyes and nostrils begin to discharge. In some cases long streams of saliva may hang from the cat's mouth and it may begin to cough. Secondary infections may set in to further complicate matters, adding to the severity of the disease and the animal's misery: conjunctivitis is common and bronchopneumonia may set in. Young cats and kittens may be more severely affected than older cats, and about 25 per cent of those treated for FVR each year die of the disease.

FCV infections caused the second component of the cat 'flu syndrome. There are a number of strains of *Calicivirus*, compared with the single strain of FVR, and they manifest themselves in a wide range of symptoms. Affected cats may have a severe upper respiratory infection such as is seen with FVR, or they may merely show a mild subclinical infection. Ulceration of the mouth is a typical feature of *Calicivirus* infection, and in some cases the ulcers may be the only sign that there is anything wrong with the cat. A cat with FCV infection does not usually show the discharge of the eyes, nose and mouth so characteristic of FVR, but the mouth ulceration may be so severe that hand feeding is necessary until it can again eat without pain.

No time should be lost in getting expert attention for the cat showing the first symptoms of upper respiratory disease. Antibiotics are given to prevent and cure secondary bacterial infections, and vitamin injections are often administered to counteract the depression and loss of appetite. The sick cat should not be taken to the clinic or surgery without an appointment, for it is inexcusable to put other cats at risk by taking an infectious animal into a crowded waiting-room.

The cat with cat 'flu must be isolated from other felines unless they are also infected. It must be kept

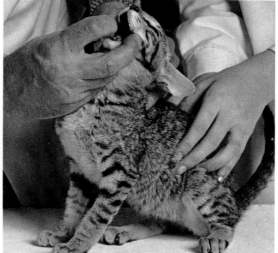

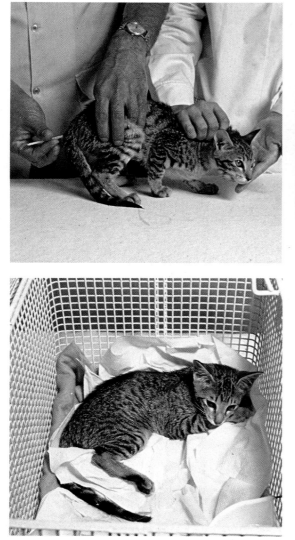

Above left A kitten suspected of starting a respiratory illness is examined by the veterinary surgeon who takes its temperature and examines the mouth and throat, *above right*.

Left After injection of antibiotics, the kitten is encouraged to rest confined within a warm carrier, wired to prevent contact with other cats. Toilet tissue may be used as napkins or diapers if diarrhoea is a symptom of the specific disease.

warm in a dry atmosphere, out of draughts but in a room with a flow of fresh air. Good nursing is of prime importance, and the cat's recovery to complete health may depend on attention to the small details of care which keep up its strength and boost its morale through the peak period of the illness (see Home Nursing). The sick cat is unwilling or unable to eat or drink, and must be fed by hand or syringe-fed with liquids. The veterinary surgeon will advise and may also prescribe an electrolyte solution to help the regulation of the water balance in the cat's body. It is of utmost importance to keep the animal's face as clean as possible. The discharges from the eyes and nostrils soon cake into lumps if neglected, and then removal leads to sore or even bleeding areas which may be slow to heal. Saliva and food dribbled from the mouth soil and mat the hair of the chin, throat and chest and should be cleaned away regularly. The cat may be unable or unwilling to use its toilet tray, but should be placed upon it after feeding, and encouraged and stroked. A very sick cat may be incontinent, and must be kept clean and dry, nursed on disposable napkins (diapers) designed for human babies.

Many cats overcome cat 'flu, even if they have also had pneumonia, and are completely restored to health. Others are left with permanent after-effects such as sinusitis, permanently damaged eyelids or conjunctiva, 'snuffles' or noisy breathing, or a persistent cough. Some cats have periods when they seem perfectly well, only showing these signs in cold, damp weather, or when subjected to any form of stress.

It seems that the majority of animals that recover from infection with the FVR virus remain as carriers of the disease, and any stress such as oestrus (estrus), parturition, exhibition at a show or a stay in a boarding cattery initiates a period of virus shedding. The cat often shows 'flu symptoms itself at these times. Carriers of *Calicivirus* appear to shed viruses constantly, while appearing to be in the best of health, and so are persistently infectious to other cats and kittens.

Vaccines are available to immunize cats against respiratory disease, and should be used intelligently to set up and maintain 'flu-free breeding colonies, as well as for any cat or kitten likely to be exposed to infection, for example at a show or in a cattery. Healthy kittens, from the age of 3 months, may have the vaccine at the same time as the injection against feline panleucopenia, and, depending on the type, it may be administered intranasally or by intramuscular injection.

The Mouth: In the course of infection with viral respiratory diseases, the mouth may become ulcerated. This condition may also be seen when the cat has *nephritis*, and long streams of saliva hang from the mouth. Ulcers appear on the lips, gums, tongue and palate as blisters, red spots or rings, sometimes covered by a cloudy membrane. The first signs of trouble in the mouth are usually noticed when the cat refuses food, and no time should be lost in seeking professional advice. Tooth decay does occur in the cat, but, more commonly, deposits of tartar form on the teeth and may build up to such an extent that the cat cannot eat. Chronic nephritis in the cat may also be associated with a build-up of tartar and the cat often has a strong odour from the mouth. Regular checking of the mouth is an essential part of cat care for neglected teeth and gums can result in the development of *periodontal disease*. Deposition of tartar, vitamin deficiencies or other unknown cause may produce the characteristic sore, red gums found in the condition known as *gingivitis*. Perhaps the soft, prepared foods which form the bulk of the pet cat's diet are causative factors in the high incidence of this disease. All problems of the mouth should be treated as serious, for the cat that refuses all food soon loses condition and is susceptible to secondary infections.

Stomach and Intestines: *Gastritis* may be caused by faulty diet; irritant substances ingested by the cat from its coat or paws during self-grooming and washing; bacterial infection; or internal parasites in kittens. The principal symptom of gastritis is vomiting, often clear and frothy, sometimes bright yellow, occasionally bloodstained. The cat should be kept warm and quiet, with food and water withheld until professional attention is available. Some cats, especially those of the long-haired varieties, often accumulate matted clumps of hair in their stomachs as the result of self-grooming. This 'hair-ball' may produce a mild gastritis in the cat, which refuses to eat until it has vomited the obstructing hair cluster. This condition is best avoided by regular grooming, and giving mildly laxative food to such cats during the seasons they are shedding their hair.

Enteritis is inflammation of the intestine, and when the stomach is also affected, the animal is said to have *gastroenteritis*. The first signs of enteritis in the cat are a typically staring coat and diarrhoea. Some cats are constipated and may vomit in the early stages, then develop diarrhoea. The diarrhoea may be very pale and milky, it may be bright yellow or it may be very much darker than a normal stool, possibly with signs of blood. There are many causes of enteritis in the cat, but the symptoms must not be ignored. If the animal passes a loose stool but otherwise appears well, it should be observed for twenty-four hours, and given plenty of fluids but no solid food. If the cat also vomits, then small drinks only should be given. The chances are that the cat will be back to normal the following day and was merely reacting to having eaten something disagreeable such as a poisoned flying insect. Some common household cleaning agents, polishes, disinfectants and fresh-air sprays produce these enteric symptoms in cats. Any animal that is regularly seen to have mild attacks of diarrhoea or vomiting should be presented to the veterinary surgeon for examination and a discussion of the probable cause.

As we have seen, feline infectious enteritis (page 130) is a most serious and often fatal viral disease, but non-specific enteritis can also be serious, especially if neglected in the early stages. The temperature may fall to 96°F and the cat may dehydrate rapidly. The animal's anus and surrounding area may become scalded with the liquid stools and secondary infections may set in. Cats with enteritis need expert and constant veterinary care plus very dedicated home nursing. It is vitally important to keep the animal very clean, warm and fed exactly as instructed (see Home Nursing).

Escherichia coli is a bacterium found in the intestines of most animals, including humans. Certain strains, however, may be harmful and a condition known as *Escherichia coli infection* may occur. Kittens with *E. coli* infection succumb to

Right In diseases of the digestive system, loss of appetite often occurs and the sick animal is given vitamins by injections under the skin.

Centre right It is essential to massage the site of such injections for a minute or two in order to disperse the substance completely.

Far right The veterinary surgeon checks the tail end of the sick kitten to ensure that diarrhoea is not causing scalding of the delicate tissues.

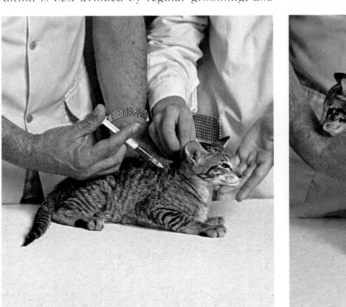

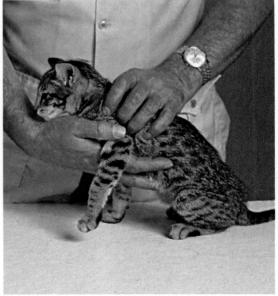

During serious disease it may be necessary to force-feed the sick cat. Any nourishing liquids can be used and a large disposable syringe makes an excellent feeding tube.

the disease very rapidly, having constant pale and very offensive diarrhoea; they lose condition quickly, dehydrate and may die despite every possible care and treatment. It was thought that *E. coli* infection caused such breeding problems as failure to conceive, abortion, production of dead kittens or litters fading away soon after birth. So much doubt has been thrown on this idea, however, that a large scale research programme has recently been started. Unfortunately, such work takes a long time and, at the time of writing, it is too early to know what the result will be.

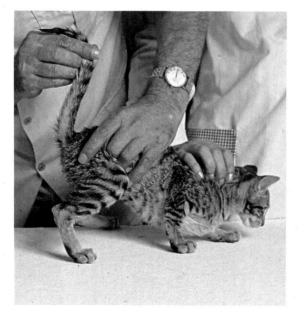

Enteritis in the cat may be caused by a group of bacteria also associated with food-poisoning in humans. These are the Salmonellae, which are common in slightly tainted foodstuffs, especially undercooked poultry, and reheated meats. *Salmonella typhimurium* can cause dysentery and death in cats fed raw, minced poultry from unreliable sources. Following illness in which broad-spectrum antibiotics have been used over a long period, the bacterial balance of the cat's intestines may be disturbed sufficiently to allow the excess formation of natural yeasts. This upset balance may also result in a form of enteritis.

Infestation with parasites such as roundworm and, more rarely, coccidia may also be the cause of enteritis, especially in kittens (see Parasites). At weaning, breeders often experience problems with diarrhoea, sometimes combined with vomiting, in their litters. It seems that an imbalance occurs in the digestive enzymes as the kittens make the transition from the milk diet to that of meat. The enteritis is so severe in some cases that fluid faeces drip almost continuously from the kittens. It is essential that the kittens are professionally treated without delay, kept warm and have their tail-ends washed, dried and lubricated whenever necessary. They are usually taken right away from the mother cat at this stage and carefully nursed back to health. The veterinary surgeon can provide hydrolysed beef extract on which to feed them, and nutritious meat jellies can be home-made. Special electrolyte solutions might be prescribed to be syringe fed each day, and binding foods such as hard-boiled egg whites might aid recovery.

The Kidneys: Some forms of poisoning, especially with phenol derivatives, may cause *acute nephritis* in cats. The symptoms of the disease are depression, increased thirst, loss of appetite, occasional vomiting and the production of small amounts of highly concentrated urine. The cat usually sits in a typical, hunched-up position, crying when touched or lifted. Ulceration of the mouth may prevent the cat from drinking, and immediate treatment is required for this often fatal disease. The FPL virus is another chief cause of acute nephritis, for it attacks the tubules of the kidneys, rapidly destroying the renal tissues. After successful treatment the cat makes a long slow recovery and needs special care. It is usually maintained on a special low-protein diet. *Chronic nephritis* is frequently seen in old cats and is due to changes in the structures of the kidneys. The cat drinks excessively, and is particularly partial to water from puddles, fish-ponds and flower vases. Large quantities of pale urine are passed, the cat may have offensive breath, tartar builds up on the teeth and gums, and the mouth becomes ulcerated. The condition known as *uraemia* sets in when the kidneys fail to filter waste products from the blood, and the cat begins to vomit, and appears anaemic.

Cats with nephritis can be fed on a special canned diet supplied by the veterinary surgeon. They need special care, and a watchful eye must be kept for any signs of deterioration in condition.

The Bladder: *Cystitis* in the cat may result from a simple bacterial infection. Most cases, however, are due to the formation of small stones, or calculi, within the bladder itself. A cat with cystitis is seen to visit its toilet tray at frequent intervals, where it squats and strains, but only manages to pass a small amount of urine each time. On examination, this urine may be found to have streaks or spots of blood. The straining action is often accompanied by a moan or cry of pain, and the uninformed owner might suspect that the animal is constipated. The cat can be gently examined, and if urinary retention is severe, the bladder can be felt like a hard, round ball. The cat must be treated

carefully and gently at this time, placed in a safe carrier and taken without delay to the veterinary surgeon. This is a critical stage at which the bladder may easily rupture with any rough treatment or undue pressure.

The Urethra: The male cat, entire or neutered, may show identical symptoms when he is suffering from a blocked urethra. As well as the constant visits to the toilet tray, sitting, straining and occasionally crying, he will be seen to wash the penis and prepuce persistently, and in a disturbed manner. *Urolithiasis* is the name given to the condition, and literally means 'stones in the urinary tract'. Whether the stones are tiny crystals in the urethra or larger calculi in the bladder, the blockage must be removed at once by the veterinary surgeon. Recovered cats are then fed on a careful diet to help avoid the formation of further stones. Salt can be added to the animal's food to increase thirst so that more water is taken, which helps prevent the urine becoming highly concentrated.

The Ovaries: Occasionally the ovaries of the cat become *cystic*, and the affected queen may call constantly. If mated, she is unlikely to produce any kittens, and the only kind and helpful solution is to have her spayed.

Left A heavily pregnant queen must be watched carefully to ensure that the pressure of the kittens does not affect her bladder function.

Constant licking of the prepuce by the neutered male could indicate some urethral obstruction and calls for expert advice.

The Uterus: After kittening, infection may develop in the uterus, due to the retention of a placenta, a very protracted labour or the passing of a dead kitten. This conditions is known as *puerperal metritis*, and the symptoms are an offensive discharge and loss of appetite. If neglected, the cat becomes stained with the discharge and walks with arched back and stiff legs. Her temperature goes up and she loses her appetite; she may vomit and quickly becomes dehydrated. The kittens cry as the queen's milk diminishes, and they become soiled with the vaginal discharge. Urgent treatment is necessary to save the queen and, hopefully, her kittens.

In older, non-breeding queens the formation of pus within the uterus is known as *pyometra*. It is an acute condition and the symptoms are general depression and loss of appetite combined with vomiting and an excessive thirst. The abdomen looks distinctly distended and the affected cat has a raised temperature. Prompt veterinary attention is essential, when an ovarohysterectomy is performed. If this is carried out early enough, the queen can be expected to make a good recovery.

Endometritis, inflammation of the uterine lining, may occur for no apparent reason in queens of all ages. In the young show cat in which breeding has been deliberately deferred a low-grade endometritis may develop from the age of about two years. The cat is listless, with a raised temperature, and spends much time cleaning the vulva. Periods of oestrus (estrus) occur but it proves impossible to get the cat in kitten, and eventually the queen must be spayed. If the operation is delayed too long, the cat's health may deteriorate suddenly and she may die despite emergency treatment. In the older queen the disease is characterized by a change in the breeding pattern, with smaller litters at first, then an increase in neonatal deaths and stillborn kittens. After the following matings, abortions occur. It is generally at this stage that an acute endometritis is diagnosed, and the cat spayed.

Above Passing urine in the normal way, the cat squats in a relaxed manner.

Below Often mistaken for constipation, this cat is most probably suffering from urolithiasis as he strains with arched back, probably crying with pain. This denotes serious trouble and urgent veterinary attention is essential.

There are several causes of nervous symptoms in the cat, including the presence of parasites in the brain tissue, certain poisons, bacterial infections and trauma. The central nervous system consists of the brain and spinal cord, and this is commonly injured in road accidents, which may result in concussion, brain damage, and laceration of the spinal cord due to dislocation and fracture of the vertebrae.

Epilepsy can be hereditary and is sometimes seen in colonies of closely bred semi-wild cats. It is a functional disease of the brain, and the affected cat suffers from convulsions, with a loss of consciousness. There are varying degrees of severity in epilepsy, but the cat is usually seen to froth at the mouth before falling over onto its side, the limbs making running movements. As the cat lapses into the unconscious state, it may urinate and pass faeces quite involuntarily. The cat usually recovers fairly quickly and sits up. Apart from being a little unsteady for a while, the animal appears perfectly normal and will wash itself and eat and drink. Epileptic cats can be treated with anticonvulsant drugs. They should never be used for breeding and are better neutered.

The haemorrhage or thrombosis of a blood-vessel in the brain may cause the cat to have a *stroke*. This can happen very suddenly without prior warning, usually in the very old cat. The cat may cry out as it falls on its side and may lose consciousness for a few minutes. It may also vomit. After coming round and sitting up, the animal's eyes are seen to flick rapidly from side to side and the cat is unable to stand steadily. Following a stroke, the cat may hold its head permanently on one side and there may be paralysis of one side of the face. Rest in a quiet, dimly lit room is essential for the patient following a stroke. The veterinary surgeon may prescribe sedatives, and will hope to see an improvement in the condition within three weeks or will consider the changes in the cat to be of a permanent nature.

A cat showing nervous symptoms is confined in a safe pen while under observation.

Lactational tetany, eclampsia or *milk fever,* is always associated with parturition of the cat, although usually considered to be a uro-genital disease. It is fairly rare in the cat but it is essential that breeders are aware of the symptoms, for no time must be lost in getting veterinary treatment for the disease. It is a condition which affects nursing queens, when a sudden drop in the critical blood calcium level occurs, producing excitability of the spinal cord, with corresponding nervous symptoms. The disease occurs most frequently in queens nursing litters of five or more kittens 3–8 weeks of age (see Having Kittens).

At first the queen is restless and leaves the kittening box. Her hind-legs may seem stiff and drag a little, and her forelimbs seem uncoordinated; often she runs a high temperature. Muscular spasms may pass along her flanks and her pupils are dilated. The queen's breathing becomes faster and she may then vomit, after which she is unsteady and may fall over onto one

susceptible as dogs. It is transmitted in the saliva from the bite of an infected animal. When introduced to the body, the virus invades the nervous tissues, producing the disease and culminating in a particularly dreadful death.

Some countries are free from the menace of rabies – notably Britain, Australia, New Zealand and the US state of Hawaii. All have imposed strict quarantine regulations on imported animals that could carry the disease. Rabies in the cat has an incubation period that is usually 3–8 weeks, but may be as short as 10 days or as long as 6 months; hence the long periods of confinement in quarantine quarters enforced by various governments.

There are two forms of the disease – *excitative* or *furious rabies* and *dumb rabies.* In cats it is the former that is most common.

The first symptoms of rabies are subtle changes in the animal's temperament, a slight temperature rise and dilation of the pupils. This stage lasts for about three days, after which the excitative stage

Normal behaviour patterns in the cat:
Left A kitten counters the aggressive hissing of the older cat with a defensive posture and half-hearted growl.

Right Burmese kittens play-fighting.

side. When she returns to her kittens, she is reluctant to feed them, holding herself hunched above them rather than settling her body around the litter in the normal way. The veterinary surgeon usually injects a solution of calcium borogluconate into a vein and beneath the skin, and if this is given early enough, the response in the cat is quite dramatic. If treatment is delayed, the cat develops severe muscular spasms before collapsing into a coma leading to death. A queen that has suffered from lactational tetany should be rested before further breeding and should only be allowed to rear a small litter under veterinary supervision with calcium supplements.

Rabies is a viral disease to which cats are as

develops. During the next four days the cat becomes increasingly nervous and irritable, showing exaggerated responses to sounds and lights. The cat becomes increasingly aggressive and will attack and bite other cats, dogs or humans that are foolish enough to approach it. Eventually all muscular control is lost; the jaw droops and the cat salivates uncontrollably; paralysis spreads throughout the body; and death follows two or three days later. In dumb rabies the excitative stage does not occur and the cat is withdrawn and nervous before lapsing into the paralytic stage.

There is no effective treatment for this disease at present, but it is possible to have cats protected by vaccination in countries where it occurs.

Non-parasitic Diseases of the Skin: Non-parasitic diseases of the skin cause a great deal of controversy between veterinary surgeons, cat breeders and pet owners. A disease of our time that is becoming increasingly common is known variously as *nutritional dermatitis, fish eczema* or *miliary eczema.* Veterinary experts are often in disagreement about the cause and treatment of this condition in the cat, and some cases fail to respond to a whole spectrum of drugs, diets and topical applications. It seems that problems are experienced in differentiating between miliary eczema, skin conditions caused by hormonal imbalance and various allergies, such as those due to the wearing of a flea collar. Some veterinary surgeons are of the opinion that a combination of factors is involved in producing these unsightly and irritating conditions in the cat, and treat them accordingly.

In miliary eczema the early signs consist of a rash of small scaly spots along the spine towards the base of the tail. The condition is very irritating and the cat licks and bites at the affected area, soon reducing it to a raw, weeping wound. There is some hair loss also, and the surrounding hair becomes discoloured owing to the excessive licking of the cat.

The cat should be presented for a veterinary examination as soon as the spots are noticed, along with a list of the items in the cat's normal, everyday diet. Various vitamins may be prescribed, and a course of hormone tablets or cortisone injections given. It may be necessary for the animal to wear an Elizabethan collar or a small jacket, to prevent it from inflicting further damage on the affected areas. The skin should be thoroughly groomed each day to remove any loose hair; then the scabs can be bathed away with warm water and soap. After drying the lesions carefully, a soothing antibiotic dressing can be applied, but the cat must not be able to reach this with its tongue. If the treatment is successful, no further scabs appear and new hairs can be seen to be growing on the bare areas after about 10–14 days. Sometimes the condition fails to respond to the initial treatment and something else has to be tried. In any case the area affected must be kept clean at all times.

Hormonal alopecia is sometimes seen in cats, especially neuters. There is considerable hair loss on the back of the affected animal's thighs. The bare areas are usually quite symmetrical and seem to be without inflammation and irritation in some cats, while others obviously find the condition extremely irritating.

Hormone and vitamin treatment is generally prescribed for this type of alopecia, but in some cats the condition recurs at frequent intervals, sometimes in cycles, sometimes when the animal has access to extra warmth. Many cats respond well to their initial treatment and remain free of the complaint.

Parasitic Diseases of the Skin

Causative Parasites:	Signs of Infestation:	Treatment:
Fleas:	Cat scratches neck; may twitch muscles along spine or turn to bite at base of tail. Small black grits can be found on the skin at base of ears and along spine near tail root.	Fleas are removed with fine toothed comb. Coat and bedding are treated with insecticidal powder, spray or bath recommended by veterinary surgeon. Cat must be checked regularly for signs of re-infestation.
Lice:	Cat scratches head and neck. Lice may be seen in the coat, small and slow-moving, looking like scurf. Tiny, clear, bead-like eggs (nits) are cemented to individual hairs.	Coat is sprayed, dusted or bathed with insecticidal preparation recommended by veterinary surgeon. Hairs with nits are combed out and burned. Cat must be checked regularly for signs of re-infestation.
Ticks:	Do not seem to cause any irritation or distress. First noticed during grooming as a blue-grey wart-like growth attached to the skin.	Suck blood, so are debilitating. A drop of surgical spirit is applied to the point of attachment to the cat's skin to cause the tick to relax its jaws, when it can be removed with tweezers and the sore area washed and dried.
Harvest Mites:	Cat may hold ears down or scratch at the head or bite at the toes. On examination the tiny mites can be seen as orange-red specks clustered closely together, usually on the ear flaps or between the toes.	A pest powder or spray as recommended for fleas quickly kills these mites.

Observation of scratching behaviour:
Right Scratching the neck could indicate the presence of fleas.

Centre right Scratching the ears could indicate fleas, ear-mites or harvest-mites.

Far right Scratching the forehead possibly denotes the presence of mange-mites.

Cheyletiella parasitovorax: Cat scratches continuously but no sign of parasites can be found. Owner may develop rash on wrists, chest and stomach. Mite is identified from skin scrapings.

Insecticide provided by veterinary surgeon and used carefully as directed quickly kills these mites, although application may need to be repeated after an interval.

Mange Mites: Cat scratches vigorously and is depressed. The hair breaks off in the affected areas of the head, face and ears, and brown scabs appear. The cat soon becomes generally ill and the scaly areas become thickened with corrugated skin which exudes a strange odour.

Cat must be isolated and the affected areas washed with soap and water to soften the skin before the application of special skin preparations. The treatment is repeated at regular intervals as instructed by the veterinary surgeon until new growth of hair indicates the final destruction of the mites.

Above The sites of parasitic infestation.
1 Ear mite
2 Miliary eczeana
3 Flea infestation
4 Hormonal Alopecia
5 Mange mite
6 Ringworm

Ringworm: Small lesions are noticed usually around the nose, lips, forehead, front legs and claw-beds. Some look like pimples with small scabs, and the lesions are often circular or oval. On examination, broken hair shafts can be seen within each 'ring'. This disease sometimes shows as apparent clumps of dandruff spread like cigarette ash on the skin, or as small white scales clustered around small clumps of hair. Lesions are sometimes discovered on human members of the family before the disease is suspected in the cat.

The veterinary surgeon must first confirm the diagnosis, then the disease is treated with a fungicidal antibiotic given orally for up to 6 weeks. Topical applications of fungicidal dressings are applied to the lesions, after the hair has been clipped away. All hair, and the animal's bedding should be burned, and other equipment should be disinfected in a formalin solution as instructed by the veterinary surgeon. Strict isolation and quarantine procedures must be carried out when cats are affected with this serious disease.

Above To prevent a cat from scratching raw areas around the head and neck, a jacket is easily made from an old sock by cutting off the toe and neatening the raw edge.

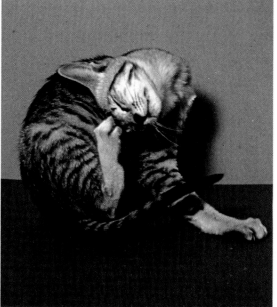

Apart from the parasites which cause skin diseases in the cat, there is another common and troublesome mite which infests the ear canal. This is the *otodectic mange mite*, which produces the condition commonly known as ear canker. This mite lives and breeds deep inside the ear of the cat and causes intense irritation to the animal, which shakes its head from time to time and vigorously scratches at the back of its ears. On inspection the ears may be found to have deposits of a dark brown exudate in the ear canal, and if this is removed, it may be possible to see the tiny white parasites with the naked eye. Secondary infections quickly attack the inflamed areas within the ear, so no time should be lost in seeking professional advice. The veterinary surgeon usually cleans most of the exudate from the ear before applying an ascaricidal lotion, plus some antibiotic cream if there is any sign of secondary infection. In a severely inflamed ear the antibiotic treatment may have to be commenced before the mites can be eradicated. It is essential to carry out the veterinary surgeon's instructions to the letter, for the mites' life cycle is such that the treatment must be repeated at the correct intervals. The cat's ear is very delicate within and should not be probed too

Above A cat showing the typical deposits within the ear caused by *otodectic mange mites*, commonly known as canker.

Below from left to right Harvest Mite – *Trombicula autumnalis.* Ear Mite – *Otodectes cynotis.* Flea – *Ctenocephalides felis.* Tick sp. – *Ixodes* sp. Louse – *Felicola subrostrata.*

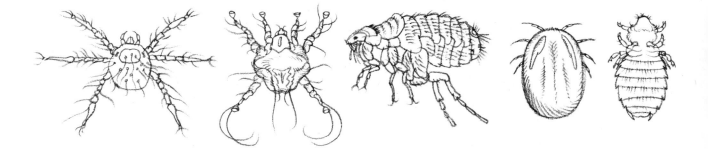

deeply. The lotions are best warmed before being dropped into the cat's ear. The best way to do this is to draw a little lotion into a plastic syringe, and then stand the syringe in water at blood heat for a few moments before applying it to the ear. Applying the lotion on the skin inside one's wrist is an excellent test of temperature.

Internal Parasites: *Roundworms* are quite common in the domestic cat, where they live mostly in the intestines. In adult cats they do very little harm, although infested animals rarely look in good condition. In kittens, however, a heavy worm burden can be serious, especially if the kitten then contracts any sort of infection. Roundworms in the stomach are often vomited by the cat and curl up like thin corkscrews of spaghetti. Intestinal worms are passed in the faeces. Queens should receive worming pills in a planned course well before mating takes place, to eliminate any roundworms from their bowels. Young kittens can be wormed under veterinary

supervision only, while still nursing, if necessary. Cats which are likely to be infected can have doses of worming medicine at regularly spaced intervals. The presence of roundworms may be suspected if a cat or kitten has diarrhoea or a pot-belly, loses condition and seems fussy with its food. There may also be a distinct odour from its breath.

Tapeworms live in the small intestines of cats. Tapeworm eggs are ingested by an intermediate host such as the flea, which, in turn, is eaten by the cat, and the worm can then develop to adulthood. The head of the worm attaches itself to the inside wall of the bowel, where it remains, feeding and growing. Ripe segments of the worm are shed from time to time and pass from the cat in its faeces. They may be seen occasionally on the fur around the anus or on the ground where the cat has been sitting. A segment is white and shaped rather like a cucumber seed, and will change shape as it moves, eventually drying up to become brittle and straw-coloured. These segments contain the

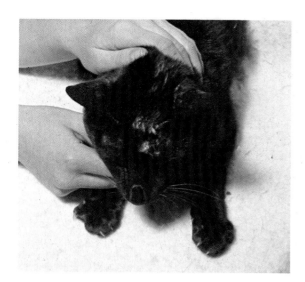

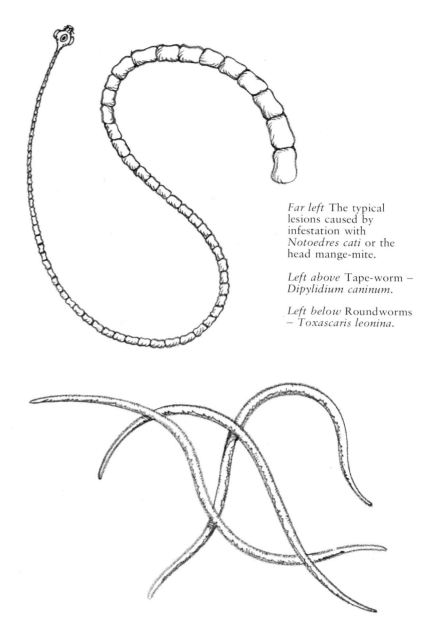

Far left The typical lesions caused by infestation with *Notoedres cati* or the head mange-mite.

Left above Tape-worm – *Dipylidium caninum*.

Left below Roundworms – *Toxascaris leonina*.

eggs of the tapeworm and will settle on the ground to await a flea in order to begin the cycle once more. A cat with a tapeworm must be carefully dosed in order to remove it, complete with head. It is important to have this carried out under veterinary supervision. By ensuring that cats are kept free from fleas, and preventing them from eating carcases of wild animals, it is possible to keep them free from infestation with a tapeworm. A cat harbouring such a worm eats a great deal but never seems to put on condition. Its coat is inclined to stand out in an unkempt fashion and the animal often seems restless and disturbed.

If a cat is difficult to get into good condition, it is a simple matter to have it tested for worms.

Having contacted the veterinary surgeon to determine a suitable day for the test to be carried out, the cat should be isolated with a clean toilet tray. After the animal has passed some faeces, a sample should be placed in a small clean glass jar and the lid screwed in place. This is taken for analysis, and any worm eggs present in the sample can be identified. Each type of worm needs different treatment; roundworm doses must be repeated at intervals to ensure that all stages in the parasite's life cycle are destroyed as they reach maturity. A dramatic improvement in the cat's condition may well be seen after a successful course of worming treatment.

Coccidia are parasites which burrow into the lining of the intestine and cause the disease known as *coccidiosis*, a condition fairly common in kittens kept in poor conditions where hygienic measures are practically non-existent, and there is overcrowding. Affected kittens often vomit, especially on awakening in the morning, and they have offensive diarrhoea, sometimes bloodstained. They look pale around the lips owing to anaemia and, unless treated, become increasingly listless and emaciated and may eventually die. Kittens with this disease must be isolated, treated by the veterinary surgeon daily and kept as clean as possible, so that they stop re-infecting themselves with the contaminated faeces.

Toxoplasmosis in the cat is very rare, but because the symptoms are so dramatic and unpleasant cat owners may be unduly worried by the thought of it. It is caused by an organism which may inhabit the body cells without any ill-effect, then suddenly becomes pathogenic. The lungs are usually affected: the cat begins to breathe heavily and laboriously, and then develops a high temperature with the onset of broncho-pneumonia. The toxoplasms may attack the abdominal organs; these become inflamed, and hepatitis and pancreatitis result. The sick cat deteriorates rapidly, with vomiting, diarrhoea and jaundice, and may die within a few days of the onset of the disease. In older cats the course of the invasion by the parasites is less dramatic. The first signs of trouble might be vomiting, diarrhoea and slight anaemia; then the parasites attack the central nervous system and the cat becomes unsteady and unable to coordinate its movements, and may develop the slight paralysis known as paresis. Obviously the veterinary surgeon will try to combat this parasitic disease with all his skill, but it is often difficult to treat, and the sick cat succumbs very easily.

Right Even the most independent of cats soon learns to get around quite well with both hindlegs in plaster.

Even in the best-managed homes and catteries accidents do happen to cats and kittens. Many cats spend much of their time in the kitchen, and their natural curiosity sometimes get them into trouble. From early kittenhood, pet cats should be discouraged from jumping onto tables, shelves and working surfaces, for a cat used to jumping up to investigate each and every tempting smell may well end up on the searing hotplate of the stove. Blistered pads are difficult to treat and cause great pain to the cat.

Sputtering hot oil may splash an inquisitive cat, scalding the skin and resulting in deep painful burns and loss of hair. Cats have also been known to tip hot fat all over themselves by jumping up and knocking the pan handle. Boiling water splashes are also dangerous, and it is a good plan to banish the cat from the kitchen while cooking is in progress.

Another kitchen hazard is the refrigerator, for the cat may decide to explore the interior if the door is accidentally left open, and may inadvertently be shut inside, with fatal consequences. Similarly, washing machines and clothes driers should never be left unattended with doors or lids open if the cat is around. Clothes driers are particularly tempting, as cats are attracted by the smell and warmth of the freshly dried clothes.

Kittens are especially attracted to electric wires and cables and will play with any draped across the floor from appliance to wall socket. They pat at the cable, roll over and kick at it, grasp it in the paws and then bite hard in a mock 'kill'. If the end of the wire is connected to a live socket and the sharp little teeth pierce the casing, contact is made and the kitten will be electrocuted.

Many household cleaning materials and disinfectants are toxic to felines, and cats have been known to die after licking or walking through such substances. Air fresheners and insect sprays can also poison cats, and all such products should be chosen and used with the utmost care, especially when there are young kittens around.

Cats allowed their freedom to roam may be accidentally poisoned by pesticides such as slug bait, which is a mixture of metaldehyde and bran, and which cats find strangely attractive. If ingested by the cat, this substance causes convulsions, arrested respiration and death. The rodenti-

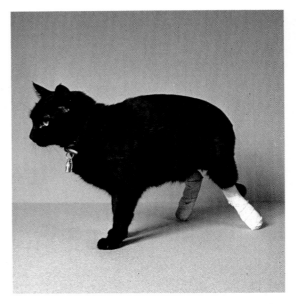

cides are also dangerous to cats, especially those which interfere with the blood-clotting mechanisms. Cats may become ill and possibly die after eating the bait, or animals killed by the poison.

Sprays used for treating garden plants may contain organophosphorus compounds, which in high concentrations prove fatal to cats. The affected animal has acute diarrhoea and muscular tremors before collapsing. In the garage antifreeze compounds made for car radiators spell death for the cat. For some inexplicable reason, cats find the substance strangely attractive, and attempt to lick the can. The toxic component is ethylene glycol, which poisons the system of the cat, causing a rapid death (see also 145).

Cats may be stung by flying insects while hunting in the garden. This usually happens when they attack the insect and attempt to bite at it; therefore most stings are in or around the mouth.

A cat that is seen frantically clawing at its mouth may have been stung, in which case the area will be seen to swell fairly quickly. It may, however, have a piece of bone, or some other foreign body, wedged across its palate or embedded in its tongue or inside the lips, and the owner should carefully inspect the mouth.

Although most cats are not fond of getting wet, they may occasionally fall into a water-butt or tank, a swimming-pool or fish-pond, and be unable to get out again. After swimming for some time, the exhausted animal may start to drown. Pools should always have some sort of sloping ladder or a raft, if there is a risk of cats falling in, and water tanks and other deep containers should be covered.

Road accidents claim many feline victims each year. Some animals are killed instantly and some are injured in various ways. The animal may be stunned and bruised, or it may have severe internal injuries. It may have single or multiple fractures. Whatever its injuries, the cat may lie unconscious at the side of the road, or it may try to drag itself back home. Worst of all, it may crawl away to die, so that its frantic owner never knows exactly what happened to it.

Right Bathing the paw to relieve stings, abcesses or strains is best done by holding the cat in a comfortable position while it stands in the soothing solution. Extra hot water can be added to keep the temperature at blood heat.

First Aid

Burns and Scalds: Cool burned area with ice-water, cover with clean cloth such as a handkerchief or tea-towel, place in warm carrier and take animal to veterinary surgeon.

Electrocution: Switch off power supply, using rubber gloves or some wooden item to prevent rescuer being shocked. Get the animal warm by rubbing its body and wrapping in warm blankets until professional help can be obtained. Artificial respiration may be necessary if the cat stops breathing (see below).

Poisoning – external: Poisonous substances on the coat or feet of the cat should be washed off immediately with plain soap (not detergent) and warm water. Professional advice is essential.

Poisoning – internal: Keep the animal as warm as possible and seek professional advice without delay. Take any suspect products along, so that the correct antidote may, if possible, be given.

Stings: Look for the presence of the sting and remove it. Bee stings are acid and can be neutralized by gentle rubbing of the site with household soda. Wasp stings are alkaline, and the wound should be bathed with vinegar or lemon juice. Keep the cat warm and quiet. If the area swells alarmingly, or the cat becomes feverish or distressed, veterinary advice should be sought.

Drowning: Lie the cat on a table with the head hanging over the edge, and allow the water and mucus to drain from the mouth while rubbing the body fairly vigorously. If breathing stops, artificial respiration is necessary until professional help is to hand.

Road Accidents: An injured and unconscious cat found in the road should be carefully eased onto a towel, blanket or jacket so that it can be lifted without disturbing its limbs, or internal organs, which may be damaged. The injured animal should be taken to a veterinary surgeon without delay, and kept warm and quiet on the journey. If the cat is haemorrhaging from the mouth, attempt to keep the airways open on the journey.

Bleeding: If blood is spurting from a wound, it may be coming from an artery and must be controlled. A folded handkerchief can be pressed firmly over the bleeding point until professional help is available. If the bleeding is from a limb, a tourniquet may be used as a temporary measure. A handkerchief is tied around the limb above the wound and a piece of stick or a pencil is placed beneath it, then twisted until the material is tight enough to stop the haemorrhage. After ten minutes the tourniquet must be gently released or tissue damage may occur. A cat haemorrhaging from the mouth, nose or ears must receive urgent veterinary attention and should be kept warm and still until help is available.

Fractures: A cat that has one or more fractures should be moved with the utmost care onto a tray or piece of board before one attempts to transfer it to the veterinary hospital. It should be covered with warm blankets and kept still and calm.

Foreign Bodies: Bones stuck across the palate can be removed by prising them off with the handle of a plastic spoon. Sewing-needles may be stuck in the tongue, lips or throat and need expert attention for safe removal. Burrs and thorns may be causing trouble in the cat's pads, and can be removed with tweezers before bathing the affected paw in a solution of Epsom salts to reduce the tenderness and swelling. Grass seeds sometimes get under the eyelids of the cat and must be flushed out with a syringe and warm saline solution.

Artificial Respiration: Necessary only in extreme cases to save the life of a cat, artificial respiration can be carried out in two ways: (1) Place the cat on its side, head slightly forward, so that the air-ways are clear. Ensure that mouth and throat are clear and that the tongue is forward (in cases of drowning allow the cat's head to hang over the edge of the table). Gentle pressure is applied to the chest of the cat, then released. This is repeated rhythmically, four seconds being taken to apply pressure and four seconds to release it, until the cat takes a breath. (2) The cat is held head down by its hind-legs grasped firmly, close together and swung in a wide half-circle, gently and smoothly until the cat breathes.

Above left Applying a bandage to an injured limb. This must be bound on firmly but not so tightly that it restricts the circulation.

Above right An injured and unconscious cat is carefully eased onto a towel, jacket or rug before being lifted and taken for veterinary attention.

Below left To stop serious bleeding in a limb a handkerchief and pencil can be used to make a tourniquet as an emergency measure only.

Below right Splints may be applied to fractured limbs before the cat is transported to the veterinary surgery, but no attempt should be made to set the limb at home.

In most cases of feline illness the efficiency of the home nursing plays as important a part in the cat's recovery as the veterinary treatment. The three essentials of good nursing are: (1) providing adequate liquids and nourishing food; (2) keeping the patient clean and warm; and (3), last but by no means least important, trying to keep its interest alive.

There is no set of hard and fast rules for nursing sick cats. Each patient and each illness has characteristics which make it unique, and so slightly different procedures may be necessary. Ill, injured or recuperating cats may need to be confined indoors or perhaps to one room. Windows and cat flaps must be securely closed. In all cases, however, it must be possible to provide a quiet area for the animal's bed, which can be shielded from light whenever necessary. Heat can be provided either by keeping the whole room at a suitable temperature or by having a dull emitter infrared heating

here also. Presented with such a sick cat, many owners just give up in despair and ask the veterinary surgeon to hospitalize the animal. If it is possible to nurse the cat at home, however, the close proximity of friends and familiar smells and surroundings sometimes permeate the animal's senses and go a small way in aiding recovery.

The first thing to be done is to clean the cat up and make it as comfortable as possible. The veterinary surgeon injects antibiotics, vitamins and other substances to help maintain the balance of the delicate systems in the cat's body. As the body begins to waste, so the muscles become slack, and a gentle body massage helps to stimulate the circulation and promotes interest in the proceedings. Next, the discharges can be wiped away with a warm saline solution on cotton-wool balls. The eyes, nostrils and lips should be cleaned thoroughly and dried, and then some petroleum jelly is worked into the inflamed areas. Antibiotic

Right The coat of the sick kitten is cleaned with baby talcum powder, *far right* this is massaged well into the fur, *below right* then brushed out again with a fairly soft brush.

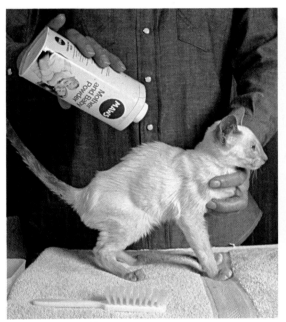

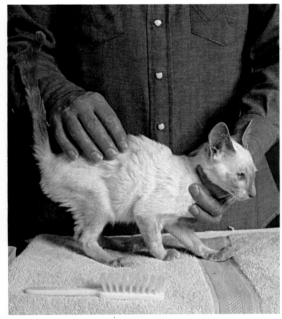

bulb suspended on an adjustable chain or cord above the patient's bed. The area used for nursing must be easy to clean and furnished with equipment that can be sterilized by heat or by immersion in strong disinfectants. It is advisable to use disposable equipment if possible, especially if the disease involved is highly infectious or contagious.

Cat 'flu cases are perhaps the most demanding in terms of time and patience. The seriously affected cat becomes so depressed and miserable that it resents any form of help and handling, and gives the impression that it would rather be left alone to die. In severe cases the mouth may be so ulcerated that even syringe-feeding with liquids causes pain, and the nostrils and lips may become ulcerated, bleeding every time the discharge is bathed away. The eyes are usually affected also, discharging and with red and swollen lids, which may also become ulcerated and bleed when bathed. The cat is probably stricken with severe diarrhoea, too, and the anus and surrounding area becomes so sore that some bleeding may be seen

ointment supplied by the veterinary surgeon can be applied to the eyelids and nostrils, and should be worked into the ulcerated areas to prevent new discharges drying and caking there. After the face has been cleaned, feeding should be carried out while the nostrils are as clear as possible. The cat may well be mouth-breathing at this stage and resents anything that interrupts this. The food, drawn into a plastic syringe, is administered by raising the cat's head, inserting the nozzle between the teeth at the side of the animal's closed mouth and depressing the plunger gently, dispensing a few drops of food. Allow the cat to swallow and take a breath before continuing. It is best to feed warm liquids, and it may be necessary to wrap the cat in a towel to prevent it struggling and becoming exhausted, or choking. As feeding can be such a traumatic procedure at this stage in the illness, highly concentrated mixtures should be used, and the veterinary surgeon will recommend suitable products.

After feeding, the mouth should be cleaned again; then the cat, if well enough, may be placed on its toilet tray and stroked to encourage it. Gentle grooming all over the body makes the sick animal relax somewhat, and it is beneficial to apply talcum powder, as used for human babies, to the easily soiled regions of the throat and chest as well as around the tail-end of the cat. This helps to keep the skin dry. The powder should be worked in, then gently brushed out. If the cat has diarrhoea and is incontinent, disposable napkins (diapers) designed for human babies can be used. These can be torn to a convenient shape and wrapped neatly around the cat's tail-end. They are very absorbent and help to keep the animal clean if changed frequently. Very depressed cats seem to appreciate having their paws and legs massaged, and the hind-legs should be stretched and flexed from time to time. It is important to change the

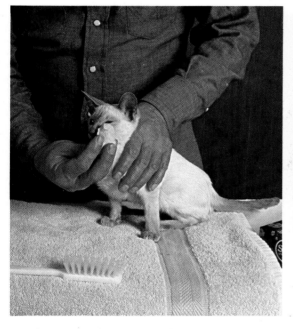

It is important to clean the corners of the eyes, *far left*, and the lips should be wiped with damp cotton-wool, *left*.

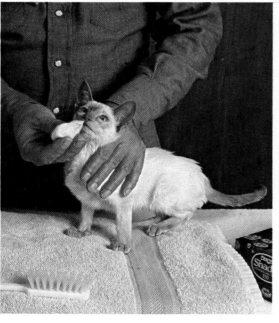

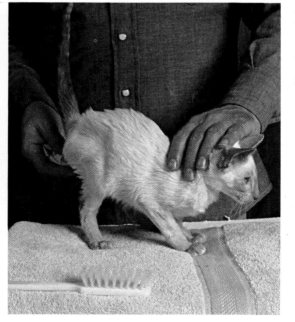

Far left Caked nostrils are bathed before applying petroleum jelly.

Left The genital area is washed, dried and powdered.

very sick cat onto a different side each time it is attended, to prevent it developing sores on the pressure points. Each day an attempt should be made to get the cat to eat voluntarily by offering tasty strong-smelling things such as kipper or herring. The best way to do this is to buy tiny pots of pastes so that refused food is not totally wasted.

When the discharges seem to be clearing up, some of the paste may be smeared along the cat's lips and nose, and one day, with luck, it will lick it off. This is a wonderful sign and a good time to wrap the cat up in its blanket and take it for a walk, preferably outside. Sometimes the stimuli of fresh air, birds singing, the warmth of the sun and the thousands of subtle sounds that humans cannot hear does the trick and the cat decides to cooperate in the saving of its life.

During nursing, the nasal passages may be relieved by putting the sick cat over an inhalant for short periods at intervals during the day. A suitable inhalant is made up by adding boiling water to any proprietary product that produces a suitable non-toxic vapour. In Britain it is usual to use Friar's Balsam, and in the United States Vicks can be obtained. The liquid can be placed in a small heat-retaining bowl inside another larger bowl or box, firm enough to take the weight of the cat contained within a mesh carrier. A plastic sheet or thick towel is draped over the carrier to keep in the vapours, which soon permeate the atmosphere, inside and around the sick cat. Before submitting the cat to the inhalant, petroleum jelly should be applied to the eyelids and nostrils to prevent any additional irritation and soreness. Five minutes over the inhalant usually proves sufficient to cause streams of mucus to flow from the nostrils of the cat. The animal should be cleaned up and replaced in its bed to rest, and the treatment can be repeated two or three times each day if it seems to benefit the sick cat.

Right To give liquid medicine it is best to use a small plastic syringe containing the correct dose. The nozzle is inserted between the side teeth of the sick animal, keeping its mouth closed and the chin slightly raised. The liquid is slowly dispelled and should be swallowed without any problems.

Far right Pills are given by opening the kitten's mouth, pressing on the lower jaw with the ring finger, and dropping the pill to the back of the throat to cause an involuntary swallowing action.

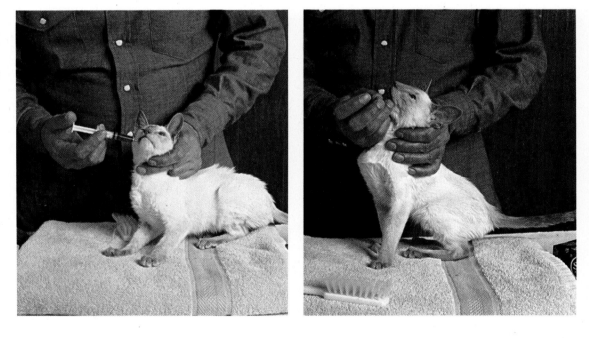

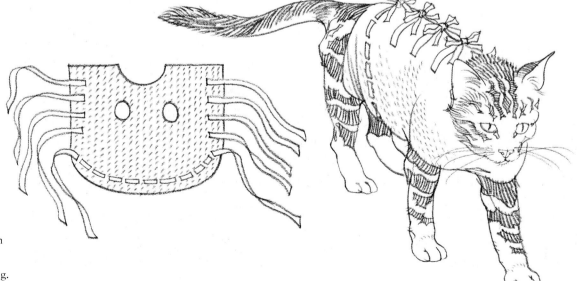

Right A pneumonia jacket is easily made from flannel or woollen material, or, in really desperate cases, from special thermal wadding.

Cats recovering from dislocations, operations or fractures may need special nursing care so that they do not injure themselves further. Such cases are usually cared for in small pens or fibreglass cages. These cats may be immobilized by bandages, splints or plaster casts, and are often unable to exercise or groom themselves properly. It is important to keep these animals interested and alert, correctly fed and groomed morning and evening, to keep the skin and coat in good condition and to keep the muscles well toned. The injured areas must be inspected regularly to ensure that there is no new swelling or that the dressings have not become displaced. The veterinary surgeon's instructions must be carried out meticulously, and any regression reported immediately. The cat will appreciate being taken out of the pen for periods during the day, seeing new sights and hearing stimulating sounds. It may also take prescribed exercise under supervision.

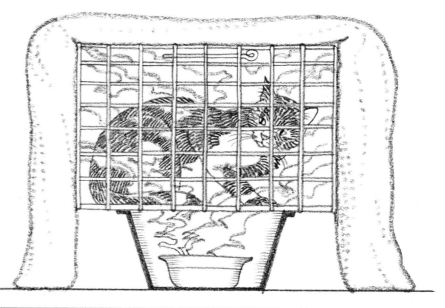

Above In severe respiratory infections, the cat can be made to inhale soothing vapours by placing it in a mesh carrier, covered with a plastic sheet, over a double bowl holding hot inhalant fluid.

Left The recovered cat benefits from fresh-air and sunshine and may be wrapped in a soft warm blanket to prevent chills.

A cattery is thought of as being accommodation specifically for cats. It can be of any size or suitable design and made to house one or one hundred animals. It may be sited indoors, out of doors or a little of each, depending upon its geographical location. It may be the ideal environment for breeding, rearing or boarding cats or it could prove to be totally inadequate and unhygienic, housing miserable animals in poor conditions.

For the general housing of a small family of cats in a temperate climate, it is usual to have cat houses made of timber or brick, sited to face south and built out-of-doors with large wired-in exercise runs. Timber is a warm and comparatively inexpensive material, and ready-made sheds and workshops of suitable size can be purchased, needing only very small adaptation to turn them into cat houses. As it is essential that cats have sanitary conditions in which to live, the timber house should be lined with smooth-faced or laminated boards. If laminated plastic board is used, no future maintenance will be required, although the initial outlay will be quite substantial. Smooth-faced hardboard or blockboard can be sealed, and then painted with a washable vinyl emulsion paint which may need a new top coat each year.

Above A carefully designed and well built cat house and run.

Far left Vinyl floor coverings are ideal in the cattery, being easy to clean and impervious to the acid content of urine and excreta.

Left Welded wire mesh is good for confining cats within their runs without obstructing their clear view of all that is going on in the garden.

It is important to line the ceiling, too, to keep the warmth in at night; and it is best to purchase a timber floor with the building rather than make a floor of poured concrete. The timber floor can have a covering of vinyl which is taken up the walls to a height of about four inches all round and fixed in place with a suitable adhesive. If required, a cat-flap can be cut in the service door, and shelves screwed around the interior walls. If the cattery is in an area where the nights can be rather cold, insulating material in strips, pads or granules can be fitted between the cladding and the interior lining of the building. Electric wiring can be run to the building from the house through a special exterior conduit made of polypropylene. This comes in all lengths and shapes, and has cat-proof fittings. Heating and lighting can then be fitted as required inside the cat house. The run should be as large as possible and high enough to allow a human adult to walk around erect. It should be constructed of stout timbers and have strong wire or mesh stapled on all the walls and the roof. Part of the roof can be covered with corrugated roofing panels if desired, and this is especially useful in areas with a high rainfall, as it enables the cats to use the run even in wet weather.

The entrance to the cat-run is the most vulnerable point. The gate must be of adequate size but not so large that the inmates can run past every time it is opened. It must be well made, with three good hinges, so that it hangs well and swings easily. There should be a strong bolt on the outside and a spring-clip to hold it shut while the attendant is inside. It is quite a good idea to have the door made with a step underneath so that mischievous kittens cannot easily run out. Double gates to the runs are ideal, but, of course, expensive. Many catteries are designed with the runs opening into an enclosed safety run or passageway.

If the run is very large and the cat population

small and static, the area can be laid out like a garden, with paved paths, grassed areas and plants, provided that the latter are not toxic to cats. Small grassed runs quickly become unkempt and unhygienic. They are difficult to clean and the grass may be impossible to cut. Small runs are best paved or concreted, and can be furnished with logs, climbing frames and shelves, so that the cats can sunbathe and exercise freely.

Inside the cattery everything necessary for grooming and attending to the cats should be neatly arranged. The animals should have comfortable, warm beds and easily cleaned toilet trays. Water and food should be in clean non-spill dishes, either on the floor or on a shelf designed for feeding. There should be a conveniently high shelf or table on which the cats can be examined or groomed, and another high shelf, or small cupboard, well away from playful paws, holding all the grooming equipment. A roll of paper towelling

in a holder fixed up high can be very handy for cleaning up odd spills and accidents, and a wastebin with a tightly fitting lid is a boon. Brushes, pans and mop can all hang on hooks on the wall.

The indoor cattery is usually favoured in areas where the temperature reaches extremes, and heating is required in the winter months and air-conditioning during the summer ones. The management of an indoor cattery must be particularly stringent, as the chance of respiratory disease spreading is always greater in such an environment. The cattery may be constructed in a spare room in the house, in a large garage or workshop, or in an outside studio. The accommodation is determined by the number of cats in the colony, and rooms or large cages are constructed accordingly. The possibilities of layout and design are endless, but the essentials are: adequate light, good ventilation, space for exercise and scrupulous sanitation.

Above Logs and branches can be arranged to provide a very natural habitat for the confined cat, allowing it to exercise its natural climbing ability and giving high vantage points.

The serious cat breeder, with several queens, may well decide to construct suitable accommodation in which calling queens can be housed so that they are safe from marauding toms, and do not disturb the neighbours with their wailing. The normal cat house or indoor cattery cage is usually quite adequate. It may also be feasible to construct kittening pens for parturition and rearing the kittens to weaning age, plus an adventure playground for developing kittens and young stock of show potential.

The kittening pen must be warm and draughtproof, and it must be constructed so that it is easily cleaned. There should be a dark, private area in which the queen can produce and nurse her family without stress, and plenty of room for her to exercise, to accommodate her toilet tray and her food and water bowls. A kittening pen may be portable and collapsible, with various removable interior components, or it may be a specially constructed unit with many refinements of design. The most important aspect of such a pen is that it meets the psychological demands of the lactating queen and her young litter. It must also be constructed so that each and every part of the pen is accessible for cleaning and disinfecting from the outside by means of small doors, panels or partitions.

If the breeder allows the cats to run in the house as well as the cattery, the kittening pen may well be sited in a living room, bedroom or study, or even in the kitchen. Then the queen can be let out

for periods of exercise each day. If the house is forbidden territory, the breeder will have alternative exercising areas for the queen and probably a special pen for weanling kittens. From the age of six weeks the kittens need the stimulation of toys, and a play area should be provided. There should be plenty of tunnels and caves, made of cartons and boxes, through which they may climb and crawl, strengthening their limbs and sharpening their reflexes. The queen can be taken away for longer periods each day until the youngsters are independent, eating well, using their toilet tray and grooming themselves.

In the large cattery litters are wormed early, and vaccinated, then sorted according to potential at about thirteen weeks of age. The very best kittens may be run on, perhaps one from each litter, and these are housed together, after a short introductory period, carefully fed and groomed ready for their first shows. The other kittens will be sold, and buyers usually like to see the mother and the rest of the cattery's stock.

Large catteries usually have a suitable play room for displaying their weanlings to buyers. The kittens are accustomed to it and romp happily while they are admired and assessed.

Above Breeding stock may have to be confined for safety, and large buildings can be divided into compartments for individual queens or growing youngsters. The addition of an outdoor run for use in fine weather is an added bonus.

Far left Weanling kittens benefit greatly from the opportunity to play and exercise in the open air.

Left Cat-sized pop holes can be cut in convenient places along the cat house walls to enable easy access, and small shutters are easily made to secure them at night, or in bad weather.

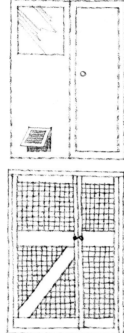

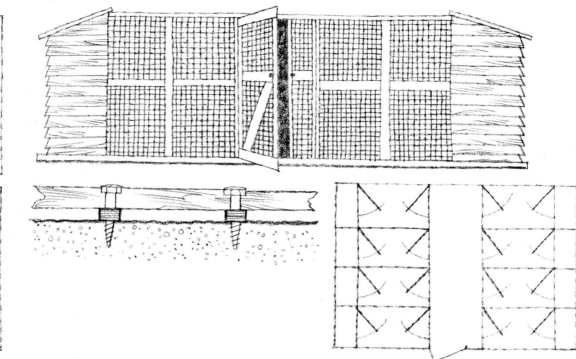

Boarding facilities must be constructed according to strict regulations laid down by licensing authorities, and these vary from country to country, and even within states and counties. It is essential that the regulations be complied with as regards construction, materials, layout and general administration, or the cattery could be closed down.

In the main the boarding cattery must provide adequate, safe and hygienic accommodation for its visitors. There must be no risk of fire breaking out, and there must be a responsible person in attendance or on call at all times. The animals must have suitable bedding, shelter and food, and room to exercise. Above all, proper precautions against the outbreak and spread of disease are of prime importance.

In countries of temperate climate the ideal boarding establishments have outdoor accommodation consisting of small timber huts and individual open-air runs. In countries which experience climatic extremes boarding units are usually built inside a larger building, heated in cold weather and cooled during the hotter months. In all catteries where there is a fast turnover of visiting cats the same essential points must be noted. First, all animals accepted for boarding must pass a basic health test. Each cat must have a normal temperature and no sign of discharge from its eyes or nostrils. There must be no sign of diarrhoea staining under the tail, and the coat and ears must be free of parasites. Second, strict attention to hygiene, with the prevention of any chance of cross-infection, must be the rule. Third, any cat showing the slightest suspicion of incubating any disease must be examined by the veterinary surgeon and placed under observation in the isolation unit. Finally, all visiting cats are fed ample amounts of good food and their progress is monitored daily.

Whatever the design and layout of the boarding cattery, it must be as airy and roomy as space permits. It should be remembered that the local authorities' requirements are set out as minima; there is nothing to stop you making each unit larger. On the other hand, cats feel secure in fairly small areas, so making the living quarters too large and spacious is just as bad as making them too small and cramped. Each cat must have room in its quarters for its bed, toilet tray, food and water dishes and perhaps a scratching-post and toys. There should be larger units available, too, for family groups of two or more cats which are better and happier when boarded together than housed separately. Two or more cats from different homes must NEVER be housed together.

Because of the risk of upper respiratory tract infection being spread by apparently healthy carrier cats, it is essential that solid partitions or wide corridors are provided between adjacent boarding pens. Indoor catteries should have extractor fans working at all times, to prevent the spread of infection.

Good catteries insist on seeing a current certificate of vaccination before accepting a cat into the boarding unit. There may be an indemnity form to be signed by the owner, who should also fill in all details of the cat, including its name, age, diet and idiosyncrasies, plus a telephone number of a friend who can be contacted in emergencies. If the cat is taken ill, the owner may wish his own veterinary surgeon to be contacted, or he may prefer the cattery to make its own arrangements. The cat's owner is generally expected to pay for any extras involved in caring for the cat in such a case. Boarding fees vary a great deal, but really good catteries feeding a varied selection of food and providing expert care in fine, clean accommodation are worth searching out, whatever the cost.

Boarding accommodation is best made on a convenient modular system for ease of maintenance and administration. The construction must be strong and catproof as well as easy to clean. The bottom timbers should be raised above the paved or concrete base to allow hosing, and the run door should preferably open into a safety zone. There should be solid partitions between each compartment.

The stud cat may spend his entire life confined within his special accommodation, so it can be seen that it is important to ensure that his unit is adequate and comfortable from all angles. The male cat's habit of spraying his highly pungent urine all around his territory makes the ideal site for his quarters out in the open air, away from the house, but not isolated. In some areas the climate makes this impossible, and stud quarters are built indoors. In this case the living and exercise areas for the entire male must be of impervious and easily washed material, and there must be no crevices or cracks into which the sprayed urine can seep. In this way, and with a good airflow and daily cleaning, the stud's accommodation can be kept fresh and pleasant.

Whenever possible, outdoor quarters are to be preferred, and they should be sited so that there is plenty for the cat to watch. Queens seem to call on some invisible signal, and the stud may be called upon to service three in one week, and then have several weeks of boredom before the next group arrives.

The outdoor stud-house should be large enough for the cat to live in, and to exercise himself adequately, if the weather is too inclement for him to use his run. There must be room for all his belongings – a bed, toilet tray and dishes, plus a grooming shelf. A pen to hold the visiting queen can be built in as a permanent unit, or, as some

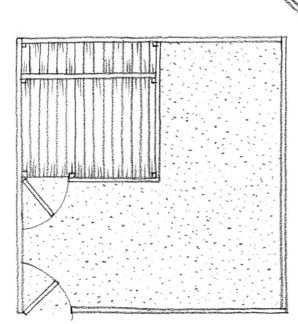

Above The stud cat must have his own large and well planned accommodation with some provision made for the temporary housing of visiting queens. This wooden house is well constructed with an internal, built-in pen, electric light and heating and a secure open-air run, raised on rag-bolts for ease of cleaning.

Left Plan view of stud accommodation.

breeders prefer the stud to have as much room as possible between queens, a collapsible wire pen can be used. It is usual to have timber housing for male cats, as this material is warm and aesthetically pleasing. In some areas existing brick or stone buildings are converted into stud quarters, but, whatever the material, the interior should be insulated if necessary and lined with smooth facing boards, covered with laminated plastic or painted with washable, impervious emulsion. The floor is usually treated with poured or sheet vinyl, and this is extended up the walls for about 4 inches for ease of cleaning. Everything in the stud-house should be easily washed, and it should be routine to swab the entire house interior every day with a solution of household bleach.

The young stud may spray a great deal during the main breeding season of early spring, and, to help in keeping the house clean, newspapers can be spread around the perimeter of the floor to soak up the urine.

Experienced breeders soon get to know the favourite sites for spraying and fit 'spray-shields' to protect the paintwork. A row of cup-hooks is screwed into the wall of the stud-house on which can be hung strong bulldog clips. Large sheets of

Paving or concrete is better than grass or earth, as it is easier to wash down. It is important to clean and sterilize the whole of the stud's accommodation after each visiting queen returns home, as well as the daily sweeping and swabbing with a mop and bucket.

In some catteries the stud's accommodation is kept very warm; in others local heat over the sleeping quarters only is the rule, with another lamp which can be used for visiting queens. A light is essential in the stud-house, and if the quarters are away from the main house, the pathway should be illuminated too. It is often necessary to visit the stud cat after dark. Visiting queens may arrive late in the evening, or may be reluctant to mate during the daytime.

To keep a stud cat takes experience, for there is a lot of work involved in looking after him correctly. His accommodation must be good, as we have seen, and he must be fed well on high-quality food. His diet should be varied and well-balanced, and he should have a little salt added to his food to encourage him to drink plenty of water so that his urine does not become too concentrated. He must be groomed correctly for his breed, and this is enjoyed by most stud cats. His

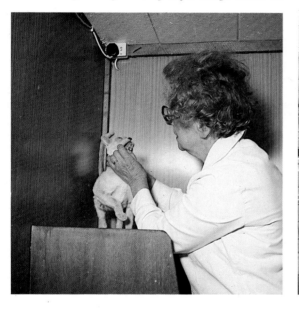

newspaper can then be clipped into place to hang down the wall in the most vulnerable spots. When soiled, it is a matter of moments to remove the damp paper and replace it with fresh.

The run adjoining the stud-house should be as large as possible and equipped with lots of shelves for sunning and logs for stropping. Some owners provide the cat with a folding wooden step-ladder and encourage him to run up and down it in pursuit of a feather or an exciting piece of string. It is important to keep the stud male properly fed and well exercised when he is not working, and this climbing activity keeps his muscles toned up. The run itself must be well constructed and the wire must be checked at regular intervals. The gate must fit well and securely, with strong bolts inside and out. Visiting queens may be nervous and try to escape.

ears and coat must be scrupulously clean, and his teeth and gums should be inspected regularly. He should have faecal samples tested every few months, and if worms are present he should be treated without delay. The stud cat must receive his booster vaccinations on the due dates, and should have a blood test analysed regularly for presence of FeLV.

The stud owner owes it to the cat to accept queens for mating only if they match up to him in health. If a suspect queen is accepted, the stud is put at risk, and so are all the other inhabitants of the cattery and future visiting queens. A sick queen may not conceive, and if she does, the kittens could be aborted or die soon after birth. The stud might well pick up an infection and be ill for some time. The visiting queen should be checked for parasites before being allowed into the studhouse.

Left The stud owner checks the health of a visiting queen.

Right The stud cat is loathe to be parted from the queen and seems to be taking a last lingering farewell.

The Lilac Burmese stud male sits on his favourite shelf and croons to the visiting queen before jumping down to get better acquainted.

If the queen is healthy and clean, she can be taken, in her carrier, into the stud-house and placed in the pen, in which she can have her own bed, a clean toilet tray and food and water bowls hooked onto the mesh wall. She may look at the stud cat with interest, but in most cases snarls and growls quite ferociously. The purpose of the pen now becomes quite clear, for the cats can be near but the queen cannot attack the male through the separating wire mesh. Occasionally a young male may 'blow-up' when the queen flies towards him, hissing. His coat becomes erect and he turns sideways-on towards her, back arched, tail curved up and round as he stretches on tiptoe to look as big and fearsome as possible.

Smacking his lips, dribbling and snarling, he may threaten the queen until she retires to her bed in the pen. The male must not be touched until he calms down or he may well bite, thinking that he is being attacked by the queen. It is at times like this that the owner remembers why the introductory pen is so essential. The older and more experienced stud takes little notice of the visiting queen's temper and tantrums. He knows only too well that within a few hours she will change her tune.

When the queen has settled down, which may take any length of time from three or four hours to three or four days, she will make soft calling noises to the male and rub her lips and cheeks against the pen. It is at this stage that she may be released into the stud-house and she should be mated immediately. If the stud is steady and gentle with the queens, the two cats may be left together after the initial mating has been witnessed (see p. 115). If the owner is unsure of the stud's behaviour patterns, the queen can be left to settle down, then replaced in the pen for a couple of hours before being allowed to mate again. It is usual to allow several matings over two or three days before the queen is collected by her owners.

A stud fee is paid to the owner of the stud, who gives a copy of the male's pedigree to the owner of the queen and a certificate giving the date of the mating and the date that the litter may be expected. If for any reason the queen fails to produce a litter, the stud's owner may give a free return mating, but there is no obligation to do this. The onus is on the owner of the queen to present her at the correct stage in her cycle, and to ensure that she is in good health. The stud cat carries out his job in mating the queen, and it is for this service that the stud fee is paid.

If a stud cat has had a good show season, with many top wins, his services will be in great demand, and there is a great temptation for his owner to accept many queens for stud service. This is a great mistake. Having a number of queens over a short period of time is very tiring to the young male cat, no matter how carefully he is managed. The risk of infection is also increased, and if one queen should prove to carry disease, the stud and several other queens could be infected before the trouble was discovered.

As we have pointed out, it is essential that the stud's accommodation be thoroughly cleaned and disinfected after each visiting queen goes home. If there are more queens waiting, it is impossible to carry out this cleaning correctly, and the next queen in line may thoroughly resent the smell of the previous female, still lingering in the pen.

A stud that has a few queens each season and is given plenty of attention and affection remains calm and contented for several years. The male that is overworked in his first season becomes irritable and restless when the inevitable happens and he loses his popularity in favour of the latest young champion of the breed. Nothing is more distressing in a cattery than to see a male cat pacing the wire walls of his pen, going to and fro, in an almost trance-like state, at a steady trot. The calm and contented stud cat, on the other hand, is a magnificent animal, affectionate and full of dignity.

After a few years the number of queens booked to the once-popular stud may dwindle, and a decision has to be made as to the animal's future. Many experienced breeders have their stud males neutered at about five or six years of age, with excellent results. The cats retain their good physique if fed correctly, and soon settle down happily. They can usually be given their freedom, and they accept all the other cats in the cattery as their friends. They make little or no attempt to mate calling queens, and often take young kittens in hand in an avuncular manner. The only problem is the habit of spraying, which they often cannot break. The spray loses its powerful smell, but the natural urge to mark out territorial landmarks seems uncontrollable. Stud males, which as entires would have fought to the death, often become inseparable friends after neutering, and are often kept on in pairs or groups by their owners, being housed in an easily cleaned room at night and given their freedom during the day.

Above The queen, apprehensive at first, soon settles and can be seen to relax.

Right Eventually the cats touch noses without growling or hissing and soon after this mating can be allowed to take place.

This cat house, with the male safe and snug under his infra-red heater, shows the damage caused to putty and timber by a severe winter. It is essential to carry out regular maintenance to keep equipment and housing in good condition.

Whether the cattery consists of one or two breeding queens, or is a large establishment with stud cats, breeding units and a boarding section, the catering arrangements are important. Animal foodstuffs, dishes, utensils and equipment should be separately stored. Larger catteries usually have a kitchen specially designed and equipped for preparing the animals' diets. A refrigerator holds fresh and prepared food – meat, fish, eggs and milk. A store cupboard holds a variety of canned foods, packets of complete diet and baby cereals. In some areas, where supplies need to be purchased in bulk, a cabinet or chest freezer is useful to hold large quantities of deep-frozen cuts of meat, and fish.

The cattery kitchen has its own range of pans, a cooking stove or hotplate, a sink, and all the dishes, bowls and trays for feeding the animals.

Strict attention must be paid to hygiene in preparing and serving the cats' meals (see p. 110). Their dishes must always be spotlessly clean, washed after use and passed through a sterilizing solution. Water bowls should also be washed daily before being refilled with fresh, cool water.

Cat breeders and cattery proprietors have their own pet methods for feeding their cats, but the most successful among them seem to agree that a good variety of quality products and fresh food produces the best results. Good boarding catteries feed individual diets to the visiting cats, exactly as requested by their owners. In this way they ensure that the homesick animal is offered its favourite food, which it usually finds irresistible. The better brands of complete dried cat diets have proved a boon for catteries. So many boarders refuse to eat during daylight hours, and fresh or canned food cannot be left down as it soon goes stale. The dried pellets remain fresh in the bowl and can be left overnight in the cat pens. The water bowl, too, must be freshly filled.

Cooked meats should be cooled rapidly and stored in the refrigerator. They must never be reheated, but neither should such food be fed too cold. It is best to take the dishes from the refrigerator about one hour before feeding time, to allow the food to rise to room temperature. Cold food can cause diarrhoea, especially in young kittens.

The cattery should be carefully and regularly maintained, and it is surprising just how much deterioration and minor damage occurs each year. Outdoor catteries suffer most, of course, being at the mercy of the weather. Extreme heat and cold blisters and cracks exterior paintwork, crumbles the putty around window panes and distorts wire, water-pipes and drains. Hinges rust if not regularly oiled, and bolts corrode. Light bulbs and heating elements burn out, timbers warp and twist, and frost may crack concrete and paving.

A routine of maintenance is carried out in the best catteries. Boarding catteries usually have an annual check-out during the slack months. The cat chalets or pens are given a fresh coat of paint or wood preservative. The flooring is checked and replaced if necessary. All bolts, fastenings and hinges are cleaned and oiled. Glass panes are refixed if required, and cracks in run surfaces are cleaned out and repointed. Roofing materials often suffer from weathering, and felt roof covering may only last one or two seasons. It is vitally

Left External timbers can be revitalized by the application of one or two coats of a non-toxic wood preservative.

Below left Bolts and hinges must be oiled regularly and, *right*, staples holding on mesh or wire must be hammered home if they have become loose due to wood expansion or shrinkage.

important to check this out, for a leaking roof can allow the whole interior of the cat-house to become saturated through the insulation material, and it may need stripping out and relining if neglected, which is expensive and very time-consuming.

Timber cat-houses should be washed off over the exterior each year. This removes any green algae on the surface of the wood. Then one or two coats of timber preservative can be applied. The run surface should be protected from splashes while this is carried out, and the cats must, of course, be removed to other accommodation until the prescribed time has elapsed for the timber to take up the preservative and *thoroughly* dry out. Such preparations can be highly toxic to cats, and must not be allowed to get onto their fur or the

pads of their feet.

The timbers of cat runs should also receive a coat of preservative each year, and the staples holding the wire mesh onto the timber frames must be checked, new ones being knocked in wherever necessary. Contracting wood often allows these staples to work free, and a cat that is determined to escape will quickly find such weak spots in the run.

All pipework carrying water and cables carrying electric current should be checked by an expert from source to supply, and all gutters and drains must receive a thorough cleaning before washing through with disinfectant. Finally, concreted and paved areas should be scrubbed with a bleach solution to remove any algal growth, which makes them slippery and dangerous in wet weather.

Left Any hair, fluff or dust trapped between the raised base timbers and the run floor are drawn out with the nozzle of the cattery vacuum cleaner.

Right To prevent any cross-infections passing between cat houses, pans of a suitable disinfectant can be placed outside the doors during routine cleaning so that the attendant may walk through the footbath.

Far right Each cat house should be provided with a set of cleaning equipment such as broom, brush and pan, mop and bucket. Here the mop is used for cleaning up spills on the vinyl floor.

Whatever the size of the cattery and whether it is an outdoor or indoor establishment, a system of routine management should be set up and followed. Cats thrive on regular meals, and those in the boarding cattery are best fed two or three small meals each day to help alleviate the inevitable boredom they experience while away from home. If meals are served at set times each day, the cats anticipate the arrival of the trays, which may well aid their digestive processes.

The general routine in the cattery is to remove and empty the litter tray from the pen or cat-house, and then refill it with litter or replace it with a fresh tray if it is soiled. Any litter spilled on the floor of the pen must be swept up, and the floor is then wiped over with a cloth wrung out in hot water containing disinfectant safe for cats. Particular attention should be paid to the angles where the floor and walls meet, as such crevices are ideal for harbouring germs. Any splashes on the walls must be cleaned off at this time; then the surfaces can be dried with a dry cloth or sponge pad.

The cat's bed, fresh toilet tray, food and water bowl can be replaced. This is a good time to check the cat over and groom it if necessary, before replacing it in the pen.

In the boarding cattery fresh disinfectant should be used for each cat-house, and each boarder should have its own equipment, such as hand-brush and sponge cloths, hanging inside the cat-house on convenient hooks. The boarder can be lifted out of the house or pen and placed in its run or confined in its carrier. The floor can be swept out after the bedding and dishes have been removed, and all the scraps can be placed neatly in the soiled toilet tray. The floor is then washed and dried and the bedding replaced, before a clean and sterilized toilet tray is added, plus clean water bowl and fresh food. The cat is then checked over and lightly groomed with its own kit, before being returned to its accommodation. All the used items are taken from the pen and disposed of, the toilet tray and bowls being stacked for washing and sterilizing.

The attendant should wash after attending to each boarding cat, and in an outdoor cattery with fresh-air runs a pan of disinfectant is generally used into which the attendant can dip his boots between entering each run. In this way cross-infection may be avoided between cats. These small details, which might appear fussy and unnecessary, can save a great deal of expense and heartbreak by preventing outbreaks of disease.

Indoor catteries are comparatively easy to clean, and the problems of wind and weather are removed. Individual equipment is still necessary for boarders, however, and the cats should not be

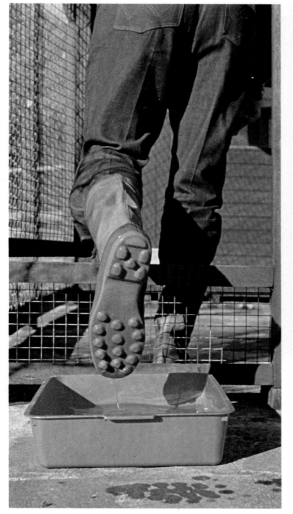

allowed to exercise in a common play area.

All sweepings and soiled litter should be disposed of carefully, the method being determined by the location of the cattery and local regulations. Incineration, if possible, is best for soiled wood-shavings or paper, while proprietary brands of cat litter may have to be packed into bins or plastic bags for disposal.

It is very important that soiled litter and waste food is covered and that it cannot be reached by flies or other insects, which could cause the spread of infection.

Outdoor catteries benefit from being cleaned at least once a week with an industrial exterior-use vacuum cleaner. The cat may not like the noise of this, so should be safely confined in its carrier while the machine is being employed. In this way every crevice of the cat-house and run can be cleaned of dirt, dust and the eggs of parasites, if these are a problem, as well as shed hairs, fluff, fallen leaves and cobwebs. The floor of the house and the paved run can then be washed and allowed to dry thoroughly before the cat is replaced. Window panes can be kept bright and sparkling with a wash-leather, and all the surfaces should be wiped down.

In a breeding cattery the routines have to be flexible, to fit in with the fluctuating population as kittens are born, reared, and then sold. Kittens must be kept in very clean quarters, but it is vitally important that the disinfectants used in cleaning their accommodation are non-toxic and that all flooring and surfaces, as well as equipment, is thoroughly rinsed and dried before the litter is allowed back in it. Small kittens explore most surfaces by licking and sniffing and even non-toxic products left on in small spots may cause ulceration of the kittens' mouths or tongues and also lead to gastric disturbances. The feeding-dishes of small kittens should be washed after each meal and should be of a material that can be sterilized with boiling water. Disposable dishes may also prove useful. The kittens should be watched to see that they are not tasting the litter in their tray, or devouring the woollen or plastic toys with which they have been provided. Some kittens go through a stage when they are not too clever at using the toilet tray, and may also have loose stools due to teething. It is important at this time to line their run with paper and to clean up after them at frequent intervals during the day. The kittens' feet may need washing off with warm water, too, until this difficult phase passes.

In the general routine it is usual to clean and tidy the animals most at risk first, such as newly born kittens and queens approaching their kittening date. Young, unweaned and unvaccinated kittens are dealt with next; then growing stock; queens; and, finally, the stud cats. Any suspect animals or those which have been exposed to the chance of infection, exhibition at a cat show or a visit to another stud, for instance, are always left until last.

With a regular programme of vaccinations, testing for disease, good feeding and carrying out good methods of husbandry, a cattery will prosper and a good reputation will be earned.

Pedigree Cats

Forerunners of today's champions, prize winning cats at the Crystal Palace Show in 1871.

One of the most expert naturalist writers on the subject of cats was Pocock (1863–1947), who regarded the study of the domestic cat as a science and made observations which still stand up today. Pocock described the earliest of domesticated cats as being of the type we know as *tabby*, in a striped or torquata pattern. He regarded the classic or blotched tabby pattern as a mutation of the wild-type tabby, and described it in his papers as *catus*. In the striped tabby the markings consist of narrow lines, either solid or broken up, which run transversely or vertically on the sides of the cat's body. Towards the hind end of the cat the markings tend to break into shorter stripes, or even spots in some cats. The tail is ringed and there are strongly etched markings on the cheeks and between the ears. In the blotched or classic tabby broad stripes spiral and loop behind the shoulders, and, usually, three strong lines run down the back of the animal. The tail, cheek and forehead markings are virtually the same as in the striped tabby.

Today tabby cats for exhibition are selected carefully for their markings and it is generally accepted that there are four types of tabby – the classic or blotched, the mackerel-striped, the spotted and the ticked or agouti.

Pocock's papers also listed varieties of domestic cat that had arisen by crossbreeding, as well as by mutation. He wrote of tortoiseshell cats from Spain, blue cats from Europe and Siberia, a red cat from the Cape of Good Hope, a Malayan cat with a twisted bobbed tail, a grey ticked animal from Abyssinia, a piebald cat from Japan, jet black cats from Russia and South Africa, a Chinese cat, tortoiseshell with lop ears, a ginger cat with very sharp features from New Spain and a fawn cat with black points from Thailand. It is easy to see how all the varieties that we have today were developed from such a selection of breeding stock as Pocock described.

Cats were encouraged in the house in preference to dogs during the nineteenth century, after Pasteur's discovery of the microbe. Cats were considered to be clean animals, taking such pains with their toilet, and prettily marked kittens were usually chosen as children's pets to live indoors. In this way, and almost by accident, humans started to intervene in the selection and breeding of cats, taking the first steps to producing pedigree animals.

The very first cat show was held in London's Crystal Palace in 1871. It was organized by a remarkable man, Harrison Weir, a skilful artist and animal lover. He decided to hold the show so that all those interested could see the different colours, markings and breeds of cat. His idea was criticized by many, but the show was such a success that it became an exciting annual event. An entry of 170 cats and kittens of all sorts filled the show hall. It included newly imported Siamese cats, a French-African cat with soft brown hair, a huge and friendly tom from Persia with long fur of black, grey and white, and an enormous English cat, a tabby, weighing 21 lb. The show had 25 classes, the cats were entered according to colour,

and there were prizes for all manner of attributes, including one for the fattest cat. By 1873 cat shows were becoming popular and were held in other English cities. Royalty visited them, and Queen Victoria, who loved cats, acquired two Blue Persians. Cat clubs were formed, some of which are still in existence, and registration procedures were instituted.

At the early cat shows the staging and cat pens were similar to those used today. Cats were given earth or sawdust for toilet purposes instead of litter trays, and hay, straw or cushions were placed at the front of the pen for their comfort. In some classes the exhibits were judged by their pens, but in the ring classes the cats were paraded by their owners on the ends of long leashes of cord or ribbon. At the early British cat shows all the exhibitors and judges wore the elegant clothes of the time – overalls were unheard of in those days – and the only disinfectant used was oil of eucalyptus. Although the cats were examined before the show by a veterinary surgeon, vaccination was unknown for cats and so infection was rife. Sometimes whole catteries were wiped out.

By the year 1889 the Crystal Palace Show was attracting over 600 exhibits, and more than 20,000 people thronged the halls to see the pedigree cats. Wealthy owners who kept large catteries took as many as 30 cats to each show. It was in this year that Harrison Weir published his book *Our Cats and all about Them*, in which he set out clear and concise standards of excellence, by which all the breeds and varieties of the time could be judged.

The breeds officially recognized for registration and exhibition purposes at the turn of the century were as follows:

Breed or Colour	SH	LH
Abyssinian	×	
Bicolour	×	×
Black	×	×
Blue	×	×
Chinchilla		×
Cream		×
Foreign	×	
Manx	×	
Orange		×
Sable	×	×
Siamese	×	
Smoke		×
Spotted	×	×
Tabby	×	×
Ticked	×	
Tortoiseshell	×	×
Tricolour	×	×

PRIZE CATS AT THE CRYSTAL PALACE

It was at the time of the first cat shows held in Britain and America that planned cat breeding began. The owners of unusual cats began to keep careful records, and so the first written pedigrees came into being. Groups interested in the same types of cat formed clubs and societies, and the Cat Fancy had begun.

Any cat that has a known, recorded ancestry can be called a pedigree animal, but this does not necessarily mean that it will be pure-bred, or even of an established breed. Each Cat Fancy, or governing body, has its own official list of recognized varieties and sets of rules for the way in which these must be bred. There are also carefully drawn up standards of perfection for each variety, with a points score allocated for each of the cat's features. These sometimes vary between countries, and in some instances even between Fancies within the same country.

Pedigree cats are basically of two types and conformation. The first type is heavily built, with a large round head, full round eyes and a short thick body, limbs and tail. The second type is more streamlined in appearance, with a long head, almond or oriental eyes and a svelte body, elegant limbs and a long thin tail.

The large, stocky cats may be longhaired, when they are known as Persian or Longhaired cats, or may have short, thick coats when they are known as British, European, American, Domestic or Exotic Shorthairs, depending on their country of origin. For convenience, in this book, they are referred to as Shorthairs.

Cats of the second type are generally known as Foreign or Oriental Shorthairs, and conformation varies in degree from the extreme type of the top flight show Siamese to the understated but unique structure of the beautiful Korat.

Apart from the two basic divisions, there are breeds and varieties which have intermediate type, such as the foreign-type longhaired cats, the Turkish, the Birman and the Balinese. These have longer, finer bone structure than the Persians, but also have coats of long silky hair.

In the large cobby Shorthairs the conformation is fairly uniform whatever the variety, except for

the breeds produced by spontaneous mutations – the tailless Manx and the bent-eared Scottish Fold. Standards and type are consistent for these cats in most countries of the world.

Conversely, the Foreign Shorthairs have diversified, each breed having developed its own special characteristics, and great variation can be seen, even in those breeds which have sprung from the same roots (see Glossary). The Havana Brown of the United States, which is descended from cats imported from Britain in 1954, provides a good example. It looks totally different from today's British Havana, and kittens of the variety taken to America nowadays have to be re-registered as Oriental Chestnut. Indeed, the American Havana Brown is not allowed to be used in the breeding programmes of the Oriental Chestnut.

The curly coats of the rexed cats are caused by at least two separate genes which spontaneously mutated in different parts of the world. Crossing and back-crossing to other shorthaired cats has enabled curly cats of all colours to come into being, but all have to comply with the strict standards of shape, coat quality and conformation laid down for the breeds.

Most of the varieties of cat are known by their descriptive names or colours, and have correspon-

Above Foreign or Oriental shorthairs are long and lithe with wedge shaped heads, large ears and almond eyes.
Top left Shorthaired cats are of cobby type, short and stocky with round heads, small ears and large round eyes.

Far left Siamese cats are Foreign in type and conformation. The colour is restricted to the points and the eyes are distinctly blue.

Left The Burmese is of a modified foreign type and has its own definitive standard of points.

Far left This British blue-cream shows her strong and sturdy conformation.

Left In the Himalayan or Colourpoint the Siamese type colouring is combined with extreme Persian conformation.

dingly acceptable eye colour. Some of the basic colours of the cat are simply called black, white, cream and silver, but others are more obscure.

Blue, for example, refers to any shade of cold-toned grey, from the palest to the darkest shade of slate. Lilac is a very pale warm-toned grey.

Brown can refer to any shade of dark brown, except in the brown tabby, when it refers to a cat that is genetically black, having black markings on an agouti background. The Brown Burmese, also genetically black, is called Sable in the United States of America.

Chocolate refers to a rich warm brown coloration.

Red refers to all shades of ginger, in the cat, although the deeper coppery tones are most sought after.

Tortoiseshell is the name given to a cat with two colours in the coat, patches of black and red. The name is often shortened to Tortie, or if the cat has white patches and so is tri-coloured, it is called a Tortie-and-White.

The dilute version of Tortoiseshell has a mingled or patched coat of palest grey and cream and is known as Blue-Cream. There are Chocolate-Cream and Lilac-Cream varieties of some breeds as well.

Smoke cats often look plain coloured, but when the fur is parted, the undercoat is white, each hair being white at the roots and coloured at the ends. If the hairs are mainly white, and coloured only at the very tips, a sparkling effect is created and the cat is said to have a 'tipped' coat.

Tabby is the name given to the oldest and most dominant pattern of the cat; it consists of dark markings, spots or stripes on a paler background. When cat fanciers speak about the points of a cat, they are referring to the face or mask, ears, tail and paws. In some breeds the main coat colour is restricted to these points, while the rest of the cat's body is of a much paler shade. Such cats are said to be Himalayan in pattern, and breeds with this coloration include the Siamese and the Birman.

Tabby is the oldest and original pattern of the domestic cat. The term covers a range of acceptable patterns, including the mackerel-striped, the spotted and the classic or blotched pattern, each of which has a defined set of standards. Tabbies can be of practically any colour, but not all are acceptable to all groups of pedigree cats.

The startling diversity of the breeds seen on the show benches today, is the result of planned permutations of the colours, coats and patterns that arose by natural mutation.

more colours as Parti-Color Persians. The self-longhairs include Black, White, Blue, Cream and Red Persians, and the Whites can be either Orange-Eyed, Blue-Eyed or Odd-Eyed (see also pages 91–2). There are Brown, Red and Silver Tabbies, and unusual Smoke Persians in Black or Blue, with hair shading down to the pure white undercoat. Cameo Persians are similar to the Smokes, but in shades of red. Parti-colours can be Tortoiseshell, Tortie-and-White, Blue-Cream or Bi-Coloured. The Chinchilla is perhaps the most photogenic of all longhaired cats, and its sparkling appearance, caused by the elusive silver gene, is due to each white hair being lightly tipped with black. The nose leather and incredible emerald or aquamarine eyes are also outlined with black.

The Himalayan factor was introduced into Persian cat breeding programmes by a few dedicated breeders, and resulted in the production of the Colourpoint Persian, or Himalayan cat. This cat has full Persian characteristics coupled with the distinctive coat pattern of the Siamese, complete with blue eye-colour.

Longhaired cats are divided for convenience into Self-coloured and Non Self-coloured. *Far left,* a Colourpoint which comes into the second category, being two toned, and *below,* a magnificent Self-coloured Black Persian.

Today's longhaired cats are said to be descendants of those brought in the sixteenth century from Ankara in Turkey, and Iran, which were known as Angora and Persian cats, respectively. The Angora cats were mainly white in colour, had long silky fur and were fairly slight in build. Their faces were rather long by today's standards, and their ears quite large and pointed. The Persians were of much stockier structure, and had thick coats of black or blue hair, round heads and small ears. The two types of longhaired cat were mated together quite indiscriminately, and the type of the Persian gradually superseded that of the Angora.

Each of the longhaired breeds has its own set standard of points or set list of desired features, and each feature is allotted a number of points, out of a total of one hundred points for a perfect specimen. The standard of points for each variety is decided by the breed's society, and points are usually allocated to encourage the development of any feature needing emphasis. Despite slight deviations in the points allowance, the general standard for most longhaired cats is the same, and calls for a broad head, with tiny tufted ears, full round cheeks, a short broad nose and very large round eyes. Obviously, the coat is of great importance, and should be dense, soft and silky. The short stocky body is supported by sturdy legs, and the tail, or brush, must be short and full, without thickened vertebrae or kinks. The 'ruff' of long fur around the head is usually brushed up to form an elegant frame for the face.

Many of the longhaired varieties are known by their coat colour: for instance, a plain black longhaired cat is known simply as the Black Longhair or Black Persian. Under the rules of GCCF cats with fur of one colour are known as the self-longhairs, while those with two or more colours are classified as non-self longhairs. In the US Persian cats with a coat of one colour are known as Solid Color Persians; those with two or

Persian cats can be delightful, but they do need daily grooming to keep their long, flowing coats free from troublesome knots of hair, and anyone contemplating the purchase of a Persian kitten must be prepared to undertake this regular brushing and combing. In the USA it is common practice to bath a Persian before showing. In the UK it depends more on the preference of the exhibitor and the colour of the cat. If it is one of the paler breeds a bath may be necessary to present the cat in perfect condition; therefore, in choosing a show specimen full consideration must be given to temperament, as well as to health and beauty.

Points of perfection for the Shorthair emphasize the sturdy body, short, well-proportioned legs, powerful neck and short thick tail (see page 180). The well-rounded, head has full cheeks and is topped with tiny wide-apart ears. The wide eyes must be large, round and lustrous, and the short nose should not be as flattened as in Longhaired cats.

Shorthairs are generally known by their coloration, such as Black, White, Blue, Cream and Red in the self-colours, and the British White can also be Orange-Eyed, Blue-Eyed or Odd-Eyed. This is in addition to the Brown, Red and Silver Tabbies, as found in the Persian breeds. The tabby markings of the shorthaired can be modified to clearly defined spotting. These cats may be of any colour, and all are known as Spotted Cats.

Parti-coloured Shorthairs also include the Tortoiseshell, Tortie-and-White, Blue-Cream and Bi-Coloured. Tortoiseshell cats must have patched coats of black and red with no blurred or tabby markings, and a red blaze bisecting the face between the orange, copper or hazel eyes is

Shorthaired cats make delightful and undemanding pets, living happily with the family, they get along well with children and most breeds of dogs. They are excellent hunters and clean in their habits, but, in contrast to their Oriental cousins, do not do so well when completely confined to the house. The Shorthairs can be kept in show condition by daily hand grooming, the coat being merely rubbed with the fingers to remove dead hair, then smoothed with firm even strokes. Loose hairs can be combed out weekly, when the ears and claws also receive any necessary attention. Before a show the cat may be given a bran-bath.

Breeding Shorthairs can be very rewarding, if frustrating at times, as the colours and patterns can be very elusive in some varieties. Generations of careful selection have produced the perfection of form now seen on the show benches. The selection of the stud male is important, for his outstanding features should be those lacking or deficient in the queen. For example, a female silver tabby with outstanding markings but a little too long in the nose, and with large ears, should be

The Shorthaired cats are also divided. The Non-Self group includes tabbies such as the Red Tabby male, *below left*, while the Self group covers such breeds as the British Cream, *below*.

desirable for show animals.

The Tortie-and-White has additional white areas, good specimens have all colours equally distributed over head, tail and body, with a white blaze. Blue-Cream cats are dilute tortoiseshells, but in England the colours of this variety are required to be softly intermingled, while patches are preferred in America. Bi-coloured cats are cats of two colours, with up to two-thirds of the coat being of any recognized colour and not more than one-half being white. Black-and-White Bi-Coloured cats were shown in the earliest cat shows, and known as Magpie cats.

mated with a male chosen for having a superb head, even if his markings are not perfect. With luck, some of the kittens may combine the best features of both sire and dam, and can be retained for breeding further generations.

Shorthaired queens usually have small litters, with three kittens on average, but these are sturdy and grow on quickly. Eyes open at about 7–10 days, and weaning onto solids can begin at around 4–5 weeks. Shorthaired queens enjoy hunting for prey for their kittens, and if not allowed access to the garden, they should be provided with some strips of raw meat to present to their offspring.

The Foreign or Oriental cats are quite different from the Shorthairs: with minor exceptions within the breeds, they must have long slim bodies, legs and tails, small feet and long, wedge-shaped heads with large pricked ears and oriental eyes. Medium in size, they are all short-coated, and each variety has its own completely separate standard of points of perfection.

Some of the Orientals sport evocative foreign names; many were, in fact, bred to their present standard in Britain and then exported all over the world. There are exceptions, for instance the Burmese travelled the opposite way, having been developed in America and then exported to Britain in 1947. Some breeds have connections with the country of their title, but these are often difficult to substantiate, and in any case are not really important. It was the judicious interbreeding and outcrossing by selective breeders during the past century that has given us all the delightful foreign and oriental shorthairs that we see today.

In determining which cats should be used for developmental breeding programmes, discerning breeders have given much thought and care to the eradication of undesirable feline features. This has shown up particularly in the most recent results, for the newest varieties are noticeably free from the defects so apparent in their ancestors. Kinked tails, cleft palates, projecting sterna, squints, bone defects and faulty dentition are all on the decline. The new wave of Oriental cats appear to have everything – health, stamina, fine temperament and outstanding show quality.

The latest additions to the ranks of Foreign and Oriental breeds are the Siamese-derived shorthairs, including the Foreign White, Lilac and Black and the Oriental Tabby. All are extremely typey, looking very like the top-class Siamese stock from which they are descended.

Foreign and Oriental shorthairs are easy to breed, usually producing large even litters twice a year, and prove to be exceptional parents. The kittens are usually very precocious and open their eyes at 3–5 days. They toddle early and may be out of the nest box and sampling their mother's food by the age of four weeks.

The kittens are generally smaller than Longhaired or Shorthaired kittens of identical age and may suffer teething setbacks therefore they should never go to new homes until at least twelve weeks old. Great escapologists, Foreign queens have to be carefully confined during their very vocal periods of oestrus (estrus). If not kept for breeding, both males and females should be neutered at about six months of age.

Other Foreign Shorthairs have completely separate standards and breeding policies; these include the Abyssinian, Burmese, Korat, Rex and the Russian Blue.

Breeds and varieties have been deliberately produced by manipulating the few mutant genes by selective breeding. In this way coat colours and patterns, conformation and anomalies such as long hair, rexing and taillessness have been combined, giving almost endless permutations as may be seen on the breed chart overleaf:

Opposite top left The elegant Foreign White resulted from deliberate breeding programmes and is genetically a white Siamese.

Left The Cornish Rex is descended from mutant stock and has a densely waved coat and fine bone structure.

The Abyssinian, *above left*, and the Egyptian Mau *above right*, are said to closely resemble those cats first tamed and revered by the Ancient Egyptians.

Above The Red Burmese is a comparatively recent addition to the varieties accepted by the GCCF.

Right **Champion Czarist Nickolenka** is a fine example of a Russian Blue, a Foreign breed with a modified standard.

Breeds and their derivations

x – recognised   exp – experimental

Acceptable eye colour	Coat pattern	Colour	Longhaired	Shorthaired
Key	**Self colours**	Black	● X	● ● X
● blue		Blue	● ● X	● ● X
● yellow		Chocolate	● exp	● ● exp
● gold		Lilac	● exp	
● orange	**Tabby series**	Brown (Black)	● ● X	● ● ● X
● amber		Blue		
● green		Chocolate		
● hazel		Lilac		
● copper		Red	● X	● X
Blue	**Red series**	Red	● X	
Aquamarine		Cream	● X	● ● X
Yellow		Tortoiseshell (Black)	● X	● ● X
Gold		Blue Tortoiseshell	● ● Blue-Cream	● ● Blue-Cream
Orange		Chocolate Tortoiseshell	● exp	
Deep orange		Lilac Tortoiseshell	● exp	
Amber	**Silver series**	Silver Tipped	● Chinchilla	●
Green		Silver Shaded	● ● Shaded Silver / Pewter	
Hazel		Smoke	● ● X	● ● X
Copper		Blue Smoke	● ● X	
		Chocolate Smoke		
		Lilac Smoke		
		Silver Spotted		● ● X
		Silver Tabby	● ● X	● ● X
	White	White – Blue eyes	● X	● X
		White – Orange eyes	● X	● X
		White – Odd eyes	● X	● X
		Bi-Coloured	● ● X	● ● X
		Tri-Coloured	● ● Tortie & White – UK / Calico – USA	● ● Tortie & White
	Himalayan		● Colourpoint – UK / Himalayan – USA	

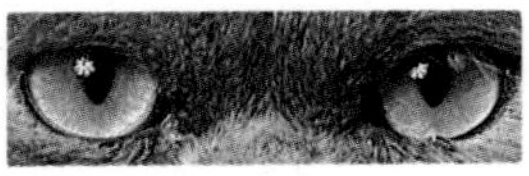

Blue

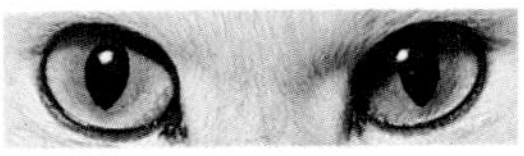

Aquamarine

Yellow

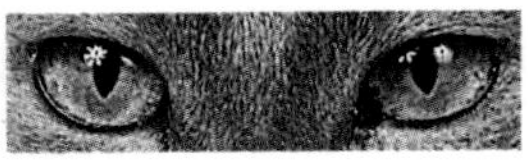

Gold

Orange

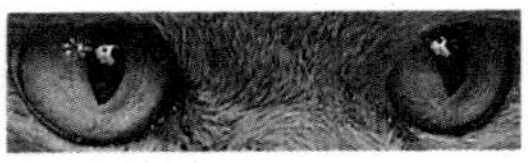

Deep orange

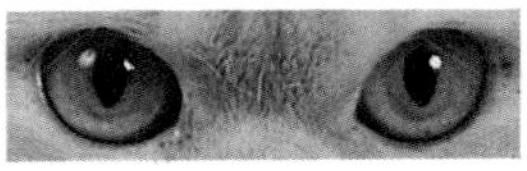

Amber

Green

Hazel

Copper

Siamese	Abyssinian	Burmese	Siamese-derived Oriental	Others
Seal Point		brown – UK sable – USA	Foreign Black – UK Ebony – USA & Europe	
Blue Point		X	exp – UK Oriental Blue	Korat Russian
Chocolate Point		X	Havana – UK Oriental chestnut – USA	
Lilac Point		X	Foreign Lilac – UK Lavender – USA	Lavender – Europe
Seal Tabby Point – UK Seal Lynx Point – USA	normal – UK ruddy – USA		X	Egyptian Mau – USA
Blue Tabby/ Lynx Point	exp		X	
Chocolate Tabby/ Lynx Point	red – UK russet – USA		X – UK	Egyptian Mau – USA
Lilac Tabby/ Lynx Point	exp		X	
Red Tabby/ Lynx Point			X	
Red Point		X	exp	
Cream Point		X	exp	
Tortie Point		X	exp	
Blue-Cream Point		X	exp	
Chocolate-Cream Point		X	exp	
Lilac Tortie Point		X	exp	
			exp	
			exp	Egyptian Mau – USA
			exp	
			exp	
			exp	
			exp – UK	Egyptian Mau – USA
	Silver Abyssinian		exp – UK	
			Foreign White	
				Turkish
All Siamese				Balinese Birman – with white gauntlets on all paws

Note Manx, Scottish Folds & Rex can be of any recognised coat colour or pattern.

Persian cats of uniform colour are known as Self (Solid Color) Longhaired. They are all very similar in their massive build and are generally of excellent type and conformation.

The Black must be jet black, with deep orange or copper eyes. The Blue, most popular of all the longhaired varieties, may be of any shade of blue, although the lighter tones are preferred, and has copper eyes.

White Persians may be Blue-Eyed, Orange-Eyed or Odd-Eyed, when one eye is blue and the other eye is orange. The Blue-Eyed White may be deaf, as the eye colour is allied to a genetic defect in the hearing mechanism of the ear. Orange-Eyed Whites are rarely, if ever, deaf, and if hearing problems exist in an Odd-Eyed White, it is the ear adjacent to the blue eye that is affected. This tendency to deafness is thought to trace back to the earliest Angora cats, some of which were recorded as seeming rather dull, and were later found to be entirely or partially deaf.

The Red Self Longhair is a rare breed, difficult to produce without tabby markings, so when a good specimen does appear on the show bench, it usually takes top awards. The Cream Longhair is very popular. Originally called 'fawn', it has a clear sound coat of a rich cream shade, without any tabby bars or stripes, and the eyes are of a deep copper tone.

Black – GCCF Variety 1

Colour Lustrous raven black to the roots and free from rustiness, shading, white hairs or markings of any kind.

Coat Long and flowing on body, full frill, and brush which should be short and broad.

Body Cobby and massive, without being coarse, with plenty of bone and substance, and low on the leg.
Head Round and broad, with plenty of space between the ears, which should be small, neat, and well covered; short nose, full cheeks and broad muzzle. An undershot jaw is considered a defect.
Eyes Large, round and wide-open, copper or deep orange in colour, with no green rim.

NB Black LH kittens are often a very bad colour up to five or six months, their coats being grey or rusty in parts, and sometimes freely speckled with white hairs. Fanciers should not condemn them on this account if good in other respects, as these kittens frequently turn into the densest Blacks.

Blue-Eyed White – GCCF Variety 2

Colour Pure white, without mark or shade of any kind.

Coat Long and flowing on body, full frill, and

brush which should be short and broad; the coat should be close and soft and silky, not woolly in texture.

Body Cobby and massive, without being coarse, with plenty of bone and substance, and low on the leg.
Head Round and broad, with plenty of space between the ears, which should be small, neat and well covered; short nose, full cheeks and broad muzzle. An undershot jaw is considered a defect.
Eyes Large, round and wide-open, deep blue in colour.

Orange-Eyed White – GCCF Variety 2a
As for Blue-Eyed White except for eye-colour, which should be orange or copper.

Odd-Eyed White – GCCF Variety 2b
As for Blue-Eyed White except for eye-colour, which should be one eye deep blue and one eye orange or copper.

NB Whites are very liable to get yellow stains on their tails from accumulated dust, etc. This very damaging peculiarity should be carefully attended to and stains removed before showing.

Far left In the Blue Longhair, breeders prefer the paler coat. *Left* A typically Persian profile.

White Persian cats may have blue eyes, *far left*, orange eyes, *left*, or one of each colour, when they are said to be Odd-Eyed Whites.

Blue – GCCF Variety 3

Coat Any shade of blue allowable, sound and even in colour; free from markings, shadings or any white hairs. Fur long, thick and soft in texture. Frill full.

Head Broad and round, with width between the ears. Face and nose short. Ears small and tufted. Cheeks well developed.
Eyes Deep orange or copper; large, round and full, without a trace of green.
Body Cobby, and low on the legs.
Tail Short and full, not tapering (a kink is considered a defect).

Red-Self – GCCF Variety 4

Colour Deep rich red, without markings.

Coat Long, dense and silky; tail short and flowing.

Body Cobby and solid; short thick legs.
Head Broad and round; small ears well set and well tufted; short broad nose; full round cheeks.
Eyes Large and round; deep copper colour.

Cream – GCCF Variety 5

Colour To be pure and sound throughout without shading or markings, pale to medium.

Coat Long, dense and silky; tail short and flowing.

Body Cobby and solid; short thick legs.
Head Broad and round; small ears well set and tufted; short broad nose; broad round cheeks.
Eyes Large and round; deep copper colour.

Comparative Points Scores (GCCF)

	Black	White	Blue	Red	White
Colour	25	25			30
Coat	20	20	} 20	} 50	
Condition			10		} 20
Body	20	20	15	15	15
Head	20	20	25	20	20
Eyes	15	15	20	15	15
Tail			10		
	100	100	100	100	100

Right, above **Champion Oxus Tarquinius Superbus** Smoke male.

Right, below **Trefleur Toinette** Shaded Silver female.

The non-self longhaired cats spring from the same roots as the self-coloured varieties and fall into several categories. The Red Tabby and the Brown Tabby have clearly etched classic markings on a lighter ground colour. Both breeds are fairly rare on the show bench. In the US there are also Cream and Blue Tabby Persians. The Silver Tabby is a more popular breed and forms part of the silver series of longhaired cats. The first in this genetic series is the exotic Chinchilla which is basically white, but the end of each hair is tipped with black giving a sparkling appearance. A similar cat with heavier black tipping is the Shaded Silver, and both these cats are very beautiful and particularly photogenic. The last in the genetically based silver series is the Black Smoke, a cat of contrasts. It has a shiny black coat hiding a pure white undercoat which, except around the frill and eartufts, only shows when the cat moves. Blue Smokes turned up in matings from Smoke and Blue Persians, and are now recognized by several governing bodies.

When the orange factor was introduced to the silver series, a new range of attractive cats was born and christened the Cameo Persian. The palest is the Shell Cameo, a white cat delicately tipped with palest apricot. The Shaded Cameo is more heavily tipped, and the Red Smoke is basically red, with a pure white undercoat.

Blue-Cream Persians are always female, due to the sex-linked orange factor (see Genetics). In Britain the standard calls for intermingling of the pastel blue and cream hairs, but in the US the coat should be clearly patched. Bi-coloured cats may be of any colour with white, but must be evenly marked on the body and face, and under GCCF rules the white must not predominate. The Tortoiseshell is another female variety, strikingly patched in red and black. When white is also present in the coat, the cat is known as the Tortie-and-White Longhair or, in the US, the Calico Persian.

The Colourpoint of Britain is known as the Himalayan in the US. It is bred in all the usual colours – seal, blue, chocolate, lilac, red, tortie and tabby, but not all are recognized by all governing bodies. This cat is Siamese in pattern and coloured only on its points, but truly Persian in type and conformation.

Brown Tabby – GCCF Variety 8

Colour and Markings Rich tawny sable, with delicate black pencillings running down face. The cheeks crossed with two or three distinct swirls, the chest crossed by two unbroken narrow lines, butterfly markings on shoulders. Front of legs striped regularly from toes upwards. The saddle and sides to have deep bands running down, and the tail to be regularly ringed.
Coat Long and flowing; tail short and full.
Body Cobby and massive; short legs.
Head Round and broad, small, well placed and well tufted ears; short broad nose; full round cheeks.
Eyes Large and round, hazel or copper colour.

Red Tabby – GCCF Variety 9

Colour and Markings Deep rich red colour, markings to be clearly and boldly defined, continuing on down the chest, legs and tail.

Coat Long, dense and silky; tail short and flowing, no white tip.

Body Cobby and solid; short thick legs.
Head Broad and round, small ears, well set and well tufted; short broad nose; full round cheeks.
Eyes Large and round, deep copper colour.

Silver Tabby – GCCF Variety 7

Colour Ground colour pure pale silver, with decided jet black markings; any brown tinge a drawback.

Head Broad and round, with breadth between ears and wide at muzzle; short nose, small, well-tufted ears.
Shape Cobby body; short thick legs.
Eyes Green or hazel colour.

Coat and Condition Silky in texture, long and dense, extra long on frill.
Tail Short and bushy.

Far left, **Oxus Holly Blue** Blue Tabby Longhair female neuter.

Left, **Champion Karnak Mailoc** Silver Tabby Longhair male.

Left below, **Oxus Fair Florence** Chinchilla female.

Right below, **Oxus Mountain Ringlet** Brown Tabby Longhair male neuter.

Chinchilla–GCCF Variety 10

Colour The undercoat pure white, the coat on back, flanks, head, ears and tail being tipped with black; this tipping to be evenly distributed, thus giving the characteristic sparkling silver appearance, the legs may be very slightly shaded with the tipping, but the chin, ear tufts, stomach and chest must be pure white; any tabby markings or brown or cream tinge is a defect. The tip of the nose brick-red, and the visible skin on eyelids and the pads black or dark brown.

Head Broad and round, with breadth between ears, which should be small and well tufted; wide at the muzzle; snub nose.
Shape Cobby body; short thick legs.
Eyes Large, round and most expressive; emerald or blue-green in colour.
Coat and Condition Silky and fine in texture, long and dense, extra long on frill.
Tail Short and bushy.

Tortoiseshell–GCCF Variety 11

Colour Three colours, black, red and cream, well broken into patches; colours to be bright and rich and well broken on face.

Coat Long and flowing, extra long on frill and brush.

Body Cobby and massive; short legs.
Head Round and broad; ears small, well placed and well tufted; short broad nose; full round cheeks.
Eyes Large and round, deep orange or copper.

Tortoiseshell-and-White–GCCF Variety 12

Colour Three colours, black, red and cream, or their dilutions to be well distributed and broken and interspersed with white.

Coat Long and flowing, extra long on brush and frill.

Body Cobby and massive; short legs.
Head Round and broad; ears small, well placed and tufted; short broad nose; full round cheeks.
Eyes Large and round, deep orange or copper.

Toanje Blossom Shaded Cameo female, a variety in which the combination of red and silver genes produces an exquisite pink, shot-silk effect in the coat.

Smoke–GCCF Variety 6

A Smoke is a cat of contrasts, the undercolour being as ash-white as possible, with the tips shading to black, the dark points being most defined on the back, head and feet, and the light points on frill, flanks and ear-tufts.

Colour Body: black shading to silver on the sides and flanks. Mask and Feet: Black with no markings. Frill and ear tufts: silver. Undercolour: as nearly white as possible.

Coat Silky texture, long and dense, extra long frill.

Head Broad and round with width between the ears, which should be small and tufted; snub nose.
Body Cobby, not coarse but massive; short legs.
Eyes Orange or copper in colour, large and round in shape, pleasing expression.
Tail Short and bushy.

NB An obvious under, or over-short jaw shall be considered a defect.

Blue Smoke–GCCF Variety 6a
The above is also the Standard for Blue Smokes, except that where the word 'black' occurs, 'blue' should be substituted.

Blue-Cream–GCCF Variety 13

Colour and Markings To consist of blue and cream, softly intermingled; pastel shades.

Coat Dense, very soft and silky.

Body Short, cobby and massive; short thick legs.
Head Broad and round, tiny ears, well placed and well tufted; short broad nose; colour intermingled on face.
Eyes Deep copper or orange.

Bi-Colour–GCCF Variety 12a

Colours and Distribution Any solid colour and white, the patches of colour to be clear, even and well distributed. Not more than two thirds of the cat's coat to be coloured and not more than a half to be white. Face to be patched with colour and white.

Coat Silky texture; long and flowing, extra long on frill and tail.

Far left, **Champion Huntley Havoc** Chocolate Colourpoint.

Left, **Champion Wynmoor Diorama** Tortoiseshell LH Female.

Right below, **Omicron Peaseblossom** Blue-Cream Colourpoint Persian.

Left below, **Champion Frallon Creampoint Apache** Cream Colourpoint male.

Head Round and broad with width between the ears which should be small, well placed and tufted; short broad nose; full cheeks; wide muzzle and firm chin (level bite).
Body and Legs Body cobby and massive; short thick legs.
Eyes Large and round, set well apart, deep orange or copper in colour.
Tail Short and full.

Serious Faults Tabby markings. A long tail. Yellow or green eyes.

Colourpoint–GCCF Variety 13b

Coat Fur long, thick and soft in texture, frill full.

Colour (i) Seal points with cream body colour.
    (ii) Blue points with glacial white body colour.
   (iii) Chocolate points with ivory body colour.
   (iv) Lilac points with magnolia body colour.
    (v) Red points with off white body colour.
   (vi) Tortie points with cream body colour.
   (vii) Cream.

 (viii) Blue Cream.
  (ix) Chocolate Cream.
   (x) Lilac Cream.

Colours i–v incl. Points to be of a solid colour and body shading, if any, to tone with the points.

Colour vi. Points colour of Tortie Points to be restricted to the basic Seal colour, body shading, if any, to tone with points.

Head Broad and round with width between the ears; short face and short nose with distinct break or stop; ears small and tufted; cheeks well developed.
Eyes Large, round and full; clear, bright and decidedly blue.
Body Cobby; low on leg.
Tail Short and full, not tapering. A kink is a defect.

NB Any similarity in *type* to Siamese, in particular a long straight nose, is undesirable and incorrect.

Pedigree shorthaired cats usually have deep-chested sturdy bodies with short, stocky legs and fairly short, thick tails. Heads are massive, round and with full cheeks, topped by tiny, wide-set ears. Their eyes must be full, round and lustrous. Most are known by their colours, and the self-coloured shorthairs may be Black, Blue, Cream or White.

The Black Shorthair is difficult to breed to perfection as extremes of weather affect the coat and cause it to have a rusty appearance. The British Blue is, perhaps, the most popular of all the shorthaired breeds, affectionate, totally independent and very hardy. Cream Shorthairs are comparatively rare and are difficult to breed with the clear, unmarked coat required by the standard. White Shirthairs, like their Persian cousins, may have orange, blue or odd eyes.

All British Shorthair cats have the same basic standard of points:

This British Cream Shorthair neuter is of the desired soft colouring and sports a fine set of whiskers.

Below Possibly the most popular of the Self Shorthaired cats is the attractive and chunky British Blue.

Scale of Points

Head	20
Eyes	10
Body	20
Legs and paws	10
Tail	10
Coat, Colour and Condition	30
Total	100

British Shorthairs

The British cat is compact, well balanced and powerful showing good depth of body, a full broad chest, short strong legs, rounded paws, tail thick at base with a rounded tip. The head is round with good width between the ears, round cheeks, firm chin, small ears, large round and well opened eyes with a short straight nose. The coat is short and dense.

Head Round and massive, with good breadth of skull; round face with round underlying bone structure, well set on a short thick neck.
Nose Short, broad and straight.
Chin Firm and well developed.
Ears Small, rounded at tips, with good width between and well furnished.
Eyes Large, round, well opened, set wide apart and level.
Body Well knit and powerful. Level back and a deep broad chest.
Legs Short, well boned and strong. Straight forelegs.
Paws Round and firm.
Tail Short and thick but in proportion to body length with a rounded tip.

Coat Short and dense.

Condition Hard and muscular.

Faults Tail defects. Definite nose stops. Overlong or fluffy coat.

Black–GCCF Variety 15

Colour Jet black to roots, no rusty tinge. No white hairs anywhere. *Rusty tinge permissible in kittens.*
Nose Leather black. Pads brown or black.

Eyes Deep copper or orange with no trace of green.

With-hold certificates Incorrect eye colour. Green rims.

Blue–GCCF Variety 16

Colour Light to medium blue. Even colour and no tabby markings or white anywhere.

Eyes Copper or orange.
Nose leather and pads Blue.

Faults Unsound coats. Silver tipping to coats.

With-hold certificates Incorrect eye colour. Green rims.

Cream– GCCF Variety 17

Colour Lighter shades preferred. Level in colour and free from markings. No sign of white anywhere.

Eyes Copper or orange.
Nose leather and pads Pink.

With-hold certificates Incorrect eye colour. Green rims. Heavy tabby markings.

White Blue-Eyed–GCCF Variety 14

Colour Pure white, untinged with yellow. *Dark mark on head permissible in kittens.*

Eyes Very deep sapphire blue. No green rims or flecks.
Nose Leather pink. Pads pink.

With-hold certificates Incorrect eye colour. Green rims.

White Orange-Eyed– GCCF Variety 14a

Colour White to be pure, untinged with yellow.

Eyes Gold, orange or copper. No green rims or flecks.
Nose leather and pads Pink.

With-hold certificates Incorrect eye colour. Green rims.

White Odd-Eyed–GCCF Variety 14b

Colour Pure white, untinged with yellow.

Eyes One gold, orange or copper. One blue. No green rims or flecks.

Nose leather and pads Pink.

With-hold certificates Incorrect eye colour. Green rims.

Above This massive British Black exhibits the desired head type of the Shorthaired varieties, with his short nose and full apple-cheeks.

As in the longhaired breeds, the White Shorthair may also show the Odd-Eyed syndrome.

Taishun Silver Spot
British Silver Spotted
male neuter.

All the non-self shorthairs conform to the same basic standard of points as the self shorthairs. The tabbies may be Brown, Red or Silver and as well as the classic or blotched pattern, mackerel tabbies are also permitted. One form of tabby is the Spotted, in which the mackerel stripes are broken up to form discrete spots. Spotted cats may be brown, red or silver, and occasionally cream and blue specimens are bred. The spots may be of any size or shape, round, triangular, rosette, lozenge or star-shaped, but they must be clearly defined.

Parti-coloured shorthaired cats include the Blue-Cream, the Tortoiseshell, the Tortie-and-White, the Bi-Colour, the Smoke and the newly recognized British Tipped. The Exotic Shorthair of America closely resembles the British Shorthair, but has more extreme head type with an exceptionally short profile achieved by selecting for the flat face effect. Exotic Shorthairs are not recognized in Britain or Europe, and British Shorthairs are only recognized by some associations in the US.

Classic Tabby Pattern

All markings to be clearly defined and dense. Legs barred evenly with bracelets going down from the body markings to the toes. Ground colour and markings should be equally balanced. Evenly ringed tail. On the neck and upper chest there should be unbroken necklaces, the more the better. On the forehead there should be a letter 'M' made by frown marks. There should be an unbroken line running back from the outer corner of the eye. There should be pencillings on the cheeks.

There should be a vertical line which runs over the back of the head and extends to the shoulder markings, which should be shaped like a butterfly. Both the upper and the lower wings should be defined clearly in outline with dots inside this outline.

On the back there should be a line running down the spine from the butterfly to the tail, and there should be a stripe on each side of this running parallel to it. These stripes should be separated from each other by stripes of the ground colour. On each flank there should be a large solid oyster or blotch which should be surrounded by one or more unbroken rings. The markings on each side should be identical. All Tabby cats should be spotted in the abdominal region. In all Tabby cats the tails should be evenly ringed.

Silver Tabby—GCCF Variety 18

Clear silver ground colour should include chin and lips. Markings dense black. Eye colour green or hazel. Nose leather brick red for preference, although black is permissible. Pads black. Soles of feet from toes to heel black.

Faults Brown on nose or paws. Brindling.

With-hold certificates Incorrect eye colour. White anywhere. Incorrect Tabby pattern.

Red Tabby—GCCF Variety 19

Red ground colour and markings of deep rich

red. Lips and chin red. Eye colour, brilliant copper. Nose leather, brick red. Pads, deep red. Sides of feet dark red.

Faults Brindling.

With-hold certificates Incorrect eye colour. White anywhere. Incorrect Tabby pattern.

Brown Tabby–GCCF Variety 20

Brilliant coppery brown ground with dense black markings. Back of legs from paw to heel should be black. Eye colour, orange, hazel or deep yellow. Nose leather, brick red. Pads black or brown.

Faults Brindling.

With-hold certificates Incorrect eye colour. White anywhere. Incorrect Tabby pattern.

Mackerel Tabby Pattern

Head, legs and tail as for Classic Tabby. There should be a narrow unbroken line running from the back of the head to the base of the tail. The rest of the body to be covered with narrow lines running vertically down from the spine line and to be unbroken. These lines should be as narrow and as numerous as possible.

Type faults As for Classic Tabby.

Pattern faults Solid back, broken tail rings,

solid sides, white tip to tail and white anywhere. Spotting on back. Brindling.

With-hold certificates Incorrect eye colour. White anywhere. Incorrect Mackerel pattern.

Spotted–GCCF Variety 30

Head markings As Classic Tabby. Body and legs good, clear spotting essential. Spots as numerous and distinct as possible.
Tail Spots or broken rings desirable.

Colour Silver with black spots. Brown with black spots. Red with deep rich red spots. Any other recognized ground colours acceptable with appropriate spotting.
Eye colour Silver spotted, green or hazel. Brown spotted, orange, hazel or deep yellow. Red spotted, brilliant copper.
Nose leather and paws As for Classic Tabby.

Faults Solid spine.

Pattern faults Linked spots. Brindling. White tip to tail. White anywhere.

With-hold certificates Incorrect eye colour. Incorrect pattern. White anywhere.

Premier Brynbuboo Spotty Muldoon British Spotted Neuter.

Vectensian Busted British Classic Red Tabby male.

Tortoiseshell—GCCF Variety 21

Black with brilliant patches of cream and red. All these patches should be clearly defined and well broken on the legs and body. A red or cream blaze on the head is desirable. Nose leather pink and/or black. Pads pink and/or black. Eyes, brilliant copper or orange.

Faults Tabby markings. Brindling. White anywhere. Colour unbroken on paws. Unequal balance of colour.

With-hold certificates Incorrect eye colour. White anywhere. Green rims.

Tortoiseshell and White—GCCF Variety 22

Black, cream and red on white, equally balanced. Colours to be brilliant. The tri-colour patchings should cover the top of the head, ears and cheeks, back, tail and part of the flanks. Patches to be clear and defined. White blaze desirable. The colour of the of the eyes should be copper or orange. Nose leather and pads as for Tortoiseshell.

Faults Tabby markings. Brindling. Colour unbroken on paws. Unequal balance of colour. White must never predominate; the reverse is preferable.

With-hold certificates Incorrect eye colour. White predominating. Green rims.

Blue Cream—GCCF Variety 28

Colour Blue and cream to be softly intermingled. No blaze.

Grand Champion Brynbuboo Bosselot British Brown Tabby male.

Eyes Copper or orange.
Nose leather Blue.
Pads Blue and/or pink.

Faults Tabby markings. White anywhere. Colour unbroken on paws. Unequal balance of colour.

With-hold certificates Incorrect eye colour. Green rims. Solid patches of colour.

Bi-Colour–GCCF Variety 31

Any accepted colour and white. The patches of colour to be clear and evenly distributed. Not more than two thirds of the coat to be coloured and not more than one half white. Face to be patched with colour. White blaze desirable. Symmetry in design is also desirable.

Eyes Brilliant copper or orange.

Faults Brindling or tabby markings.

With-hold certificates White patching on solid colours. Incorrect eye colour. Green rims.

Smokes–GCCF Variety 36

Colour Black or blue. Undercoat pale silver.

Eyes Yellow or orange.
Nose leather and pads Blue or black to correspond with coat colour. (Kittens should not be penalized for ghost markings.)

Faults White guard hairs. Overlong coat.

With-hold certificates Incorrect eye colour. Tabby markings in adults. Overlong coat.

Right The Shorthaired Smoke has a pale silver undercoat and the top coat may be blue, or black as seen in this young female.

Below, left **Cramar Chilison** British Tipped male, a new variety of Shorthair.

Below, right **Cherrywood Suzi** British Blue-Cream, an all-female variety.

The Abyssinian cat may be 'normal' in colour and is known as the Ruddy Abyssinian in the US. This is the basic variety and is recognized by its beautiful coat in which each hair is distinctly banded with black or very dark brown on a warm brown background. This banding causes the breed's unique ticked appearance. Red Abyssinians turned up in litters of 'normal' parents and in 1963, these were recognized as a separate colour variety. In this instance the red appearance is not caused by the sex-linked orange gene which produces red cats of other varieties, but by a factor similar to that which converts black to chocolate in other breeds.

Recently, other colours have been produced in the Abyssinian, including blue and lilac, plus a colour which is said to be cream, but the Blue Abyssinian is the only one to have official recognition by GCCF at present.

In 1868, the first Abyssinian cat was brought out of its native land by a military expedition returning to Britain, and is said to be the founder of the breed. By the turn of the century, Abyssinian cats very similar to those of today were being shown, and in the year 1909, a breeding pair were sent to the US.

Abyssinian–GCCF Varieties 23, 23a and 23b

Type Foreign type of medium build, firm, lithe and muscular, never large or coarse. The head broad, tapering to a firm wedge set on an elegant neck. Body of medium length with fairly long tapering tail. A 'cobby' cat is not permissible.

Head and Ears Head a moderate wedge of medium proportions, the brow, cheeks and profile lines showing a gentle contour and the muzzle not sharply pointed. A shallow indentation forming the muzzle is desirable but a pinch is a fault. Ears set wide apart and pricked, broad at base, comparatively large, well cupped and preferably tufted. In profile the head shows a gentle rounding to the brow with a slight nose-break leading to a very firm chin.
Eyes Well apart, large, bright and expressive in an oriental setting. A squint is a fault. Colour, amber, hazel or green. A light eye colour is undesirable.
Tail Broad at base, fairly long and tapering. Neither a whip nor a kink is permissible.
Feet Small and oval.

Coat Short, fine and close lying with double, or preferably, treble ticking, i.e. two or three bands of colour on each hair.

Markings The appropriate darker hair colour should extend well up the back of the hind legs; also showing as a solid tip at the extreme end of the tail, and the absence of either is a fault. A line of dark pigmentation is required round the eyes and absence of this is also a fault.

Undesirable markings are bars on the legs, chest and tail. An unbroken necklet is not permissible. The Abyssinian cat has a tendency to white in the immediate area of the lips and lower jaw and it is a fault if this white area extends on to the neck. A locket and other white markings are not permissible.

Taishun Abigail Normal Abyssinian female showing her beautifully ticked coat.

Colours

Usual–GCCF Variety 23

The body colour to be a rich golden brown, ticked with black and the base hair ruddy-orange or rich apricot. A pale or cold colour is a fault.

The belly and inside of legs to be a ruddy-orange or rich apricot to harmonize with the base hair on the rest of the body. Any spinal shading to be of deeper colour. The tip of the tail and the solid colour on the hind legs to be black. Nose leather brick red and pads black.

Left An exciting litter of Abyssinian kittens bred by the **Chezchats** cattery showing the four basic colours. Left to right lilac, normal, blue, red.

Arolan Blue Smenkhare Blue Abyssinian male.

Arolan Herkles Abyssinian female.

Red – GCCF Variety 23a

The body colour to be a lustrous copper-red, ticked with chocolate and the base hair deep apricot. A pale or sandy colour is a fault.

The belly and inside of legs to be a deep apricot to harmonize with the base hair on the rest of the body. Any spinal shading to be of deeper colour. The tip of the tail and the solid colour on the hind legs chocolate. Nose leather and pads pink.

Blue – GCCF Variety 23c (Provisional Standard)

The body colour to be blue-grey with a soft warm effect, ticked with deeper steel blue and the base hair pale cream or oatmeal.

The belly and inside of legs to be pale cream or oatmeal to harmonize with the base hair on the rest of the body. Any spinal shading to be of deeper colour. The tip of the tail and the solid colour on the hind legs steel blue. Nose leather dark pink and pads mauve/blue.

Scale of Points

Colour	
Body colour	25
Ticking	20
Type	
Body shape, tail, feet, coat, carriage and general condition	30
Head and ears	15
Eyes	10
Total	100

NB Any cat displaying a feature which is *not permissible* (i.e. cobby type; whip tail; kink in tail; unbroken necklet; locket; other white markings) shall not be awarded a first prize, nor as a result of this, can it be considered for either a challenge certificate or a premier certificate.

Any cat displaying a *fault* may be awarded a prize but any cat displaying two or more faults shall not be awarded a challenge certificate nor a premier certificate.

Above **Champion Sidarka Henry Hotfoot** Brown Burmese male.

Far right **Champion Sidarka Delta Dawn** Blue Burmese female.

Burmese cats come in many colours, all of which are recognized in GCCF and other associations throughout the world. In the US only the original Brown Burmese is recognized by CFA and called the Sable Burmese. Some of the other American associations recognize the blue, chocolate and lilac varieties, which they call Blue, Champagne and Platinum Burmese respectively.

The type of the Burmese varies considerably on either side of the Atlantic, as is shown by the standards on page 191.

In 1930, a small brown cat called Wong Mau was taken from Burma to the US by a retired ship's doctor. Wong Mau was a hybrid Siamese and from her offspring came the first Burmese cats. The Burmese and Siamese breeds are closely related (see Genetics), and intermating between the two varieties produces the interesting Tonkanese. Mated *inter se*, Tonkanese then produce Burmese and Siamese offspring with some intermediates like themselves.

The Burmese breed soon became popular and was officially recognized by CFA in 1936. In 1947 the breed received a severe setback when recognition was withdrawn for six years by CFA, following confirmation that breeding methods outside the terms of their constitution were being used.

In 1949, Burmese breeding stock was exported from the US to Britain, and in 1952, after three generations of pure Burmese had been bred to their satisfaction, GCCF gave the breed official status.

Standard of Points for Burmese

The Burmese is an elegant cat of a foreign type, which is positive and quite individual to the breed. Any suggestion of either Siamese type, or the cobbiness of a British cat, is regarded as a fault.

Body, legs and tail The body should be of medium length and size, feeling hard and well-muscled, and heavier than its appearance indicates. The chest should be strong, and rounded in profile, the back straight from shoulder to rump. Legs slender and in proportion to the body: hind legs slightly longer than front: paws neat and oval in shape. The tail straight and of medium length, not heavy at base, and tapering only slightly to a rounded tip without bone defect. A visible kink or other bone defect in the tail is a fault, precluding the award of a challenge certificate, but an invisible defect at the extreme tip may be overlooked in an otherwise excellent specimen.

Head, ears and eyeset The head should be slightly rounded on top, with good breadth between the ears, wide cheek bones and tapering to a short blunt wedge. The jaw

should be wide at the hinge and the chin firm. A muzzle pinch is a bad fault. Ears should be medium in size, set well apart on the skull, broad at the base, with slightly rounded tips, the outer line of the ears continuing the shape of the upper part of the face. This may not be possible in mature males who develop a fullness of cheek. In profile the ears should have a slight forward tilt. There should be a distinct nose break, and in profile the chin should show a strong lower jaw. The eyes, which must be set well apart, should be large and lustrous, the top line of the eye showing a straight oriental slant towards the nose, the lower line being rounded. Round or oriental eyes are a fault.
Eye Colour Any shade of yellow from chartreuse to amber, but golden yellow preferred. Green eyes are a serious fault in Brown Burmese, but Blue Burmese may show a slight fading of colour. Green eyes with more blue than yellow pigmentation must preclude the award of a challenge certificate in Burmese of all colours.

Coat The coat should be short, fine, satin-like in texture lying close to the body. The glossy coat is a distinctive feature of Burmese, and is indicative of good health.

Colours

General Considerations In all colours, the underparts will be lighter than the back. In kittens and adolescents, allowances should be made for faint tabby barring and, overall, a lighter colour than adults. The presence of a few white hairs may be overlooked in an otherwise excellent cat, but a noticeable number of white hairs, or a white patch, is a serious fault, precluding the award of a challenge certificate.

Brown—GCCF Variety 27

In maturity, the adult should be a rich warm seal brown, shading almost imperceptibly to a slightly lighter shade on the underparts; apart from this and slightly darker ears and mask, there should be no shading or marking of any kind. Very dark colour, bordering on black, is incorrect. Nose leather rich brown, foot pads brown.

Blue—GCCF Variety 27a

In maturity, the adult should be a soft silver grey only very slightly darker on the back and tail. There should be a distinct silver sheen on rounded areas such as ears, face and feet. Nose leather very dark grey, foot pads grey.

Top right **Cheronia Oliver** Red Burmese male.

Right **Yamsar Rainbow** Blue-Cream Burmese female.

Chocolate – GCCF Variety 27b

In maturity, the overall colour should be a warm milk chocolate. Ears and mask may be slightly darker, but legs, tail and lower jaw should be the same colour as the back. Evenness of colour overall very desirable. Nose leather warm chocolate brown, foot pads brick pink shading to chocolate.

Lilac – GCCF Variety 27c

In maturity, the coat colour should be a pale, delicate dove-grey, with a slightly pinkish cast giving a rather faded effect. Ears and mask may be slightly deeper in colour. Nose leather lavender pink, foot pads shell pink in kittens, becoming, with the onset of adulthood, lavender pink.

Red – GCCF Variety 27d

In maturity, the coat colour should be light tangerine. Slight tabby markings on the face and small indeterminate markings elsewhere (except on sides and belly) are permissible in an otherwise excellent cat. Ears should be distinctly darker than the back. Nose leather and foot pads pink.

Brown Tortie – GCCF Variety 27e
(Normal Tortie)

The coat should be a mixture of brown and red without any obvious barring. The colour and markings are not as important as the Burmese type, which must be excellent. Nose leather and foot pads plain or blotched, brown and pink.

Cream – GCCF Variety 27f

In maturity, the coat colour should be rich cream. Slight tabby markings on the face and small indeterminate markings elsewhere (except on the sides and belly) are permissible in an otherwise excellent cat. Ears should be only slightly darker than the back coat colour. Nose leather and foot pads pink.

Blue Tortie–GCCF Variety 27g (Blue Cream)

The coat should be a mixture of blue and cream without any obvious barring. Colour and markings are not as important as the Burmese type, which should be excellent. Nose leather and foot pads will be plain coloured or blotched, blue and pink.

Chocolate Tortie–GCCF Variety 27h

The coat should be a mixture of chocolate and red without any obvious barring. The colour and markings are not as important as the Burmese type, which should be excellent. Nose

leather and foot pads plain or blotched, chocolate and pink.

Lilac Tortie–GCCF Variety 27j (Lilac Cream)

The coat should be a mixture of lilac and cream without any obvious barring. The colour and markings are not as important as the Burmese type, which should be excellent. Nose leather and foot pads plain or blotched, lilac and pink.

Distribution of Points

	General	Torties
Body shape, legs, tail, feet	30	35
Body colour, coat texture and condition	25	20
Head and ears	20	20
Shape and set of eyes	15	15
Colour of eyes	10	10
Total	100	100

NB In the case of the four tortie colours 27e, 27g, 27h and 27j, the coat may display two shades of its basic colours and *may thus appear to display three or even four colours*. The colours may be mingled or blotched: blazes, solid legs or tails are all permissible: therefore additional marks are awarded for type, which is of far greater importance than coat colour and markings.

Above **Champion Typla Yercum Zea** Chocolate Burmese female.

Left **Champion Kanzam Lilac Lana** Lilac Burmese female.

It is said that the first Siamese cats were brought out of Siam in 1884, having been presented to the British Consul General by the King of Siam. The following year, a Siamese cat caused much interest when it was exhibited at the Crystal Palace show, and during the next few years the breed gained in popularity.

Pictures of the first Siamese cats show that they had rounded heads and heavier bodies than their counterparts of today. They often had kinked, knotted or shortened tails as well as squinting eyes, which have now been virtually bred out. These early imports were often very delicate and difficult to rear, but stronger stock was eventually developed and today the breed is among the most popular of all.

The Seal-Pointed or Royal Cat of Siam was first officially recognized by the newly formed Siamese Cat Club in 1901, long before the formation of the Governing Council of the Cat Fancy. The Blue-Pointed Siamese was the second variety to be recognized and soon became popular, but the Chocolate-Pointed Siamese, although recorded since the turn of the century, was not recognized by GCCF until 1950. The American associations followed suit in 1951.

The Lilac-Pointed Siamese arrived naturally enough when cats with both chocolate and blue genes intermated. The Tabby-Pointed series and the red group were man-made when initial crosses were made with tabby and red cats to introduce the desired colour characteristics. Back-crossing to top Siamese stock soon restored the ideal type, and as each variety achieved its standards of perfection, it was given official recognition.

In the US the tabby and red series of Siamese are known as Colorpoint Shorthairs by some associations, including CFA, although ACFA acknowledges them as Siamese.

Standards for Siamese Cats

Siamese (Seal-Pointed)–GCCF Variety 24

Shape (Body and Tail) Medium in size, body long and svelte, legs proportionately slim, hind legs slightly higher than the front ones, feet small and oval, tail long and tapering and free from any kink. A visible kink disqualifies. The body, legs, feet, head and tail all in proportion, giving the whole a well balanced appearance.

Head and Ears Head long and well proportioned, with width between the eyes, narrowing in perfectly straight lines to a fine muzzle, with straight profile, strong chin and level bite. Ears rather large and pricked, wide at the base.
Eyes Clear, brilliant deep blue. Shape oriental and slanting towards the nose. No tendency to squint.

Body Colour Cream, shading gradually into pale warm fawn on the back. Kittens paler in colour.

Left **Champion Meikleriggs Minima** Blue Tabby Point Siamese pictured at seven months and showing excellent Siamese type.

Below A young Chocolate Pointed kitten just developing his points' colour. Siamese kittens are all born white and colour slowly appears after a few days.

Points Mask, ears, legs, feet and tail dense and clearly defined seal brown. Mask complete and (except in kittens) connected by tracing with the ears.

Coat Very short and fine in texture, glossy and close-lying.

Notes and Definitions Definition of Squint: When the eyes are so placed that they appear to look permanently at the nose.

NB The Siamese cat should be a beautifully balanced animal with head, ears and neck carried on a long svelte body, supported on fine legs and feet with a tail in proportion. The head and profile should be wedge shaped, neither round nor pointed. The mask complete, connected by tracings with the ears (except in kittens), the eyes a deep blue, green tinge is considered a fault. Expression alert and intelligent.

White toes or toe automatically disqualify an exhibit. It is important to note that the Standard with regard to Type is the same for all Siamese Cats.

Scale of Points

Type and Shape	
Head	15
Ears	5
Eyes	5
Body	15
Legs and Paws	5
Tail	5
Total	50

Colour	
Eyes	15
Points	10
Body Colour	10
Texture of Coat	10
Condition	5
Total	50

Siamese (Blue-Pointed)–GCCF Variety 24a

The Standard is the same as for Seal-Pointed with the following exceptions:

Colour Points blue; the ears, mask, legs, paws and tail of the same colour; the ears no darker than the other points.

Eyes Clear, bright, vivid blue.

Body Body colour: glacial white, shading

gradually into blue on back, the same cold tone as the points, but of a lighter shade.

Texture of Coat As for Seal-Pointed.

Siamese (Chocolate-Pointed)–GCCF Variety 24b

The Standard is the same as for Seal-Pointed with the following exceptions:

Colour Points milk chocolate; the ears, mask, legs, paws and tail of the same colour, the ears no darker than the other points.

Eyes Clear, bright, vivid blue.

Body Ivory colour all over. Shading, if at all, to be colour of points.

Texture of Coat As for Seal-Pointed.

Siamese (Lilac-Pointed)–GCCF Variety 24c

The Standard is the same as for Seal-Pointed with the following exceptions:

Eyes Clear, light vivid blue (but not pale).

Body Colour Off white (Magnolia) shading, if any, to tone with points.

Points Pinkish grey, nose leather and pads faded lilac.

Siamese (Tabby-Pointed)–GCCF Variety 32

Type and Shape As Seal-Pointed.

Body Colour Pale coat, preferably free from body markings including back of head and neck and conforming to recognized Siamese standard for the particular colour of points.

Points Same colour essential, but varied tones of same colour acceptable, i.e. seal, blue, chocolate, lilac, red and cream. The standard for Tortie/Tabby Points is listed in the information below.

Ears Solid, no stripes. Thumb marks as clear as possible.
Nose leather Conforming to recognized Siamese standard for the particular colour of points, or pink.
Mask Clearly defined stripes, especially around the eyes and nose. Distinct markings on cheeks, darkly spotted whisker pads.
Eyes Brilliant clear blue. The lids dark rimmed or toning with the points.
Legs Clearly defined varied sized broken stripes. Solid markings on back of hind legs.
Tail Many varied sized clearly defined rings ending in a solid tip.

Coat Very short and fine in texture. Glossy and close lying.

The Blue-Pointed Siamese has been recognised for many years and appeared as a simple dilution of the black gene which gives Seal-Point.

The paler colouring of the Lilac-Pointed is produced by the effect of two genes chocolate and blue, which together produce the ethereal effect of this variety's points and coat.

Tortie/Tabby Points

As above with the following exceptions:

Ears Mottled.
Nose and pad leathers Mottled.
Tail As above but mottling permissible.

Points Patched with red and/or cream over tabby pattern. Distribution of patching on points immaterial (as in standard for Tortie Points).

NB These cats usually resemble Tabby Points rather than Tortie Points.

Scale of Points

Type and Shape (as for Seal-Pointed Siamese)	50
Colour and Condition	
Ringed Tail	10
Eyes	10
Body Colour	15
Points and Thumb Marks	10
Texture of Coat General Condition	5
Total	100

Siamese (Red-Pointed)–GCCF Variety 32a

Type As for Seal-Pointed Siamese.
Colour Restricted to points.

Body White, shading (if any) to apricot on the back, kittens paler.

Nose Leather Pink.
Ears Bright reddish-gold.
Mask Bright reddish-gold.
Legs and Feet Bright reddish-gold or apricot.
Tail Bright reddish-gold.
Eyes Bright vivid blue.

NB Barring or striping on mask, legs and tail is not deemed a fault.

Siamese (Tortie-Pointed)–GCCF Variety 32b

Type As for Seal-Pointed Siamese.

Colour Restricted to points as in all Siamese: basic colour seal, blue, chocolate or lilac, as in Breeds 24, 24a, 24b, 24c.

Body As in equivalent solid colour Siamese.

Nose Leather As in equivalent solid colour Siamese (see note).
Mask Seal, blue, chocolate or lilac as in Breeds 24, 24a, 24c; patched or mingled with red and/or cream.
Ears Basic colour as in mask, patched or mingled with red and/or cream, which must be clearly visible.
Legs and Feet Basic colour as in mask, patched or mingled red and/or cream.
Tail Basic colour as in mask, patched or mingled with red and/or cream.
Eyes Blue, as in equivalent solid colour Siamese.

Coat Very short and fine in texture, glossy and close lying.

NB Distribution of patching on points colour and leathers of all tortie point Siamese is random and immaterial. Barring and ticking is a fault.

Cream Point Siamese Provisional Breed Number 32c

Provisional Standard of Points

Type	
As for Seal Point Siamese	50
Colour	
Restricted to points as in all Siamese	
Body	
White, shading (if any) to palest cream	10
Nose Leather	
Pink	
Mask	
Cream, with tracings to ears, except in kittens	
Ears, Legs and Feet	
Cream	10
Tail	
Cream	
Eyes	
Bright vivid blue	15
Coat	
Very fine and short in texture, glossy and close lying	10
Condition	5
Modification	
Barring and striping on mask, legs and tail, is *not* to be deemed a serious fault.	

NB A hot cream is not desirable.

Whatever the colour of their points, all Siamese cats have blue eyes. The blue colouring is generally deeper in the darker varieties and this is covered in the relevant standard of points. (*top left*) An elegant Cream-Point awaits his judges. (*top right*) In the Tortie-Point, the black and red areas are patched and mingled in a random pattern unique to each cat. (*centre*) A composed Cream-Point. (*below*) a dark-phase Chocolate-Point.

Far left **Solitaire Aniani** elegant Havana queen with her three-week-old son **Solitaire Solo**.

Left **Kalaya Black Creole** Foreign Black neuter.

From the Seal, Blue, Chocolate and Lilac-Pointed Siamese, self- or solid-coloured equivalent varieties have been bred. The first of these to become established was the self chocolate which was officially recognized in 1958 as the Chestnut Brown (Foreign) Shorthair. In 1956 cats of this variety had been sent to the US with their breeder's preferred choice of breed name – Havana, and in America the breed became established as the Havana Brown. From these beginnings, the breed developed along different lines and two distinct types of cat have arisen on either side of the Atlantic. In 1970, GCCF allowed the name of the breed to be changed to Havana. This is a svelte and charming cat of Siamese type, with a glossy, chocolate brown coat. In the US, however, the Havana Brown is less extreme, and its distinctive head has a sharply dipped profile, a whisker break, rounded ears and oval eyes.

The Foreign Lilac, or Foreign Lavender, is similar to the Havana, but has a pinkish-grey coat. The variety was first recognized by GCCF in 1974. The Foreign or Oriental Blue has been bred over the years, but due to the existence of other blue breeds, has not been developed to recognition point. The Foreign Black, on the other hand, caught the public imagination. Looking like a miniature black panther, a good specimen with its raven black coat and emerald eyes can be a show-stopper. In any case sufficient numbers of high quality were bred for GCCF to grant a provisional breed number in 1978.

Breeding programmes for the development of a cat similar to the cats of the Ancient Egyptians were formulated in Britain and eventually strikingly marked spotted tabbies were produced and called 'Egyptian Mau'. Oriental tabby cats of ticked, classic and mackerel patterns were also bred, but to date, only the spotted varieties of all colours except silver, are recognized by GCCF. Other associations in some countries do recognize all patterns and colours of Oriental Tabby, some regard all foreign tabbies as experimental breeds only.

In the Foreign White, the dominant white coat overlays the basic conformation and colouring of the Siamese Cat. Foreign White cats were carefully and methodically developed by a group of British breeders, backcrossing to top quality Siamese at each stage until the desired type was achieved and the breed received its official number in 1974. Unlike the other green-eyed Orientals, the Foreign White has eyes of sapphire blue.

Standard of Points for the Foreign Black Shorthair Cat
Foreign Black – GCCF Variety 37

Shape (Body and tail) Medium in size, body long and svelte, legs proportionately slim, hind legs slightly higher than the front ones, feet small and oval, tail long and tapering and free from any kink. A visible kink disqualifies. The body, legs, feet, head and tail all in proportion, giving the whole a well balanced appearance.

Head and Ears Head long and well proportioned with width between the eyes, narrowing in perfectly straight lines to a fine muzzle, with straight profile, strong chin and level bite. Ears rather large and pricked, wide at the base.
Eyes Green. Shape oriental and slanting towards the nose. No tendency to squint.

Body colour Jet black to the roots. No rusty tinge. Nose leather black. Paw pads black or brown.

Coat Very short and fine in texture, glossy and close-lying.

Notes and definitions Definition of a squint. When the eyes are so placed that they appear to look permanently at the nose.

NB The Foreign Black cat should be a beautifully balanced animal with head, ears and neck carried on a long svelte body, supported on fine legs and feet with a tail in proportion. The head and profile should be wedge shaped, neither round nor pointed. Expression alert and intelligent. Scattered white hairs and rusty or other shadings in the coat are often present during kittenhood and should not be too severely penalized in an otherwise good kitten.

Scattered white hairs are undesirable in adults.
White locket, white chin or white belly spots
are serious faults.

Havana–GCCF Variety 29

Havana Foreign shorthaired cats are of the
Siamese Type. Fine in bone, lithe and sinuous
and of graceful proportions. The coat is a rich
brown in colour, even and sound. Whiskers and
nose leather to be the same colour as coat. The
pads of the feet are a pinkish shade of brown.
The eyes are green.

Coat Rich chestnut brown, very short and fine
in texture, glossy and close lying, even and
sound throughout.

Head and ears Head long and well
proportioned, narrowing in straight lines to a
fine muzzle. Ears large and well pricked, wide
at base with a good width between. Strong
chin.
Body, legs and tail Medium size body, long and
lithe, well muscled, graceful in outline. Slim
and dainty legs with small oval paws, hind legs
slightly longer than front legs. Long whipped
tail. No kink.
Eyes Oriental in shape and setting. Green in
colour. No squint.

Faults Tabby or other markings. White spots or
hairs. Any tendency to British type. Yellow or
copper eye colour. Kinked tail. 'Ghost' tabby
markings should not be held against an
otherwise good kitten.

With-hold certificates Incorrect eye colour.

Foreign Lilac–GCCF Variety 29c

The same standard and scale of points applies
to the Foreign Lilac, except for coat colour.
Coat colour should be a frosty-grey with a
distinct pinkish tone. Nose leather and pads
should be pinkish. Coat colour too blue or
fawn is a fault. Otherwise the same faults apply
to the Foreign Lilac as to the Havana.

Standard of Points for the Oriental Spotted Tabby Shorthair

Oriental Spotted Tabby (Standard colours)–GCCF Variety 38

Shape (Body and tail) Medium in size, body
long and svelte, legs proportionately slim, hind
legs slightly higher than the front ones, feet
small and oval, tail long and tapering, and free
from any kink. A visible kink disqualifies. The
body, legs, feet, head and tail all in proportion,
giving the whole a well balanced appearance.

Head and ears Head long and well
proportioned with width between the eyes,
narrowing in perfectly straight lines to a fine

Left Oriental Silver
Tabby kitten showing
the dense black
markings on a silver
ground, offset with
green eyes.

Below In the lilac
Oriental Tabby the
markings are much paler
and diffuse into the
mushroom colour of the
base coat.

muzzle, with straight profile, strong chin and
level bite. Ears rather large and pricked, wide
at base.

Eyes Shape oriental and slanting towards the
nose. No tendency to squint.

Colour and pattern On the head should be a
clear scarab marking. There should be
unbroken lines running back from the outer
corners of the eyes and there should be
pencillings on the cheeks. Thumb prints on the
ears are desirable. Good clear spotting on the
essential on the body. Legs should be barred
and/or spotted. A broken spine line is desirable.
The tail should be ringed.

Colours: Brown Dense black spotting on a
sable brown agouti ground. Nose leather black
or pink rimmed with black. Paw pads black or
brown. Eye rims black. Eye colour green.

Blue Blue spotting on a beige agouti ground.
Nose leather blue or pink rimmed with blue.
Paw pads and eye rims blue. Eye colour green.

Chocolate Rich chocolate brown spotting on a
bronze agouti ground. Nose leather chocolate
or pink rimmed with chocolate. Eye rims
chocolate. Paw pads chocolate. Eye colour
green.

Lilac Lilac spotting on a beige agouti ground. Nose leather faded lilac or pink rimmed with faded lilac. Paw pads and eye rims faded lilac. Eye colour green.

Red Rich red spotting on an apricot ground. Nose leather pink or pink rimmed with red. Paw pads pink. Eye rims pink or red. Eye colour – all shades of copper to green.

Cream Rich cream spotting on a paler cream ground. Nose leather pink or pink rimmed with cream. Paw pads pink. Eye rims pink or cream. Eye colour all shades of copper to green.

Coat Very short and fine in texture, glossy and close lying.

Notes and definitions Definition of a squint. When the eyes are so placed that they appear to look permanently at the nose.

NB The Oriental Spotted Tabby should be a beautifully balanced animal with head, ears and neck carried on a long svelte body, supported on fine legs and feet with a tail in proportion. The head and profile should be wedge shaped, neither round nor pointed. Expression alert and intelligent. The term 'clear spotting' defines spots that are not elongated to become broken stripes and exhibits should not be penalized for

lack of colour contrast between the spotting and ground colours. This particularly applies to Blue, Lilac and Cream Spotted Tabbies.

Foreign White–GCCF Variety 35
The body of the Foreign White cat should be lightly built, long and lissom and the cat should have a well proportioned and graceful appearance. The overall type should be similar to that of Siamese Cats. The head should be long and wedge-shaped in profile, and the face should narrow in straight lines to a fine muzzle. The eyes should be clear, brilliant blue and oriental in set; the ears wide at base, large and pricked. The coat should be completely white and the paw and nose leather pink. Coloured hairs and spotting on paw and nose leather are disqualifying faults.
Coat Pure white, short, silky, even and close-lying.
Head Face narrowing in straight lines to a fine muzzle, wedge-shaped profile with strong chin; even teeth and bite; head set well on graceful neck.
Ears Large, pricked with a good width between.
Eyes Almond-shaped and slanting, clear brilliant blue.
Body Long and slender, the rump carried higher than the shoulders. Well muscled, elegant.
Legs Long and proportionately slender; paws neat and oval.
Tail Long and tapering, whiplike, without kink.

Above, left **Solitaire Hapi** Lilac Oriental Spotted Tabby male showing the desired body type and balance.

Above, right Seemingly made of porcelain, Foreign White females **Chawalet Shimmering Lace** and **Chawalet White Fanfare**.

Two very unusual breeds make up the Foreign-type Longhaired section of the Cat Fancy. They are the Birman, or Sacred Cat of Burma, and the Turkish Cat.

The Birman has a pale body and coloured points, caused by the Himalayan factor and may be seal, blue, chocolate or lilac, although not all of these colours are recognized by all bodies. The outstanding feature of the breed, however, is the presence of pure white paws on all four feet. On the fore feet, the white line is sharply defined and is cut off, like a white glove, at the wrist. On the hind feet the white areas come to points at the heels, rather like gauntlets. This breed was first recognized in France in 1925, but did not receive official status from GCCF until 1966, and CFA in 1967.

In 1955 an Englishwoman travelling in Turkey acquired a pair of rare cats. They were white with long, silky hair and bright auburn markings. As they were commonly found in the region of Lake Van in south-eastern Turkey, they were originally called Van Cats. Eventually a breed was established and the name was changed to Swimming Cat when it was discovered that the animals enjoyed an occasional swim. In 1969 the breed was officially recognized by GCCF under the name of Turkish Cat, and numbers are increasing on the show benches of the world.

Comparative Points Scores (GCCF)

	Birman	Turkish
Body	20	10
Head	20	25
Eyes	5	10
Coat	25	} 35
Colour	} 20	
Condition		10
Tail	10	10
Total	100	100

Birman–GCCF Variety 13c

Body Long but low on the legs. Short strong paws. Four white paws, the white on the rear paws to go up the back of the legs to a point like a gauntlet.

Head Wide, round but strongly built, with full cheeks.
Fur Long with good full ruff, bushy tail, silky texture, slightly curled on belly.
Eyes Bright china blue.
Tail Bushy (not short).

Colour and Condition The colour is the same as Siamese, Seal and Blue but face (mask), tail and paws are dark brown in the seals, and blue/grey in the blues. However, the beige of the coat is slightly golden. The paws are white gloved, this being the characteristic of the Birman cat.

Turkish–GCCF Variety 13d

Colour and Coat Chalk white with no trace of yellow. Auburn markings on face with white blaze. Ears white; nose tip, pads and inside ears a delicate shell pink. Fur long, soft and silky to the roots; no woolly undercoat.

Head Short wedge; well feathered large ears upright and set fairly close together; long nose.
Eyes Round, colour light amber, rims pink-skinned.
Body Long but sturdy, legs medium in length; neat round feet with well tufted toes. Males should be particularly muscular on neck and shoulders.
Tail Full, medium length, auburn in colour with faint auburn rings in cats, more distinct ring markings in kittens.
NB This is the ideal, some cats may have small auburn markings irregularly spaced but this should not disqualify an otherwise good specimen.

Two breeds of foreign-type shorthaired cats are the Russian Blue and the Korat, and both are attractive and popular varieties.

The Russian Blue was once called the Archangel Cat, said to have been brought to Britain from the port of Archangel in the reign of Queen Elizabeth I. Whatever its beginnings the breed was well

Right **Champion Czarist Nickolenka** Russian Blue male.

Top left **Ramiro Labelle Versaille** Korat kitten.

established until the hardships of the Second World War severely depleted the breeding stock in Britain. Crosses with Siamese were made to save the breed and to increase the numbers, but unwanted Siamese characteristics were also introduced. With careful selective breeding, the Russian Blue is now being bred to its original type and with its unique dense coat like sealskin.

The Korat originated in Thailand where it is considered to be a lucky charm and is known as the Si-Sawat. In 1959 a pair was taken to the US and carefully controlled breeding programmes were established to prevent the infusion of any other blood into the breed. In 1966, the American associations accepted the Korat as an official breed, and they have become popular for showing and breeding, and as delightful pets. A few selected specimens have been exported to other countries, and breeders are asked to sign a pledge, ensuring that the breed will be kept pure. To date the breed has not been granted championship status by GCCF.

Russian Blue–GCCF Variety 16a

Colour Clear blue and even throughout. In maturity free from tabby markings or shading. Medium blue is preferred.

Coat Short, thick and very fine, standing up soft and silky like seal skin. Very different from any other breed. Coat is double so that it has a distinct silvery sheen. The texture and appearance of the coat is the truest criterion of the Russian Blue.

Body Long and graceful in outline and carriage. Medium strong bone.
Tail Fairly long and tapering.
Legs and Feet Long legs. Feet small and oval.
Head Short wedge with flat skull; forehead and nose straight forming an angle. Prominent whisker pads. Strong chin.
Nose leather and pads Blue.
Eyes Vivid green, set rather wide apart, almond in shape.

Ears Large and pointed, wide at base and set vertically to the head. Skin of ears thin and transparent, with little inside hair.

Faults White or tabby markings. Cobby or heavy build. Square head. Yellow or blue in eyes. Siamese type is undesirable.

With-hold certificates White anywhere. Incorrect eye colour. Siamese type.

Korat Cats–GCCF Variety 34
This variety does not carry challenge certificate status

Head and Ears Heart-shaped when viewed from the front of the head with breadth between and across the eyes gently curving to a well-developed but neither sharp pointed nor squared muzzle. Forehead large, flat. Ears are large and with a rounded tip and large flare base, set high on head, giving an alert expression. Inside ears sparsely furnished.

Eyes, Colour and Shape Large and luminous, particularly prominent. Wide open and oversized for the face. Eye aperture, which appears as well-rounded when fully open has Asian slant when closed or partially closed. Colour, brilliant green, but amber cast acceptable. Kittens and adolescents up to 2 years have yellow, amber or amber-green eyes. *Nose* Short and with slight downward curve. Profile shows a stop between forehead and nose. *Chin and jaw* Strong.

Body and Tail Medium-sized body, strong, muscular and semi-cobby. Medium bone. Back carried in a curve. Tail medium in length, heavier at the base, tapering to a rounded tip. Non-visible kink at extremity permissible.

Body Colour Silver-blue all over, tipped with silver, the more silver tipping the better. Without shading or tabby markings. When the coat is short the silver sheen is intensified. Silver tipping develops through kittenhood and adolescence to full intensity at about 2 years.

Nose leather and lips Dark blue or lavender.
Paw pads Dark blue ranging to lavender with pinkish tinge.

Coat Single. Hair, short to medium in length, glossy, fine and lying close to body. The coat over the spine inclined to break as the cat moves.

Legs and Paws Legs should be well-proportioned to body, paws oval. 5 toes in front, 4 behind.

Condition Perfect physical condition, muscular, alert appearance.

Faults White hair or spots, wrong eye colour.

It is possible that rex genes, which cause the hair of a cat to curl, turned up many times in the past, but it was not until 1950 that an unusual curly-coated kitten was noticed in a litter born on a farm in Cornwall. The kitten grew up and was mated back to his mother, and a new breed was born. Ten years later, another curly kitten was discovered in the neighbouring county of Devon, and the interested breeders assumed that its coat was due to the same gene as that found in the Cornish Rex. Breeding tests proved this to be invalid, however, and the two types of rex cats are quite distinct.

GCCF recognize the Cornish and Devon Rex as two separate breeds and they have entirely different standards. In the US, ACFA provides classes for both Devon and Cornish Rex, but only the latter are shown in CFA Rex classes.

Rex fur is very interesting as the coat is devoid of the guard and awn hairs found in a cat with a normal coat. The hair length is only about 50% that of normal cats and there are less hairs present in the skin. The effect of this is to produce a short plush pelage which curls, waves or ripples over the body. In the Cornish Rex, the coat is generally very dense and covers the animal in the desired deep waves and curls. Even the tail is closely curled and the effect is completed by crinkled whiskers and eyebrows. The coat of the Devon Rex is slightly harsher and the cat is often a little short of fur, especially after moulting or shedding, under the belly and along the neck.

Comparative Points Scores (GCCF)

	Cornish Rex	Devon Rex
Coat	35	40
Whiskers & Eyebrows	5	
Head	15	15
Eyes	10	5
Ears	10	10
Body & Legs	20	25
Tail	5	5
Total	100	100

Cornish Rex–GCCF Variety 33

Coat Short and plushy, without guard hairs, and should curl, wave or ripple, particularly on back and tail. Whiskers and eyebrows crinkled and of good length All coat colours acceptable, but any white markings must be symmetrical, except in Tortoiseshell and white.
Head Medium wedge. Head length about one-third more than the maximum width, narrowing to a strong chin. The skull flat. Profile straight from centre of forehead to end of nose.
Eyes Oval, medium in size, colour in keeping with coat colour.
Ears Large, set rather high on head, wide at base, tapering to rounded tips and well covered with fine fur.
Body and Legs Body hard and muscular, slender and of medium length. Legs long and straight, giving an overall appearance of being high on the legs. Paws small and oval.
Tail Long, fine and tapering, well covered with curly fur.

Faults
1 Asymmetrical white markings, except in Tortoiseshell and white. 2. Shaggy or too short a coat. 3 Bare patches a fault in kittens and a serious fault in cats. 4 Shorthair type head, or too long a wedge. 5 Small ears. 6 Cobby body. 7 Lack of firm muscles. 8 Short or bare tail. 9 Kinks in tail.

Devon Rex–GCCF Variety 33a

Coat Very short and fine, wavy and soft, without guard hairs. Whiskers and eyebrows crinkled, rather coarse and of medium length. All coat colours, except bi-colours, acceptable. Any white markings other than in Tortoiseshell and white a fault.
Head Wedge-shaped with face full cheeked. Short muzzle with strong chin and whisker break. Nose with a strongly marked stop. Forehead curving back to a flat skull.
Eyes Wide set, large, oval and sloping towards outer edges of ears. Colour in keeping with coat colour, or except in Si-Rex, chartreuse, green or yellow.
Ears Large, set rather low, very wide at base, tapering to rounded tops and well covered with fine fur. With or without ear muffs.
Body, legs and neck Body hard and muscular, slender and of medium length, broad in chest, carried high on long slim legs, with length of hind legs emphasized. Paws small and oval. Neck slender.
Tail Long, fine and tapering, well covered with short fur.

Faults
1 Straight or shaggy coat. 2 Any white markings, other than Tortoiseshell and white. 3 Bare patches a fault in kittens and serious fault in cats. 4 Narrow, long or Shorthair head. 5 Cobby body. 6 Lack of firm muscles. 7 Small or high set ears. 8 Short, bare or bushy tail. 9 Kinks in tail.

NB Many Devon Rex Cats have down on the underparts. This is not classed as bareness. Si-Rex is simply a rex cat with Siamese colour restriction.

Top left **Rupasajo Barry Muscatel** beautiful chocolate brown Cornish Rex male.

Top right **Blue Betty Boop** Blue Devon Rex queen.

Above **Amaska Madame Butterfly** strikingly marked tortie-and-white Cornish female.

Two unusual breeds which mutated quite separately are the Manx and the Scottish Fold.

The Manx or 'rumpie' is a tailless cat of standard shorthaired type except that its hindquarters are high with deep flanks causing it to have a characteristic gait. Manx parents often produce kittens with full tails, or some with abbreviated tails which are called 'stumpies'. Tailless cats occur in many parts of the world, but the breed known as the Manx originated on the Isle of Man, possibly stemming from cats first landed on the island by Phoenician trading ships.

An old-established breed, the Manx is known throughout the world and recognized by most governing bodies. It is, however, a comparatively rare breed because the gene which makes it tailless may also affect the whole of the vertebrae and sometimes other malformations occur, too, which result in the kittens' death *in utero* or shortly after birth.

The first Scottish Fold appeared in a litter of kittens born in Scotland in 1961. Cats of this breed look like ordinary, stocky shorthaired cats but have distinctive folded ears. Eventually, breeding programmes were formulated and interest in these unusual cats spread to the US. In Britain, tests were carried out which indicated that the cats often had other related skeletal defects, and so GCCF refused to accept the breed, even on a provisional basis. In the US, however, the cats were recognized for registration by CFA in 1974.

Manx – GCCF Variety 25

Head As near to British as possible. Fairly round and large with prominent cheeks. Appearance, rather jowled. Nose longish without a definite nose break but with no appearance of 'snipeyness'.
Ears Wide at base, tapering slightly to a point. Taller than standard British and set more on top of head.
Eyes Large and round. Colour corresponding preferably to British standard colours.
Body Solid, compact, cannot be too short and ending on a definite round rump. Back legs higher than front making an incline from back to front. Flanks of great depth.
Legs Of good substance with front legs short and well set apart to show good depth of chest. Back legs longer with a heavy muscular thigh.
Coat Short, good texture. Double coated showing a well padded quality arising from the longer outer coat and the thicker undercoat. Coat colour and markings only taken into account when other points are equal.
Tail Absolute taillessness is essential in a show specimen and there should be a decided hollow at the end of the backbone where, ordinarily, the tail would begin.

Faults A rise of bone at the end of the spine. A non-visible joint or cartilage.

With-hold certificates Definitely visible tail joint. Incorrect number of toes.

Above **Champion Calliope Rosey Dawn** red and white Manx female.

Left **Denisla Morag** a Scottish bred Scottish Fold.

Scale of Points

Taillessness	25
Coat texture	15
Head and ears	15
Body shape	25
Eyes	5
Shortness of back	10
Condition	5
Total	100

This page, top left
Cheldene Big Mac Lilac
Pointed Balinese male.

Above Shaded Silver
male.

Above right **Tobias
Tybalt** Cameo Shorthair
male.

Right, centre **Solitaire
Silver Serval** Silver
Egyptian Mau female

Right, below **Smithway
Alfredo** Red Tabby Peke
Faced Persian.

Facing page, top Maine
Coon neuter.

Centre, right **Omicron
Ophelia** Chocolate
Tortie Longhair female.

Centre, far right
Omicron Opal Lilac
Cream Longhair female.

Below, right **Kambuku
Mariquita** Cinnamon
Oriental female.

Below, far right
Omicron Organdie Lilac
Self Longhair female.

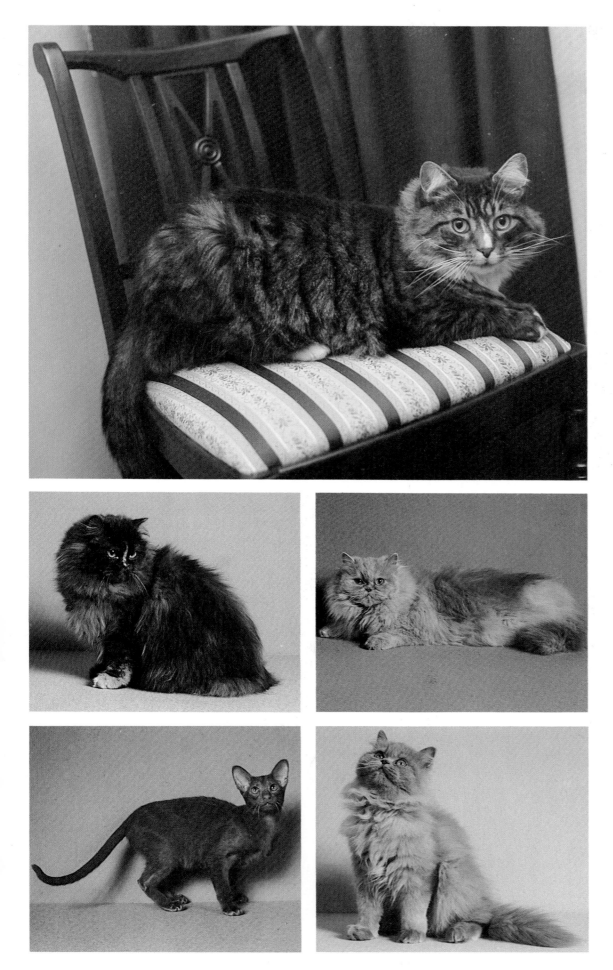

The most important function of any club is its link between its members and the governing body to which it is affiliated, and this is particularly true in the case of a cat club.

Britain Here, the Governing Council of the Cat Fancy (GCCF) is made up of delegates from its affiliated clubs, and has various integral committees to deal with such things as finance and disciplinary matters. A cat club may apply for affiliation after it has proved its necessity and efficiency by running its affairs in a satisfactory manner for a certain period of time. The membership must consist of at least 100 fully paid-up persons at the time of application, and if affiliation is granted, the club may elect a delegate to attend the four Council meetings held each year. When the membership exceeds 150, application may be made for the club to elect a second delegate to Council. Substitute delegates, formally proposed, seconded and passed by the membership of a club, may attend Council meetings if for any reason the appointed delegate is unable to be present.

It is usual for the delegates to be briefed at committee or general meetings of their clubs in any policy matters which might arise in Council. The delegate is expected to vote as instructed by the club he represents and not to reflect his own, personal views. Clubs may, after discussion in committee or general meeting, decide to raise important issues by having propositions put on the Council agenda. It is in this way that active, live clubs ensure that progressive steps are taken by governing bodies and that the welfare of cats does not get overlooked.

America Of the eight governing bodies for cats in the United States, the Cat Fanciers Association (CFA) is the largest with many affiliated clubs. As well as authorizing shows across the United States, CFA trains and appoints judges, controls a nationwide scoring system for cats winning in its affiliated clubs' shows, and produces an excellent and mighty tome each year, the *CFA Yearbook*. The oldest of the American governing bodies is the American Cat Association.

The other cat registries in the United States are:
American Cat Fanciers Association
Cat Fanciers Federation
Crown Cat Fanciers Federation
United Cat Fanciers.
NB There are reciprocal arrangements between the appropriate organizations, so that suitably qualified Canadian cats can be shown and compete in the US, and vice versa.

Australia In Australia, pedigree cats are widely and sparsely distributed across the vast continent. This has led to the formation of separate governing bodies in different states. Victoria and Queensland each have three or four governing bodies, Northern Territory, New South Wales, South Australia, West Australia and the island of Tasmania each have one. Most of these bodies have rules similar to GCCF and also follow the British standard of points. The exception to this is the governing body of New South Wales, which has an entirely unique set of rules. There are many clubs in Australia, and the fancy is very lively, with many well attended shows.

New Zealand's approach to the cat fancy and registration is very similar to Britain's, although in recent years it has taken several progressive steps in formulating breeding programmes, and the acceptance of new varieties.

The New Zealand Cat Fancy Incorporated is the governing council of the cat fancy of New Zealand and has many affiliated clubs, some of which produce excellent magazines for their members. Each year a different cat club manages the celebrated National Cat Show, sponsored by a manufacturer of pet foods.

Clubs, societies and associations in Australia, Austria, Belgium, Czechoslovakia, Denmark, Finland, France, Germany, Holland, Italy, Norway, Sweden and Switzerland are affiliated to the Federation Internationale d'Europe (FIFE). There are other bodies, too, such as the Cercle Feline de Paris, the Association Feline de France and the Association Feline du Centre. All these bodies cater for all breeds of cat and license international cat shows throughout Europe. Under the rules of FIFE the training of judges is a serious affair which produces highly qualified and respected officials. Having stewarded at four international shows and acted as a pupil-judge at six similar shows, a written and oral examination is taken before two existing and senior judges. Separate examinations are set for the judging of longhaired and shorthaired cats, and a judge that expects to officiate in countries other than his own is expected to speak at least two languages.

Most governing bodies throughout the world of cats act in a totally democratic way, electing officials and officers to be wholly representative of the cat fancy in their country. Now and again personalities and politics overshadow the main aims of the cat fancy, but the strength of the exhibitors and breeders ensures that it is the welfare of cats and the protection of policies that eventually wins the day.

In the development of new breeds or colour varieties, various governing bodies lay down rules and restrictions, mainly covering the registration of the various offspring. Even in the breeding of established varieties, certain cross-matings are allowed, while others are taboo.

It is considered quite in order to mate similar breeds together if they have the same eye-colour in some cases, or the desired type. In the Persians, Blue and Cream are mated quite frequently. A Blue female mated to a Cream male gives Blue male kittens and the ethereal Blue-Cream females. Mating a Cream female to a Blue male gives Cream male kittens and Blue-Cream females. Blue-Creams are always female, and are therefore mated to Blue or Cream males. To a Blue sire the kittens will be Blue or Cream if male and Blue or Blue-Cream if female. The same queen mated to a Cream male, however, will produce Blue and Cream males, while the females may be Blue, Blue-Cream or the coveted Cream.

White longhaired cats are often mated to Persians of other colours, while Blacks and Blues are often crossed. In the longhaired non-selfs (non-solids), some exquisite new varieties have been produced by careful manipulation of genes in breeding programmes. Just as the silver series produced the range of cats from the heavily marked Smoke, through the Shaded Silver to the delicately tipped Chinchilla, so the addition of the orange gene to the silver produced the Cameo cats. The deepest-coloured is the Red Smoke; then comes the Shaded Cameo and lastly the red-tipped Shell Cameo.

Planned programmes produced the popular Colourpoint Persians, known as Himalayans in the United States, and these are now bred in every points colour, including some with exotic tabby markings. During the development of the Colourpoints, the Chocolate and Lilac Selfs also appeared and a few very rare Chocolate-Cream and Lilac-Cream females.

In the Shorthairs, never numerically strong on the show bench, there are fewer progressive breeders to bring forward new varieties. In spite of this, Shorthaired Cameo cats have been exhibited, and the show world in Britain was entranced by the appearance of the British Tipped, a white cat with black tipping, like a shorthaired Chinchilla.

Self Chocolate and Self Lilac Shorthairs are very striking, with deep yellow to gold eye-colour and should make welcome additions to the show bench when bred in sufficient numbers to gain acceptance to the Cat Fancy.

In the Foreign Shorthairs several new colour varieties of Abyssinian are now bred, and some of the pale shades are very attractive. With the typical small litter size of the breed, however, progress is slow and the breeders have to exercise great care and patience in their programmes.

Burmese varieties now exist in all the possible permutations (see page 188), although it is conceivable that someone will attempt to gain acceptance for jet-black and pure white cats with Burmese forebears.

In the Oriental group (see page 195) every

possible colour variety is planned, with the addition of all patterns of tabby, and the silver gene, giving an awe-inspiring number of possibilities, daunting the more conservative members of the fancy. Blacks, Whites and Lilacs have joined the already established Havana or Oriental Chocolate. Oriental Blues have not found the same favour in Britain, probably because the Foreign Blue niche is already occupied by the Russian and the Korat.

Oriental Tabbies are recognized when spotted in pattern; mackerel, ticked and classic still have to be bred in sufficient numbers to gain their breed number in GCCF but are accepted by some other bodies, including CFA. Even the spotted are still classed as experimental when their body colour is silver.

When breeding programmes are drawn up by specialist clubs and followed by groups of dedicated breeders, standards for many traits are fixed and those for new coat colours or patterns decided. The foundation stock in many cases is carefully picked, not only for the desired characteristics of appearance, but also for health, strength and stamina, the breeding record of the parents and temperament. It is no accident then that some of the newly developed breeds often produce super-kittens – disease-resistant, highly intelligent, loving and beautiful animals.

Progressive breeding takes a lot of time, space and finance, and it is thanks to those who have undertaken the often controversial steps along the paths of cross-breeding that we have the wonderful diversity of pedigree cats gracing the show benches and hearth-rugs of today.

Above Last-minute grooming is vital in the presentation of longhaired exhibits. Here one of the Marisha Colourpoints receives her owner's attention.

Far left Steward holds up the Best in Show award-winning British kitten for its well deserved applause as its win is announced by the show-manager.

Having bought a pedigree kitten for showing, as opposed to one of purely pet potential, the first steps in entering a cat show are usually taken under the guidance of the kitten's breeder. A really good kitten may well have been entered in several shows before sale, and in this instance the paperwork will probably include tickets, tags or entry confirmation for an approaching cat show.

The basic ingredients for a show cat are health, good condition and conformity to the breed standard. It is important to buy a kitten of show potential if exhibiting is the aim, but many people buy a fairly inexpensive kitten and then decide to start showing it later.

The first step in showing is to apply to the governing body or check through cat magazines for a list of official shows for the current season. The list should include the names and addresses of the show secretaries, dates and venues. It must be remembered that show entries may close two months before show date in some countries, to enable the office work and catalogue to be completed in good time.

Having chosen a suitable show, a letter requesting a schedule and entry form should be sent to the secretary, enclosing a self-addressed, stamped envelope for the reply. The envelope should be fairly large, as some show schedules are bulky.

When the schedule comes, it should be checked to ascertain that there is sufficient time in which to send the entry before the closing date. GCCF show schedules give a full list of show rules, which must be carefully read and adhered to. Many club secretaries are sympathetic to novice exhibitors and are pleased to answer any queries by telephone. Show managers often publish specific times for answering telephone queries. Running shows is usually done without any remuneration. It is hard work, taking many hours of spare time and is usually undertaken by busy people working during the daytime. Therefore queries should be carefully formulated before one calls the show manager, kept as brief and succinct as possible, and the advice given followed to the letter.

Having read the rules, the entry form is filled in, using the information from the cat's registration form and copying the details carefully in block letters or else typing it. It is from this information that the judging books and catalogues are compiled, so it is vital that the information given is accurate. Most governing bodies check the show catalogues after the event, against the registration forms, and if there are any discrepancies, the cat may be disqualified.

Most show rules are fairly simple and straightforward, and when the form is completed it should be signed and sent with the entry fee to the show manager or entry clerk as instructed. In some countries an acknowledgement is made automatically; in others this is only done if a stamped self-addressed card is enclosed. Some show secretaries send out the documents and tickets prior to the show, while in other cases these are collected at the show hall on the day.

Having entered and been accepted, it is time to start on the gentle show preparation necessary to produce a winning cat. The animal should be wormed if necessary, and it is a good idea to have the veterinary surgeon check over its teeth, ears and claws. (In the US it is necessary to clip the cat's claws before it is benched.) A good, well-balanced diet should be provided, and the cat's coat should be lightly but carefully groomed every day in the way recommended for its breed. The object is to produce the cat in peak condition on show day, and so it needs building up to that event slowly.

When grooming the cat, a pad of cloth or a buffer can be used to lightly bang the muscles of the shoulders, back and thighs, promoting good circulation and a bloom on the coat. All dead hair should be taken out, and the ears and claws should be kept very clean.

The cat should be friendly with all humans and, ideally, should have been accustomed to being picked up by strangers. If a small pen can be obtained, the cat will benefit from being shut in this, perhaps at meal-times, for a few days.

Show cats need to travel well, so it is a good plan to accustom the kitten to enjoy going in its carrier and being transported without fuss. Feeding the kitten its favourite treat after releasing it from the carrier helps in this training.

As show day approaches, the show equipment as laid down in the rules must be prepared. In GCCF shows a white blanket is necessary. This should be of plain wool or man-made fibre, without any fancy trimmings or bindings. The cat also needs a plain white toilet tray or bowl and a white drinking-water container. Some shows have stalls where the equipment can be purchased, and these may also be advertised in the schedule, with details of mail-order services. Litter is required for the toilet tray, although some experienced exhibitors use torn kitchen paper towels or toilet tissue. If the show requires that a tally or numbered tag be worn by the exhibit, the necessary ribbon or elastic must be procured.

On the eve of show day the cat should be thoroughly groomed and checked over. All the equipment should be checked and packed, along with the cat's favourite food in a sealed container. It is quite a good idea to take a small bottle or flask of water for filling the water bowl. Strange water can upset the digestion of some cats.

Plan to arrive at the show hall for vetting-in as early as possible. There is often a considerable line of people waiting with their cats, and the risk of infection is obviously reduced for those who arrive first. The veterinary surgeon's steward removes the cat from its carrier, then it is checked expertly for any signs of pregnancy or lactation if it is female, entirety if male, parasites, deformities or disease. There are also strict rules on the improper preparation of exhibits by plucking, shaving or colouring any of the coat. The veterinary officer's decision is final, and the cat rejected for any reason is banned from the show hall. If all is well, the vetting-in slip is signed and the cat can be taken into the hall.

Inside the hall the array of numbered pens can be confusing, but if the numbers do not run consecutively, there is usually a floor plan on display. Stewards and officials wearing distinctive badges are generally on hand to help if asked and most shows have an information table.

Having found the pen, it may be cleaned or wiped with disinfectant if necessary, although it will have been steam-sterilized before the show. The cat's equipment is carefully arranged inside the pen, then the cat can be lightly groomed before being settled into place, with much petting and coaxing. The carrier and any spare bags must be stowed neatly out of sight under the pen.

In shows where the cats are taken to the judges it is now time to settle down to wait for the action. In shows where the judges assess the cats at their pens an announcement will be made to clear the show hall. When this comes, it is important to go swiftly, making sure that nothing that can identify the cat is left on or near the pen.

It is only a short while before the breed class results start to be posted on the awards boards, and the suspense ends as the cat's placing in the class can be seen.

After judging, or at the appointed time for the admission of the general public, it is permissible to go to the cat's pen, to feed and reassure it. In some countries judging of miscellaneous and other classes continues in the afternoon, but the hall is not cleared again.

It is forbidden to speak to the judge or stewards while judging is in progress, but most judges are pleasant and kind, and will be pleased to give you a verbal opinion on your cat, if approached courteously when it is obvious that they have quite finished judging for the day.

Far left At GCCF Shows exhibits are placed in unadorned pens and allowed only a plain white blanket, feeding bowls and litter tray. A numbered tally or disc is hung around the cat's neck with ribbon, tape or fine elastic.

Below Early morning and the first arrivals form a queue outside the show hall as they wait for the veterinary surgeons within to pass the exhibits before they can enter the exhibition area.

Cat shows in Britain are held under the rules of the GCCF, and are organized by various specialist and area cat clubs. The one exception is the Supreme Show, an annual event staged by the GCCF and limited to cats, kittens and neuters which have qualified by wins at other shows.

There are three categories of cat show – exemption, sanction and Championship – and all have slightly different rules and regulations. Exemption shows are arranged to enable newly affiliated clubs to gain experience in show management, when they may apply for a licence to stage a sanction show. Only after completing such shows to the satisfaction of Council may a licence be granted for the staging of a Championship cat show.

Although all licensed shows must engage the services of officially appointed judges, it is only at the Championship shows that the coveted challenge certificates are awarded. At exemption and sanction shows there are breed classes and many other miscellaneous and club classes, with prizes awarded for cats, kittens and neuters winning first, second and third places.

At Championship shows entire cats over the age of nine months compete in Open breed classes against other cats of the same variety. If the winner is of very high quality, the judge may also award an official GCCF Challenge Certificate. To become a Champion, a cat must win three such certificates at three separate shows, and under three different judges.

Neutered cats compete under similar rules, although varieties are grouped together in some Open classes. Winning neuters may be awarded Premier Challenge Certificates, and if a neutered cat is awarded three such certificates at three separate shows, under three different judges, it achieves the title of Premier.

Full Champion cats can compete against one another in special classes to win Grand Challenge Certificates, and the runner-up is given a Reserve ticket. Three such certificates, issued by three different judges, make the cat a Grand Champion. Full Premier neuters have similar classes which enable them to attain the rank of Grand Premiers.

Kittens may be shown from the age of three months, and have their own breed classes. All pedigree cats, kittens and neuters must be registered with GCCF in order to be shown, and their ownership must be officially transferred well before show date if the animals have changed hands.

Open class winners may compete for the title of Best of Breed at some shows, while at others a panel of senior judges makes a selection from the winning exhibits for the titles of Best in Show Cat, Kitten and Neuter.

All shows in Britain are one-day affairs. The exhibitors arrive between 8 a.m. and 10 a.m., when their cats are checked by a panel of veterinary surgeons. Each exhibit is placed in a numbered, anonymous pen with a plain white blanket, toilet tray and water bowl. A numbered disc or tally, corresponding with the number of the pen, is hung around the cat's neck on thin elastic or ribbon. At approximately 10 a.m. the exhibitors must clear the hall while the judging commences.

White-coated judges, accompanied by similarly dressed stewards, judge the classes, using a book of numerical slips, written out in triplicate. Each cat in the class is taken from its pen by the steward for the judge's inspection, and each judge has a small portable table or wheeled trolley on which to stand the cat if necessary. The judge writes a critique of each exhibit, with reference to the

official standard of points for its breed, before passing on to the next cat. Judges and stewards clean their hands with a disinfectant solution between handling the exhibits, and the steward also cleans the trolley's surface. Having assessed every cat in the class, the judge places them in order of merit, awarding first, second and third prizes, followed by a Reserve, and may also give Very Highly Commended, Highly Commended or Commended prizes, although these awards do not carry prize money or rosettes.

The results are entered on the numbered judging slips and two of the copies are taken to the show administration table, while the judge retains the third copy. At the table the results are entered into the awards book; one copy is retained by the show secretary and the other copy is posted on the awards board for the information of the exhibitors.

Judges always complete the Open breed classes first, as these are the important ones, carrying the most meaningful awards. Then they carry on to judge the miscellaneous classes such as the Breeder's, Limit and Novice, followed by the classes offered by various area and specialist clubs for their members. The club classes are often very full, and have all sorts of cats entered, taxing the judge's skill and knowledge of several breeds.

By the end of the afternoon the judge may have handled and assessed around one hundred exhibits. After the last slip is handed in, the judge receives an official show catalogue listing the names and details of the exhibits corresponding to the numbered pens.

Winning cats may receive small money prizes or rosettes, and those winning Best of Breed or Best in Show often receive silver trophies and other special prizes. Most shows close at around 6 p.m., when owners, judges and officials gather up their belongings to journey home.

Above **Grand Premier Brynbuboo Katies Lad,** British Blue, adds to his wins with a Best in Show at the unique Kensington Kitten & Neuter Cat Club's annual Premier event in London.

Below Stewards bring exhibits to the ring for judging at a show staged by the Nederlandse Vereniging van Kattevrienden.

Right In the main hall at the same show, exhibits wait their turns in their own personalized pens, attended by their owners and well away from the judging area.

Cat shows on the European Continent are usually spread over two-day periods, with the individual judging being completed on the first day, and Best in Show and the signing of the certificates by the judges on the second day.

The cats are penned in the main show hall, and judging takes place in a separate room, or a screened area of the hall. As the judges do not see the exhibits in their pens, these may be decorated with coloured curtains and draperies and adorned with ribbons, streamers and rosettes won at other shows, as well as carrying pedigree information and cattery advertising material. Stewards carry the exhibits to the judging area where clean empty pens are arranged. Each judge has a steward or two, plus a clerk in some instances and an interpreter if necessary. There are no club classes at European shows, and few if any, side or miscellaneous classes.

The exhibits come from several countries, so two types of honours are awarded. First is the Certificat d'Aptitude de Championnat or CAC, equivalent to the British Challenge Certificate. Three certificates issued by three judges complete a cat's championship. Secondly, there is the Certificat d'Aptitude de Championnat Internationale de Beaute, or CACIB, and three of these certificates won in three different countries elevate the champion cat to the status of

International Champion.

Similar awards exist for neutered cats, which can win the Certificat d'Aptitude de Premier, or CAP, three times to become a Premier, or the Certificat d'Aptitude de Premier Internationale de Beaute, CAPIB, to become an International Premier.

The Best in Show exhibits are usually selected by a panel of judges from winners of the Open class or the Best of Colour. In the longhaired section there are Best Longhair Cat, Best Longhair Kitten and Best Longhair Neuter. There are similar awards for the best shorthairs, which include both types of shorthairs and the Siamese. Winners do not receive prize money in Europe. Instead they have beautiful ribbons and rosettes, medals and trophies.

In the United States of America and Canada the majority of cat shows are conducted along the same general lines. The cats may or may not have to be vetted-in on arrival at the show hall, depending upon the relevant rules of the organizing body. They are penned in comfortable decorated cages, where they can be attended by their owners at all times.

Judging takes place in various rings placed around the show hall. There are usually four rings, each presided over by one judge assisted by clerks,

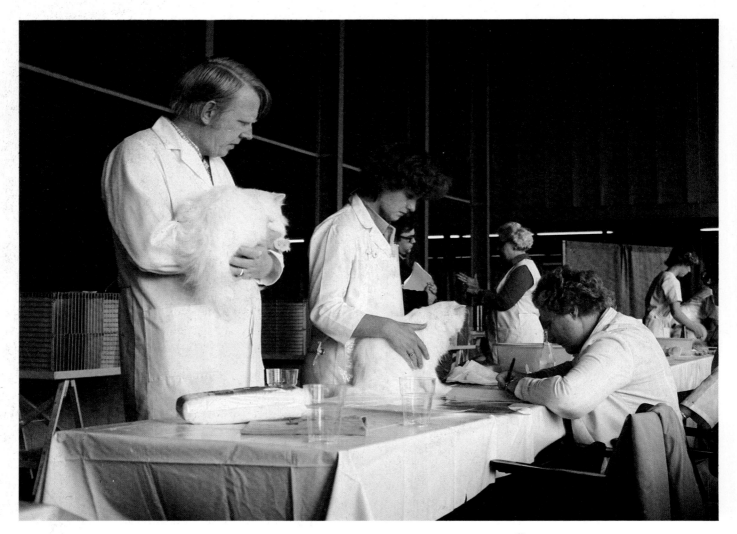

and each ring is, in effect, a small complete show within the main show. The judging ring consists of a row of pens and tables for the judge and assistants, usually arranged in a 'L'-shape. There are seats for interested exhibitors and spectators to occupy for a good view of the judging and placings.

Cats, kittens and neuters all have their own classes, in which they compete against other similar exhibits. An announcement is made telling the exhibitors the classes to be judged in each ring and the catalogue numbers of the cats in those classes. Corresponding numbers are placed on the empty pens in the judging rings, and the exhibitors are expected to carry their cats to the correct pens and place them securely inside before taking a seat to view the judging.

The judge carefully examines each cat in the class and, assessing its points score, compares it with its competitors before awarding the ribbons – the blue ribbon denoting first place, the red ribbon, second, and the yellow ribbon, third. Cats of each breed and sex are split into separate classes such as Open, Champion and Grand Champion, according to the status already achieved, to make the competition fair. If the winners of the male and

female Open classes are considered to be of very high merit, a special Winner's ribbon is also awarded. Judging then takes place between the winners in each breed to find the Best of Color, Best Opposite Sex, and so on. Various bodies have different rules for the making of Champion and Grand Champion cats, but, basically, a cat winning four to six Winner's ribbons – one in each ring at one show, or in some of the rings at two or three shows – achieves Championship status. Grand Champions achieve their exalted position by complex mathematical systems which vary between the associations concerned.

At the end of judging, each officiating judge concludes events by presenting final awards to the top-scoring cats. In the largest of the associations, CFA, these may consist of the five or ten top cats being chosen and awarded Best Cat, Second Best Cat and so on.

The judge generally announces the top finals winners in reverse order, adding to the suspense of the occasion. It is usual to have each cat taken from its pen as the award is made, and shown to the audience, with an explanation of its winning features.

When the show is a two-day one, most exhibits

An exquisite Golden Chinchilla kitten **Araenaca**, captivates Dutch judge Mevr Smeehuijzen van der Velde.

are shown in their first ring on the morning of the first day, followed by a second ring in the afternoon. Two more rings follow on the second day and complete the show.

Showing in North America is tiring for the exhibitors, as they must be constantly alert for the calling of their cat's number in order to get it to the relevant ring on time. With several exhibits at one show, it is necessary to have plenty of stamina and the ability to remain calm and organized.

Some Australian cat shows are run on similar lines to British ones; others are run on the ring system, as in the United States of America and Canada. The cats are penned either by breeds or by exhibitors. In breed grouping, exhibits are penned according to their breeds and varieties, and this more usual way of penning is better for the judges, who carry out their duties in the body of the show hall. If cats belonging to each exhibitor are penned together, the show is confusing for the visitors and tiring for the judges, although the exhibitors gain by having their cats adjacent to one another.

Cats are judged to the official standards of points, and Challenge certificates are awarded to

Open Class winners of high merit. In some associations three challenge certificates entitle the cat to become a Champion, but in New South Wales Champion status is achieved by winning a set number of points. Judges usually finish their assignments by lunchtime, when an announcement is made, and exhibitors are allowed to dress their show pens for display to the general public.

Australian cat shows are usually held to aid some charity, and the prizes are normally given in the form of trophies rather than money. The trophy tables are always eye-catching displays of the items to be won by the top exhibits.

New Zealand has a thriving, lively cat fancy, with well-attended, well-filled cat shows. The cats are judged to standards very similar to those of GCCF, and exhibits are assessed at their pens by the judge, assisted by one or two stewards. After judging is completed, exhibitors are allowed to decorate their pens. Champions and Grand Champions are made up in a way similar to that employed in GCCF shows, and cats can achieve top show awards such as Best in Show, Second Best, and so on.

Above The author demonstrates the finer points of an Oriental Spotted Tabby during a judges' symposium in London.

Comparative Points Scores (GCCF)	Brown Tabby	Red Tabby	Silver Tabby	Chinchilla	(Shaded Silver)	Smoke	(Cameo)	Blue-Cream	Bi-Colour	Tortoiseshell	Tortie & White	Colourpoint
Colour			40	25		40		30	25	} 50	} 50	10
Coat	50	50	} 15	} 15		} 10		} 20	15			15
Condition												
Head	20	20	20	20	experimental – GCCF	20	experimental – GCCF	20	25	20	20	30
Eyes – shape colour	15	15	10	15		10		15	15	15	15	10 / 10
Body	15	15	10	15		15		15	15	15	15	15
Tail			5	10		5			5			10
	100	100	100	100		100		100	100	100	100	100

Comparative Points Score (GCCF)	Foreign Black (Oriental Black) (Ebony)	Havana (Oriental Chestnut)	Foreign Lilac (Oriental Lavender)	Oriental Spotted Tabby	Foreign White
Head	15	15	15	15	20
Ears	5	5	5	5	
Body	15	15	15	15	15
Legs & Paws	5	5	5	5	10
Tail	5	5	5	5	10
Eyes – Shape	5	} 20	} 20	5	10
Colour	5			5	10
Coat – Colour	30	20	20		5
(Spotting)				30	
Texture	10	10	10	10	10
Condition	5	5	5	5	10
	100	100	100	100	100

Comparative Points Score (GCCF)	Russian Blue	Korat	
Colour	20	20	
Coat	} 25	10 { shortness	4
		texture	4
Condition		5 { close lying	2
Body & Tail	25	25 { Body	15
		Legs & Feet	5
		Tail	5
Eyes – Shape	} 15	15	
Colour		5	
Head	15	20 { Broad head	5
		Profile	6
		Breadth between eyes	4
		Ear set & placement	5
	100	100	

Even the non-pedigree pet puss can achieve top awards. At his first show tiny tabby **Fusspot** swept the board and made it to the Best in Show pen where he proceeded to sleep away the remainder of the show.

abortion   the premature expulsion of a foetus.

abscess   a localized collection of pus or matter, forming a lump under the skin – usually results from a bite or other injury. If not treated it can burst and discharge.

Abyssinian   cat of foreign type with a typically ticked coat.

ACA   American Cat Association.

ACFA   American Cat Fanciers Association.

affiliation   term applied to clubs and associations when attached to a larger governing body or other organizations.

affix   a cattery name used at the end of a cat's registered name. In the US this is known as a suffix.

afterbirth   see placenta.

agouti   the wild-type of coat pattern found in cats in which the hairs are banded, giving a ticked effect.

albino   a cat with a lack of colouring due to a recessive gene, causing the coat to appear white (not to be confused with Dominant White).

allergy   a state of hypersensitivity which may be due to drugs, parasites, food or cleaning materials.

almond   term given to eye-shape in some Foreign or Oriental breeds.

alter   to neuter (see castration and spaying).

amnion   the foetal envelope enclosing the foetus.

amniotic fluid   surrounds the foetus, cushioning it and protecting it within the amnion. This fluid is seen when the amnion ruptures during the birth process and the term 'waters have broken' is commonly used.

Angora   one of the original varieties of longhaired cat, first found in Turkey.

anoestrus   the resting period of the oestrus cycle.

anorexia   loss of appetite often associated with the onset of several feline diseases.

antibiotic   a chemical compound derived from or produced by living organisms and used in the treatment of infection.

antibody   a substance formed in the body to exert a specific destructive, restrictive or protective action on invading bacteria, foreign proteins or toxins.

AOC   Any Other Colour (term used in registrations and show literature by some bodies).

AOV   Any Other Variety (term used as above).

ataxia   a loss of control of movement resulting in an unsteady or staggering gait. Found in some feline diseases or poisoning or following street accidents or concussion.

bacteria   types of microscopic organisms, some of which cause disease.

balanced   a term given to a cat with good proportions in relation to the standard of points for its particular breed or variety.

Balinese   a longhaired Siamese which arose from a spontaneous mutation.

banding   areas of dark pigmentation in individual hairs of the cat's coat giving rise to the agouti effect.

barring   a form of tabby marking required on some tabby cats but considered a serious fault in self-coloured (solid-colored) varieties.

benching   placing a cat or kitten, with all its show equipment, in its pen at the cat show, ready for judging.

Bi-colour (Bi-color)   a cat with patches of white and any other solid colour (found in longhaired and shorthaired varieties).

Birman   the Sacred Cat of Burma. A longhaired cat of Himalayan coat pattern and distinctive white feet.

bite   the term given to the way in which the cat's jaws meet. The teeth should close together evenly when the bite is said to be 'level'.

black   the darkest of all feline colours – often has a rusty appearance during moulting or shedding periods. Found in longhaired, shorthaired and Foreign or Oriental varieties.

blaze   a distinctive, contrasting mark running down the cat's face from forehead to nostrils. Usually found in tortoiseshell or parti-coloured cats.

blotched   the term given to the tabby pattern, also known as 'classic' or 'marbled'.

blowing-up   stud males are said to be showing this behaviour when confronting another male or a female that smells of another male. The cat turns sideways on to the animal it considers a threat, its coat becomes erect and its jowls are puffed out. The ears are laid back and it growls deeply, with lip-smacking and some salivating. The cat is highly dangerous in this situation and will attack at the slightest provocation.

blue   a simple dilution of black. There are blue varieties in all categories of cat breeds. Blue colouration may vary from a very pale, soft grey colour to a dark slate tone.

blue-cream   a simple dilution of tortoiseshell in which the cat's coat has a two-toned effect of blue and cream hairs, either patched or intermingled.

bonnet-ears   the term given to an effect seen when a cat holds its ears sideways and forwards, looking rather like the brim of a bonnet. Often caused by stress at cat shows and most common in Siamese varieties.

breech birth   when a kitten is presented with its rump first. When a kitten is presented with its hindfeet first, it usually emerges without difficulty. A true breech birth may cause some difficulty in a young maiden queen.

brindling   is the effect caused when hairs of an incorrect colour are interspersed in the coat. This effect is often seen after illness in some cats. For example a Siamese may have many white hairs scattered among the coloured hairs of its mask, and is then said to have a brindled face. Brindling is usually a temporary condition and is corrected at the next moult.

British   the British Shorthairs are descended from British domestic cats and are found in most colour varieties. The term 'British' is generally used to denote a specific type of conformation with cobby body, round head, short tail and sturdy limbs, as opposed to the longer, slender build of the Foreign or Oriental Shorthairs.

brush   the tail of a longhaired cat.

Burmese   a self-coloured breed of foreign type but more heavily built than the Siamese to which it is genetically allied.

butterfly   the shape of the pattern of markings on the shoulders of blotched, classic or marbled tabby cats.

CAC   Certificat d'Aptitude de Championnat.

CACIB   Certificat d'Aptitude de Championnat International de Beauté.

CACIP   Certificat d'Aptitude de Championnat International de Premier.

caesarian section   an operation performed to remove a queen's litter when she is unable to produce them in the normal way.

Calico   an American name for the Tortie-and-White cat.

calling   the crying emitted by a female cat in oestrus.

Cameo   a series of cat varieties in which the orange and silver genes have been combined to give a beautiful two-layered 'cameo' effect in the coat.

canker   usually refers to any inflammatory condition of the cat's ears but most often associated with infestation by ear-mites.

carrier (1)   any container used for the safe transport of a cat; it can be made of any suitable material such as mesh, wickerwork, fibreglass, wood, cardboard or perspex.

carrier (2)   a cat that appears perfectly normal, but is able to infect other cats with disease, usually viral, e.g. cat 'flu. The animal may have contracted and recovered from the disease.

castration   the neutering or altering operation carried out on male cats.

catatonic state   a state of shock in which the cat is motionless and appears to be in a death-like trance.

cat flap   a small hinged door made to allow a cat ready access to the garden or its run without opening the main door.

cat-nip   Nepeta cataria, or cat mint, contains a chemical substance which is attractive to cats. The dried leaves may be used as cat-nip to stuff small toys or to impregnate scratching posts.

CC   an abbreviation for the Governing Council of the Cat Fancy's Challenge Certificate.

CCA   Canadian Cat Association (Canada).

CCFF   Crown Cat Fanciers Federation (USA).

CFA   Cat Fanciers Association (USA).

CFF   Cat Fanciers Federation (USA).

champagne   the term given by some associations to the chocolate variety of the Burmese.

Champion   status earned by cats after completing a required number of specialized wins.

Championship Show   a show at which Championship points or certificates may be won.

Chinchilla   a longhaired breed in which each white hair is tipped with black giving a sparkling appearance.

chromosome   a structure within the nucleus of the cell, carrying genetic information. A cat has 19 pairs of chromosomes in each cell.

classic   a tabby pattern (see blotched).

cleft palate   a congenital abnormality in which the new-born kitten has a fissure in the roof of its mouth.

coarse   a term used to describe a cat which is larger or heavier than indicated by its breed standard.

cobby   the short-coupled, stocky effect as seen in American, British, Domestic, European and Exotic Shorthairs.

colostrum   is the first milk secreted by the cat after parturition, through which the kittens receive maternal antibodies

Colorpoints (USA)	Red, Tortie and Tabby Pointed cats of Siamese type.
Colourpoints (UK)	Siamese or Himalayan patterned longhaired cats of Persian type.
colours of the cat	
black	from these basic colours all coat colour combinations
blue	may be made, some being modified by various coat
chocolate	pattern effects including tabby in all types, the
cream	Himalayan factor, the sex-linkage of the red series,
lilac	and so on. (*See* chart on page 90.)
red	
silver	
white	
condition	the general state of fitness and health.
cotton (USA)	soft wadding made of cotton fibres and used as swabs
cottonwool (UK)	for cleaning eyes, nostrils, wounds etc. (Also available wound as pledgets onto wooden or plastic sticks and then called cotton-buds or cotton-tips.)
cowhocked	a condition in which the cat's hocks turn in towards each other; a weakness.
cream	a dilution of the orange colouration in the cat.
cryptorchid	a male cat without descended testicles and therefore useless for breeding.
cull	to weed out weak or undesirable stock, ensuring that they go as neutered pets and are not used for breeding and perpetuating their faults.
dam	mother cat.
dehydration	rapid loss of fluids from the body tissues during the course of some feline diseases.
dentition	the conformation of the cat's teeth.
dilution	a lighter colour variation of standard feline colour.
disinfectant	a substance used for cleaning; those used for catteries and in the home where cats are present must be carefully checked to ensure that they are non-toxic to the feline species.
dome	term given to the shape of certain cats' heads (*see* Burmese standard).
dominant factor	the member of an allelic gene pair which over-rides the effects of the other (recessive) allele.
dominant genes in cats	
Tabby	is dominant to Non-Tabby.
Black	is dominant to Chocolate.
Dense Colour	is dominant to Dilute Colour.
Orange	is dominant to Non-Orange.
White	is dominant to Non-White.
Burmese	is dominant to Siamese.
Self-Colour	is dominant to Himalayan.
Shorthair	is dominant to Longhair.
Normal Coat	is dominant to Rex-Coat.
Manx	is dominant to Normal Tail.
double coat	having two thick coats in one, comprising a soft undercoat of thick, short hairs and another set of coarser, slightly longer hairs (seen in Manx).
eclampsia	milk fever or lactational tetany.
entire	male or female cats which have not been altered or neutered.
estrus	*see* oestrus.
eumelanin	black or brown pigmentation.
experimental breeds	varieties being developed by breeders wishing to modify type or produce additional colours or coat patterns within existing breeds of cat.
experimental register	a facility offered by some governing bodies to enable experimental breeds to be registered and to eventually gain official recognition.
eye-colour in the cat	*see* page 60.
fancier	one who breeds or exhibits cats as a serious hobby.
feral cat	a domestic cat which has reverted to the wild or has been born in the wild and is not domesticated.
FeLV	Feline Leukaemia Virus.
FIE	Feline Infectious Enteritis.
FIFE	Federation Internationale Feline d'Europe.
flehmen reaction	is seen when a cat savours an unusual or evocative scent. The head is raised and the mouth is held slightly open.
flyer (1)	a cat which is an exceptional example of its breed and is considered virtually unbeatable at cat shows.
flyer (2)	an announcement and full details of a cat show or other social event (USA).
foreign type	a cat with long, elegant lines and fine bones.
	which protect them against infections.
formalin	(formaldehyde solution B.P. 36%) is excellent for disinfecting in cases of viral and other disease; great care must be exercised in handling this substance and it must be diluted 1 part on 400 parts of water before use. It may also be used as a fumigant.
FPL	Feline Panleucopaenia (or Feline Infectious Enteritis).
frill	the fine hairs around the neck of a longhaired cat, forming a frame for the face and sometimes called the 'ruff'.
furball	fur swallowed by the cat during self-grooming which forms into a tightly packed ball in the stomach or bowels.
FVR	Feline Viral Rhinotracheitis.
gait	a cat's manner of walking or running.
gauntlets	the white glove-like markings on the legs of the Birman.
GCCF	Governing Council of the Cat Fancy (UK).
gene	each chromosome has many genes, each of which contributes a characteristic to the cat's makeup.
genetics	the study of heredity.
genotype	the genetic makeup of an individual cat.
gestation	the period of pregnancy from conception to birth, about 65 days in the cat.
ghost markings	the faint tabby markings which may be visible in the coats of young kittens of self-coloured (solid-colored) breeds.
gingivitis	inflammation of the gums.
gloves	white feet as seen in Birman cats.
haematoma	a blood blister.
hairball	*see* furball.
harness	specially made of soft elasticated cord or leather which can be adjusted to fit the cat, and to which a lead may be attached, a harness is very useful for travelling or when the cat needs to be restrained.
Havana (UK)	a chocolate brown cat of extreme foreign type, derived from Siamese. Known in US as Chestnut Oriental Shorthair.
Havana Brown (USA)	a unique breed descended from English stock and developed in limited gene pools in America.
haw	the nictitating membrane, or third eyelid of the cat. May be seen as a membrane protruding across the inner corner of the cat's eye during illness or in times of stress.
heat	period of oestrus.
heterozygous	a condition in which any particular characteristic has been derived from only one parent.
homozygous	a condition in which any particular characteristic has been derived from both parents.
Himalayan (USA)	a Persian cat of Siamese or Himalayan colouring (*see* Colourpoint).
hot	a term used to describe a cream cat with too much red in the coat.
hybrid	a cross between two species. As domestic cats all belong to the same species, it is incorrect to refer to crosses between the varieties as hybrids.
ICF	Independent Cat Federation (USA).
incontinence	the inability to retain the contents of the bladder and/or bowels, a condition sometimes occurring in the very old cat, or one weakened by illness or accident.
incubation period	the time which elapses between the actual infection of the cat and the appearance of the first symptoms. Most diseases have specific incubation periods.
injection	the method of introducing substances such as drugs into the body of the cat by means of a needle and syringe. Subcutaneous injections are given just under the skin; intravenous injections are given directly into a vein, intramuscular injections are given into a muscle.
inoculation	*see* vaccination.
intranasal vaccines	vaccines in liquid form instilled into the cat's nostrils with a dropper. Currently the only such vaccines are those developed for cat 'flu.
jaundice	a yellowing of the tissues caused by absorption into the blood of bile pigments. A symptom of serious disease in the cat.
jaw pinch	indentation of the line of the muzzle, a fault in cats whose standard calls for a wedge shaped head

jowls	narrowing in perfectly straight lines to a fine muzzle. the extra development of the cheeks seen in entire male cats.
kink	a bend or twist in the tail of a cat due to malformation of two or more vertebrae. Considered a fault in most breeds and heavily penalized in show specimens.
kitten	a young cat up to the age of 9 months under the rules of GCCF. Other Associations vary in their definitions, some consider them as kittens up to the age of 8 months, some up to the age of 10 months.
Korat	a unique self-blue shorthaired breed from Thailand.
lactation	the production of milk by the queen.
lavender	the term given to the lilac colouration in cats, by some Associations.
lesion	any change in an organ or tissue, but commonly taken to be a scar or scab on the skin of the cat.
level bite	see 'bite'.
lilac	the simple dilution of chocolate (see lavender).
litter (1)	a family of kittens born to one queen.
litter (2)	the substance used in a toilet tray.
locket	a white spot at the base of the cat's throat – a serious fault in most breeds (see Abyssinian standard).
mackerel	a pattern of tabby markings in which thin unbroken lines run vertically down from the spine line.
mammary glands	produce milk for the queen's litter.
marbled	the tabby pattern, also known as blotched or classic.
mask	the darker coloured areas of the face as seen in Siamese or Himalayan cats.
mats	clumps of matted hair which form in a neglected coat and may need clipping away.
mayor's chains	the lines around the neck of the classic tabbies.
melanin	see eumelanin and phaenomelanin.
melanistic	a black variety of a cat normally of some other colour.
membrane	a thin skin or sheet of connective tissue.
midline incision/ operation site	a midline incision is used in some feline operations and is made along a central line straight down the cat's belly.
monorchid	a male cat with only one testicle descended.
moribund	approaching the point of death.
moult (UK) molt (USA)	the periodic or seasonal shedding of dead hair.
mutation	a change which occurs spontaneously and gives rise to a new colour, type or species variation.
muzzle	the nose and jaws of the cat.
muzzle-break	indentation in the lines of the muzzle – desirable in some breeds but a serious fault in others.
nephritis	inflammation of the kidneys.
neuter	a castrated male or spayed female.
nictitating membrane	see haw.
non-self (non-solid)	a cat which has a coat of more than one colour.
nose leather	the smooth area of skin to be found between the cat's nostrils.
obesity	overweight.
odd-eyed	having one eye of blue and the other one of orange or copper.
oestrus	the period of heat when the queen will mate. A queen in oestrus is said to be 'on heat', 'on call', 'calling' or 'in season'.
Oriental	a group of varieties derived from Siamese, with Siamese type and conformation but without either the blue eyes or restriction of colour to the points of the body.
out of coat	refers mainly to longhaired breeds during moulting, or following a hot summer when their coats are thin, short or sparse. In other varieties, a cat is said to be out of coat when the coat condition leaves much to be desired and the animal is unfit for showing.
ovario-hysterectomy	the surgical removal of the uterus and ovaries following illness or infection, or to sterilize, neuter or spay the female cat.
overshot jaw	the upper jaw is longer than the lower jaw causing the upper teeth to overlap the lower teeth – a serious fault.
ovulation	the process by which the ovaries release ova. In the cat, this takes place after mating.
pads	the tough hairless cushions on the soles of the cat's feet.
parti-coloured	having a coat of more than one distinct colour, such as the Bi-colour.
parturition	the process of giving birth.
patching	the way in which colours are arranged in clearly defined areas on the coat, as seen in the Tortie-and-White.
pencilling	the term given to the striking fine lines seen on the cheeks of tabby cats.
phaenomelanin	orange pigment.
phenotype	in heredity, this refers to individuals showing the same characteristics of appearance.
pinch	a break in the straight lines of the muzzle – a fault in many breeds.
placenta	the afterbirth – embryonic tissue to which each kitten is attached by its umbilical cord and from which it receives nourishment before birth. It is expelled soon after the kitten's birth.
platinum	the term given to lilac colouration by some associations.
pneumonia	inflammation of the lungs – very serious in the cat.
points	the extremities of the cat's body: the mask, ears, feet and legs, and tail. In Siamese these are variously coloured giving Seal-Point, Blue-Point etc.
polydactyl	having six toes or more on the forefeet and five toes or more on the hindfeet.
poisons	chemicals which may result in illness or death if used incorrectly, indiscriminately or contacted accidentally. agricultural sprays – arsenic; nicotine; nitrites. disinfectants containing – cresol; phenol; chloroxylenol; iodine. domestic dangers – anti-freeze; caustic soda; coal gas; creosote; oils; paint; paraffin (kerosene); slug bait; sump oil; tar; turpentine; waxes. drugs prepared as painkillers for humans – aspirin; paracetamol. food preservative – benzoic acid. insecticides – Aldrin; benzyl benzoate; BHC (Gammexane); Chlordane; DDT; derris; Dieldrin; Malathion; Ronnel (Ectoral); TDE; toxaphene. plants – dieffenbachia; common house plants; philodendron; laurel; toadstools and other fungi. rodenticides – alphanaphylthiourea (Antu); sodium fluoracetate; strychnine; thallium; Warfarin.
pot belly	the typically distended belly of a kitten with a heavy worm burden or cats with dropsy.
prefix	a registered cattery name used at the beginning of the name of each cat bred and registered by that cattery.
Premier	a title attained by neutered cats which is equivalent to the title of Champion for entire cats.
pricked	a term used to describe ears when held high and alert, a desired trait in some breeds but may be considered a fault in others.
progeny	the offspring of a particular cat.
progesterone	a sex hormone, most important in the breeding queen.
pulse	the pulse of the cat at rest is about 100 beats per minute.
quarantine	a period of enforced isolation when a cat enters a foreign country or after an infectious illness. Cats entering the UK, for example, must be quarantined for a period of six months. Some countries have no such restrictions but may require certain vaccinations and health certificates.
queen	a female cat used for breeding.
quick	the sensitive area within the cat's claw.
recessive factor	the member of an allelic gene pair which is over-ridden or masked by the other dominant allele.
recognition	the official acceptance of a breed or variety by a governing body.
red	caused by the orange gene, found in most breeds.
registration	details of each animal recorded by governing body.
regurgitation	the bringing back of recently eaten food or fluid, sometimes for re-eating or feeding to the kittens.
rex	a curled effect of the coat caused by genes which resulted from separate mutations.
ribbon (USA)	a coloured ribbon, generally printed, presented to prize-winning cats.
ringed	a term used to describe the bands of darker coloured hairs on legs and tails of tabbies.
rolling	the posturing and rolling-over of the queen in oestrus usually accompanied by strident cries. A stud owner, when contacted, may well ask to be contacted again

	when the queen is 'rolling and calling' and therefore considered ready for mating.
rosette	a gathered or pleated rose-shaped ribbon ornament awarded to prize winners.
ruddy	a term used to describe Abyssinian cats.
ruff	the hair around the neck of a longhaired cat (see frill).
rumpy	a true Manx cat with a well-rounded rump and no detectable tail structure.
Russian Blue	a distinctive self-blue foreign breed.
saline solution	made by boiling one pint (550 ml) of water and using this to dissolve one teaspoon (5 ml) salt (sodium chloride). Cooled and then stored in a sterilized, tightly corked bottle, this solution should be kept for emergency use in the feline First Aid cupboard.
salivation	excessive production of saliva. May be a symptom of respiratory disease, ulcerated mouth or tongue, dental pain or inflamed gums, a foreign body in the mouth or throat, or a sign of aggression or apprehension.
scarab	the distinctive marking found on the forehead of the Oriental Tabby cats.
schedule	a printed broadsheet or booklet announcing the classes and judges of a particular cat show (see flyer).
scruff	the loose skin at the nape of the cat's neck, taken up by the male when mating the female. May be held firmly in order to restrain a difficult or fractious cat.
self	a cat which is evenly covered in hair of one colour.
Shaded Silver	a striking cat with a silver undercoat heavily tipped with black.
shedding	see moulting, molting.
Siamese	a range of foreign-type cats in which the Himalayan factor causes the colouration to be restricted to the points, and the eyes to be blue.
silver	a gene which is present in several breeds including the Cameo, Chinchilla, Silver Tabby and Smoke.
sire	the male responsible for the production of a litter.
Smoke	a variety in which there is a dark or coloured top coat, which is white or silver at the roots.
solid	see self.
spay	see ovario-hysterectomy.
Sphynx	a rare breed of hairless cat.
Spotted	a form of tabby in which the bands of colour are broken into distinct spots which may be of any regular shape.
spraying	the habit of urinating (micturating) to mark out a territory.
squint	unequal placement of the eyes so that one or both look towards the nose – a fault in any breed.
standard of points	agreed lists of points laid down by governing bodies to which exhibition cats are judged and assessed.
sternum	the breast bone. In some breeds, a projected sternum is found from time to time as a hard lump near the navel. It is an hereditary defect.
steward (USA)	a helper at cat shows employed to clean the cages in the judging rings after each exhibit has been judged.
steward (UK)	the judge's personal assistant at a cat show.
stools	faeces.
stop	a break in the straight line of the profile, desired in some breeds but a serious fault in others.
stripes	markings found in tabby cats.
stropping	the habit of sharpening the claws.
stud cat	an entire male kept for breeding purposes.
stud tail	a greasy condition of the sebaceous glands situated along the root end of the cat's tail; found in females as well as males, it should be cleaned regularly.
stumpy	a Manx cat with a short stump of a tail.
sub-mental organ	a small gland situated in the cat's chin.
suffix	see affix.
svelte	long, lithe and elegant in build, like an ideal Siamese.
Tabby	a series of striped, blotched, spotted or ticked patterns. Tabby varieties are found in longhaired, shorthaired, foreign and Siamese breeds.
tangles	knots which form in the coat, especially in longhaired breeds, when grooming has been neglected (see also mats).
tapetum lucidum	the reflective layer at the back of the cat's eye.
tartar	a concretion which accumulates on the teeth of cats and should be removed from time to time as necessary.
teat	nipple.
temperature	the *average* normal temperature of the domestic cat is 101.5°F (38.6°C).
testes	the male generative glands; the testicles.
testosterone	male hormone secreted by the testes.

thumb-mark	also called thumb-print, is the distinctive mark on the back of each ear of Tabby-Point Siamese and some other tabby varieties.
ticking	the two or three bands of colour seen in the typical agouti coat.
tipping	the contrasting colour seen at the tips of the hairs of some cats' coats. The tipping may be very slight as in the Chinchilla, Shell Cameo or British Tipped, or extend further down the hairs to give a darker effect as in the Shaded Silver and Shaded Cameo.
tom	an entire male cat.
tortoiseshell	a cat patched or intermingled with black and red; an all-female variety.
tortie-and-white	as tortoiseshell with the addition of white (see calico).
tourniquet	a band used above an injury on a limb in order to stop bleeding.
toxins	poisons.
transfer	on the change of ownership, a registered cat or kitten must have this registered with the governing body by the completion of the appropriate form and payment of a small fee.
tri-colour	a cat of three distinct colours.
tufts	small clusters of hairs at the tips of some cats' ears. Fairly common in Abyssinian cats.
type	the essential characteristics distinguishing a breed. A cat of good type conforms closely to the official standard of points for its breed.
UCF	United Cat Fanciers (USA).
umbilical cord	the cord through which the unborn kitten receives nourishment. After birth this is severed about 1 inch from the kitten's navel and after a few days it dries up completely and falls away.
undershot jaw	the lower jaw protrudes further than the upper jaw and the front teeth do not meet – a serious fault in any breed.
uterus	the womb.
vaccination	inoculation with a vaccine against infectious disease.
vibrissae	whiskers – long sensitive bristles protruding from the face of the cat.
virus	minute organism which may cause disease.
wedge	describes the head shape of some breeds, notably the Siamese varieties.
whip	describes the desired long, thin tapering tail required in some varieties such as the Siamese.
whiskers	see vibrissae.
white	a colour variety found in longhaired, shorthaired and foreign breeds and allied to variations in eyecolour – orange-eyed, blue-eyed and odd-eyed.
white hairs	scattered white hairs are a serious fault in most breeds unless they are the temporary result of illness (see brindling).
white spotting	the presence of small white areas on an otherwise self-coloured cat – a very serious fault.
Universal Antidote	a useful component of the feline first aid kit. 1–2 tablespoons should be given by mouth to the poisoned cat or kitten. *To Make:* Mix together the following ingredients: 2 parts powdered charcoal 1 part Milk of Magnesia 1 part tannic acid Store in a sterile, well-corked bottle for emergency use. In extreme emergency, burnt toast or charcoal dog biscuits may be crushed and used instead of the charcoal, and cold, strong tea may be used instead of the tannic acid.

The publishers would like to thank the following individuals and organisations for their kind permission to reproduce the photographs in this book:

The following were specially photographed by Animal Graphics Limited:

44 above right, 45 below, 46–47, 53 below, 62 below, 63 below, 67 above left, 81 above left and below, 86, 90 above, 111 above, 116, 132, 152 above, 168 below, 169, 174 above, 175 above and below left, 177 above right, 180 above, 181, 184, 185 above, 187 below left, 192 above, 194 left, 195 right, 198 above, 202 below left and above right, 203 above, 204, 207, 208 above right and left.

Animal Graphics Limited/Solitaire:

12 below, 14 above left, 44 above left, 45 above, 50, 51, 52, 53 above and centre, 54, 55, 56, 57, 58, 59, 60, 61 above, 62 above, 63 above right and left, 64, 66, 67 above right and below, 68, 69, 70, 71, 72, 73, 74 below right and left, 75, 76, 77, 78, 80, 83, 84, 85, 86–87, 87, 88, 89, 90 centre and below, 91, 92–93, 96, 97, 98, 99, 100, 101, 102, 104, 106, 107, 108, 109, 110, 111 above centre, centre, below right, below centre and left, 112, 113, 117, 120, 121, 122, 123, 124, 125, 126, 127, 130, 133, 134, 135, 136, 138, 139, 140, 141, 142, 143, 144, 145, 146, 147, 148, 149, 150, 151, 152 below left and right, 155, 156, 157, 158, 159, 160, 161, 162–163, 166, 167, 168 above, 170, 171, 174 below, 175 above and below right, 176, 177 above and below left, 177 below right, 178, 179, 180 below, 182, 183, 185 below right and left, 186, 187 above and below right, 188, 189, 190, 191, 192 below, 193, 194 above right, centre and below, 195 left, 196, 197, 198 below, 199, 200, 201, 202 above left, centre and below, 203 centre right and left, 203 below right and left, 205, 206, 208 below right, 209, 210, 211, 212, 215.

Animal Graphics Limited/Burley: 213; Daphne Negus: 6–7.

The publishers would also like to thank:

Animals Animals/Oxford Scientific Films Limited: (L Lee Rue II) 8; (Stouffer Enterprises) 36 above; (Robert Caoba) 39 below; (E Wilkinson) 40; (L L T Rhodes) 41; Ardea: (P J Green) 10; (K Fink) 28 above, 29 below right and below left, 36 below left and below right, 39 above; (M D England) 28 below right, 33 centre and below; (P Steyn) 30; (M E J Grove) 31 above; (McDougal Tiger Tops) 32 above; (J P Ferrero) 32 below; Bio-Arts: 56 below, 61 below, 74 above, 81 above right; S C Bisserot: 35; B Coleman Limited: (D & R Sullivan) 31 centre; (J Markham) 33 above; (F Erize) 38; (D Robinson) 41 above; (H Reinhard) 42; (J Burton) 43 above; (L Lee Rue II) 43 centre; Mary Evans Picture Library: 17 below, 18 below right, 24 above right; Fotomas Index: (J Freeman) 12 above, 24 above left; The Frick Collection, New York: 23; R Harding Associates: (W Rawlings) 22 below; Michael Holford: 13, 14 above right and below, 15; Jacana Agence de Presse: (Varin-Visage) 28 below left; (Vala) 43 below; F W Lane: 34 below; The Mansell Collection: 26 above and below, 164, 165; Ruth M Meyer: 16; Musee de Louvre, Paris: 22 above; Reproduced by courtesy of the Trustees, National Gallery, London: 21; Natural Science Photos: (A Lamb) 34 above; (J Hobday) 37; N.H.P.A.: (A Bannister) 31 below; Scala: 17 above, 20 below; R Sheridan's Photo Library: 18 below left, 19; Snark International: 18 above, 24 below; The Tate Gallery, London: (A Hornak) 25, 27 above and below; University College, London: 20 above.

Colour illustrations by Barry Jackson.

Black and white drawings by John Lobban.

The author and publishers are most grateful to the Governing Council of the Cat Fancy for permission to print the official standard of breed points in this book.

The author particularly wishes to thank all those cat breeders and cat lovers who have permitted their pets to be photographed for this book.